Economic Studies in and Well-Being

MW01273713

Volume Number 7

For further volumes:
http://www.springer.com/7140

Louis-Marie Asselin

Analysis of Multidimensional Poverty

Theory and Case Studies

Contributions from

Jean-Bosco Ki
Vu Tuan Anh

 Springer

International Development Research Centre
Ottawa • Cairo • Dakar • Montevideo • Nairobi • New Delhi • Singapore

Louis-Marie Asselin
Institut de Mathématique Gauss
9 Carré F.X. Lemieux
Lévis QC G6W 1H2
Canada
imgasselin@globetrotter.net

A copublication with the
International Development Research Centre
PO Box 8500
Ottawa, ON K1G 3H9
Canada
www.idrc.ca/info@idrc.ca
e-ISBN 978-1-55250-460-4

ISBN 978-1-4419-0842-1 (hardcover)   e-ISBN 978-1-4419-0843-8
ISBN 978-1-4419-0905-3 (softcover)
DOI 10.1007/978-1-4419-0843-8
Springer Dordrecht Heidelberg London New York

Library of Congress Control Number: 2009933416 (hardcover)
Library of Congress Control Number: 2009933417 (softcover)

© Springer Science+Business Media, LLC 2009
All rights reserved. This work may not be translated or copied in whole or in part without the written permission of the publisher (Springer Science+Business Media, LLC, 233 Spring Street, New York, NY 10013, USA), except for brief excerpts in connection with reviews or scholarly analysis. Use in connection with any form of information storage and retrieval, electronic adaptation, computer software, or by similar or dissimilar methodology now known or hereafter developed is forbidden.
The use in this publication of trade names, trademarks, service marks, and similar terms, even if they are not identified as such, is not to be taken as an expression of opinion as to whether or not they are subject to proprietary rights.

Printed on acid-free paper

Springer is part of Springer Science+Business Media (www.springer.com)

To an unknown Nepalese child once seen in Jumla, no more than 5 years old and already working hard, with so much sadness in his eyes.

An unforgettable face of poverty.

Il suffit qu'un seul homme soit tenu sciemment . . . dans la misère pour que le pacte civique tout entier soit nul; aussi longtemps qu'il y a un homme dehors, la porte qui lui est fermée au nez ferme une cité d'injustice et de haine.

It only takes one man consciously maintained . . . in destitution for the entire social contract to be null; as long as there is one man outside, the door shut on his face closes a city of injustice and of hate.[1]

Charles Péguy
Cahiers de la Quinzaine
Novembre 1902

---

[1] Free translation by L.-M. Asselin

Preface

Poverty is a paradoxical state. Recognizable in the field for any sensitive observer who travels in remote rural areas and urban slums and meets marginalized people in a given society, poverty still remains a challenge to conceptual formalization and to measurement that is consistent with such formalization. The analysis of poverty is multidisciplinary. It goes from ethics to economics, from political science to human biology, and any type of measurement rests on mathematics. Moreover, poverty is multifaceted according to the types of deprivation, and it is also gender and age specific. A vector of variables is required, which raises a substantial problem for individual and group comparisons necessary to equity analysis. Multidimensionality also complicates the aggregation necessary to perform the efficiency analysis of policies. In the case of income poverty, these two problems, equity and efficiency, have benefited from very significant progress in the field of economics. Similar achievements are still to come in the area of multidimensional poverty.

Within this general background, this book has a very modest and narrow-scoped objective. It proposes an operational methodology for measuring multidimensional poverty, independent from the conceptual origin, the size and the qualitative as well as the quantitative nature of the primary indicators used to describe the poverty of an individual, a household or a sociodemographic entity. It is my view that the proposed methodology should allow to integrate into the analysis of multidimensional poverty the sets of techniques already available or forthcoming in the area of income poverty. Despite this, I do not want to avoid the issue of the conceptual foundations of poverty. Thus, I propose from the start a quite comprehensive definition of poverty, whose ethical basis is briefly presented in an annex which can be skipped by readers not interested in such issues. The core of the methodology rests on a solution to the issue of the aggregation across the multiple subdimensions of poverty. The rationale of the proposed solution consists in exploring the internal structure of association between these subdimensions of poverty.

The methodology aims to be operational, by which I mean that it should be feasible with the use of computational tools that are easily accessible, as well as feasible without any specific limitation on the number and the nature of the poverty indicators used by the analyst. I also sincerely believe that the conceptual debates on the dimensions of poverty and on the measurement methodologies need to be lit with numerous empirical studies showing the strengths and weaknesses of different approaches. This explains the structure of the book. It does not try to be encyclope-dic and thus does not include an exhaustive review of the literature on multidimen-sional poverty; there is however a short overview of the main methodological trends to situate the chosen approach.

The first part, which is theoretical, develops the rationale underlying the pro-posed methodology, the concepts being illustrated with numerical examples taken from an empirical study realized in Vietnam. My co-authors join me in a second part to present two case studies using partially (first) or fully (second one) the methodology of the first part. The first case study presents a static analysis realized in Senegal under the coordination of Jean-Bosco Ki. I had the opportunity to work closely with this team and to benefit importantly from this collaboration to refine the methodology. My colleague and friend Vu Tuan Anh and I have realized the second study, a dynamic analysis of poverty in Vietnam during the period 1993–2002. This last study uses the full methodology presented in the first part. Both case studies are based on large household surveys implemented by the different national statistical offices. Many other research works realized within the Poverty and Economic Policy (PEP) network have also helped test the proposed methodology. I thank all of these developing country researchers for the fruitful discussions that have helped me much in writing this book.

I thank the International Development Research Centre (IDRC) whose support has made this book possible. I have had the privilege to be involved for 12 years in the Micro Impact of Macroeconomic and Adjustment Policies (MIMAP) program and in the PEP network, both funded by IDRC. Thirty years ago, IDRC had also wel-comed me as an associate researcher for the writing of a book that much influenced my professional and scientific life. From this institution to which I owe so much, I am particularly grateful to Marie-Claude Martin, Randy Spence, Rohinton Medhora and to their colleague managers of the above-mentioned programs, based either in Ottawa, Dakar, Nairobi, New Delhi or Singapore. Their generous and sustained trust moves me deeply. Laval University is a mother institution for me since my very first student life in the 1960s. There, I have been student, professor, student again, pro-fessional partner and now associate researcher. I have never been a long time away from the campus. I thank the numerous colleagues, professors, students and admin-istrative staff who contributed so much to my training and research work. Regarding this book, Jean-Yves Duclos, from the Department of Economics, has accompanied me from the beginning. His critical eye, always constructive, his tight review of the theoretical part and his unfailing support contributed a lot to improve the first drafts and to come to a conclusion. I thank many other MIMAP and PEP coworkers, from Laval or other institutions, for their encouragement, critique and friendship, *inter alia*: Bernard Decaluwé, John Cockburn, Celia Reyes, Cosme Vodounou, Touhami Abdelkhalek, Samuel Kaboré, Swapna Mukhopadhyay, Ponciano Intal, Abdelkrim Araar, Sami Bibi, Anyck Dauphin, Dorothée Boccanfuso, Luc Savard. I thank an unknown reviewer of the Vietnam case study from the Philippines. The Canadian Centre for International Cooperation and Study (CECI) has welcomed me during 20 years as Director of Studies, Training and Poverty unit. In this position, I have had the opportunity to be frequently in the field, which contributed in an inestimable way to develop my thinking on poverty. I thank all of my CECI colleagues, either from the headquarters, Africa, Asia or Central and Latin America.

My close family, Lise, Pierre, Marie-Claude, and Matthieu, has accepted my frequent and often long absences from home. Without their affection and generous comprehension, my professional life resulting in this book would not have been as fruitful. I thank them with much love and emotion.[2]

Lévis, Quebec   Louis-Marie Asselin
October 2008

[2] This work was carried out with financial and scientific support from the Poverty and Economic Policy (PEP) Research Network, which is financed by the Government of Canada through the International Development Research Centre (IDRC) and the Canadian International Development Agency (CIDA), and by the Australian Agency for International Development (AusAID).

Contents

Part I
Theory

Chapter 1
Introduction

The technical problem that we are facing originates from the multidimensionality of the poverty concept, which is by now universally accepted. The form given to this multidimensionality depends on the definition given to poverty, for which there is not a unique formulation; however, there is usually a significant overlap among the various meanings found here and there. We would like to share with the readers the following definition, which expresses well our own views on poverty:

> Poverty consists in any form of inequity, which is a source of social exclusion, in the distribution of the living conditions essential to human dignity. These living conditions correspond to the capabilities of individuals, households and communities to meet their basic needs in the following dimensions:

- income (1)
- education (2)
- health (3)
- food/nutrition (4)
- safe water/sanitation (5)
- labor/employment (6)
- housing (living environment) (7)
- access to productive assets (8)
- access to markets (9)
- community participation/social peace (10).

The particular faces of poverty become particularly meaningful if we consider that, at the individual level, the different dimensions mentioned above may take specific forms according to gender and age group. From this point of view, looking at individual poverty seems to be the most feasible way of implementing multidimensionality. Moreover, and even more importantly, looking at individual poverty seems a natural way of exploring poverty dynamics, perceived as a life-cycle poverty status that may be differentiated according to gender.

From a human development point of view, a poverty indicator must be significant and eventually measurable at the individual, household, or community level. It must

L.-M. Asselin, *Analysis of Multidimensional Poverty,*
Economic Studies in Inequality, Social Exclusion and Well-Being 7,
DOI 10.1007/978-1-4419-0843-8_1, © Springer Science+Business Media, LLC 2009

allow a ranking of these demographic units as more or less poor, in one of the above-mentioned dimensions.

We would like to characterize this definition as reflecting *poverty with a human face*. With reference to inequity, it obviously leads us to a discourse on ethics and moral philosophy. Such considerations are developed in Appendix I.1, *Poverty Measurement, A Conceptual Framework*.

Our objective here is not to discuss the different concepts of poverty, as this type of discussion is already found abundantly in the literature.[1] We would rather operationalize the different expressions of multidimensional poverty. Our focus is really on *measuring multidimensional poverty* using sound scientific basis, with a methodology applicable to a wide range of situations, as well as available data sets.

Our specific objective is to operationalize multidimensional poverty comparisons. But practical issues and measurement choices are quite dependent on the level of comparisons being made: are we interested in international, national, or local comparisons? Our implicit reference is at the level of national and local comparisons. By "national comparisons" we refer to socioeconomic-group (SEG) comparisons within a country or across-time comparisons, while "local comparisons" refer to comparisons between communities. International analysis is based on a much smaller universe of statistical units (that is, no more than 200 countries[2]) and with no sampling issues. On the other hand, analytical issues are different: ranking countries with composite indicators is the central aggregation issue, instead of aggregating countries through composite multidimensional indices for comparisons between groups of countries. Targeting issues are also different. At the international level, with around 100–130 identified less-developed countries, targeting is almost country-specific by definition, which is a completely different context from targeting national programs with a universe of thousands of communities or small administrative units and millions of households. Nevertheless, this approach does not prevent the possibility that some targeting concepts and methodologies developed in one context can also be applicable to another context.

It is now universally recognized that multidimensional poverty is a richer concept than the traditional unidimensional income approach. In addition to philosophical reasons for considering multidimensional poverty measurement, the technical difficulties of income measurement, especially in developing countries, have provided an impetus for looking at other poverty measures.

In the vast majority of African countries, we remain unable to make inter-temporal comparisons of poverty due the unavailability of data. And where survey data are available at more than one point in time, the determination of changes has proven problematic. First, survey designs change. It is now well established that differences in recall periods, changes in the survey instrument (e.g., the number and selection of item codes listed), and even the nature of interviewer training, can have large systematic effects on the measurement of

---

[1] A review is given in Asselin L.-M. and Dauphin A., *Poverty Measurement, A Conceptual Framework*, CECI, MIMAP Training Session on Poverty Measurement and Analysis, Laval University, Quebec, August 1999.

[2] The last UNDP Human Development Report publishes tables for 177 countries.

household expenditures. Compounding this problem, intertemporal comparisons of money-metric welfare are only as precise as the deflators used. Consumer price indices (CIPs) are often suspect in Africa, due to weaknesses in data collection and related analytical procedures. Thus, relying on official CIPs is often precarious, at best. Alternatives such as deriving price indices from unit values, where quantity and expenditure data are collected, also have serious drawbacks.[3]

The same comment certainly applies to most low-income countries.

Therefore, we must be aware that the central issue in operationally defining the concept of poverty is that poverty is completely different in the multidimensional case and in the standard income and money-metric one. In this latter case, it is usually understood that poverty needs to be distinguished from inequality by referring to a poverty line. This calls for techniques either to numerically determine the poverty line or to free comparisons from the intricacies and arbitrariness of poverty lines through the use of stochastic dominance techniques, for instance. On the contrary, in the multidimensional case, the content of the vector of indicators chosen to measure poverty is crucial to determine the poverty concept, and fixing a poverty line or indicator-specific poverty lines is not a first requirement to grasp the concept of poverty. This difference underlies the developments of Chapter 2 on indicators.

It must also be recognized that the income measurement of poverty presents a great technical advantage: it is unidimensional, and it thus allows for a complete ordering of households according to income level. This property is very important for targeting policies and programs for welfare mapping, data aggregation, inequality analysis, and more sophisticated poverty analysis. That is why there is a strong request for retrieving a similar property with multidimensional poverty measurement. There are many proposals coming out of current research work on this issue: as a well-known example, there is the set of human development and human poverty indices[4] developed and published by UNDP. The search for such an analytical property in multidimensional poverty analysis is in fact the core subject of this book and is addressed in Chapter 3 on composite indicators.

Once we have derived a composite indicator as a basic tool, the field is wide open for poverty and inequality analysis with the specificity of a multidimensional background. These analytical issues are developed in Chapter 4. These three chapters make up the first part of this book, which is on multidimensional poverty analysis theory. The second part illustrates the methodology with two case studies on Sénégal and Vietnam.

---

[3] Sahn David E. and David C. Stifel (2000), p. 1.

[4] With the terminology proposed in this book, these UNDP indices would be called "indicators", or more precisely "composite indicators."

Chapter 2
Indicators and Multidimensionality Analysis

Upstream from technical measurement issues, the selection of indicators constitutes an important conceptual step. Multidimensional poverty analysis cannot just stay at a formal level and escape the necessity to look deeply inside poverty vectors appearing here and there in the universal effort to capture the multiple facets of poverty.

2.1 Structured Poverty Vectors

Multidimensional poverty refers to a measurement of poverty which relies on a vector I of K variables, here called primary poverty indicators, with $K > 1$.

These indicators are possibly heterogeneous in their nature:

- quantitative indicators, e.g., household income, number of bicycles,
- qualitative or categorical indicators, e.g., type of toilet.

A minimal requirement for a variable to be admissible as a poverty indicator is to be ordinal. Thus, for a categorical indicator, there should be a clear consensus on the ranking of the finite set of categories, from the worst one to the best one, in terms of some type of basic welfare, e.g., for the type of toilet, nature of wall material for the house. Variables like "main occupation of household head," "place of residence (urban/rural)," and "region" are not admissible poverty indicators. Obviously such non-ordinal variables can play an important role in poverty analysis, for example as characteristics associated with poverty.

Note that all of these indicators are or can be expressed numerically, the number being a fully significant one in the case of "quantitative" indicators, and a non-significant one in the case of "categorical" ones, where it is simply a numerical code. If well chosen, this numerical code can reflect the ordinal structure of the given poverty indicator, which is normally desirable.

We are thus in the statistical domain of multivariate analysis. It does not mean that the number of poverty dimensions is K. We have to identify some more structure in the vector I. Take as an example the case of the UNDP Human Poverty Index for the developing countries, HPI-1. There are four primary indicators in the vector:

L.-M. Asselin, *Analysis of Multidimensional Poverty,*
Economic Studies in Inequality, Social Exclusion and Well-Being 7,
DOI 10.1007/978-1-4419-0843-8_2, © Springer Science+Business Media, LLC 2009

- I_1: the probability at birth of not surviving to age 40
- I_2: the adult illiteracy rate
- I_3: the percentage of the population without sustainable access to a safe water source
- I_4: the percentage of children undernourished.

Within the vector I, *poverty dimensions* will be defined as disjoint subsets of indicators covering I. For the HPI-1, there are three poverty dimensions:

- dimension 1: a relatively long and healthy life, or vulnerability to death at a relatively early age, corresponding to the subset $\{I_1\}$,
- dimension 2: knowledge, or exclusion from the world of reading and communications, corresponding to the subset $\{I_2\}$,
- dimension 3: a decent standard of living, or lack of access to overall economic provisioning, corresponding to the subset $\{I_3, I_4\}$.

Thus, a poverty dimension is defined a priori as being represented by a univariate or multivariate measurement, each variable of the subset being a poverty indicator. We can thus have the health dimension, the education dimension, the income dimension, etc. Strictly speaking, we are in the domain of multidimensional poverty if there are at least two poverty dimensions identified within the vector I. Given a vector I of K primary poverty indicators and a partition into D subsets representing as many poverty dimensions, the number $|d|$ of indicators in the subset d can already be seen as an *implicit weighting* of the poverty dimension d. In the last example with four indicators for three dimensions, the implicit relative weights of dimensions 1, 2, and 3 are respectively 25, 25, and 50%. This weighting will become explicit according to each analytical treatment of the vector I, particularly in the aggregative technique used to produce a composite indicator of the multidimensional poverty (CIP).

A primary poverty indicator can itself be represented by a multivariate measurement. The best known example is the money-metric indicator of income given usually as a vector of household expenditures and aggregated by simple addition.

Another structure we introduce within the vector I is the notion of a *poverty type* which we define as a subset of poverty indicators all positively correlated.[1] A poverty type can also be described as a *statistical poverty dimension*, expressing the fact that there is some redundancy within a subset of the vector I. It is obviously *distribution dependent*, in contrast to a normatively defined poverty dimension, and can go across many of these dimensions. Two poverty types can in fact overlap, which is not the case for poverty dimensions. This structure will appear useful in the process of exploring poverty multidimensionality and of reducing multivariateness.

---

[1] Intentionally we do not enter here into the technical definition and measurement of "correlation," which depends on the type of indicator (such as the usual Pearson correlation, the rank-order correlation like Kendall's τ, etc.).

Empirically, most multidimensional poverty micro-measurements[2] rely directly on ordinal categorical indicators, such as household sanitation, source of potable water, ownership of assets, school attendance, and child health status. Higher-level measurement is usually made of indices based on such indicators. Since quantitative indicators can always be transformed into ordinal categorical ones,[3] we are naturally inclined to pay special attention to that type of indicator. Let I_k be an ordinal categorical indicator. What should we expect of I_k as a potential good *poverty* indicator? In addition to referring to some kind of basic capability, need or right, to differ really from a welfare indicator, most of the categorical values of I_k should refer to different poverty statuses, more or less acute, instead of describing many different levels of welfare. Consider the following example of housing conditions, linked to the following six categories in a household questionnaire:

a) temporary house
b) semi-permanent house
c) one-storey permanent house
d) two-storey permanent house with one toilet
e) two-storey permanent house with two toilets
f) more than two-storey permanent house.

We can consider that the last four categories are too detailed for a good *poverty* indicator and that only the following three are really relevant:

a) temporary house
b) semi-permanent house
c) permanent house,

the last one representing the non-poverty status for basic good "decent dwelling conditions," and the first one referring to an extreme poverty status in that regard.

We thus define a *pure categorical poverty indicator* I_k, with J_k categories, as one which meets the following conditions:

I.   It has an ordinal structure.
II. The lowest category $I_{k,1}$ refers to an extreme poverty status in reference to the basic need (good, right) considered.
III. The highest category I_{k,J_k} is considered as the non-poverty status, meaning that once you reach this status, there is a general agreement that you have exited this particular dimension of poverty.

---

[2] By micro-measurement, we mean measurement at the individual or household level.

[3] There are different optimization techniques for discretizing a quantitative variable, e.g. cluster analysis. Any process of discretization should nevertheless be aware of the information loss thus involved (Kolenikov and Angeles (2004)). The information loss should not be overweighted in case of variables bearing usually significant measurement errors like household income and expenditure.

If condition III is not met, there is more than one non-poverty category, and the term "extended categorical poverty" indicator will be used.

In fact, the idea we try to catch with this definition is what is called a *censored variable* in the money-metric analysis of poverty, once a poverty line has been determined. The important point here, in the context of primary indicators for measuring multidimensional poverty, is that we should think of ensuring, at the step of the questionnaire design, the possibility of building such types of pure poverty indicators, which will prove to be extremely productive and efficient at the analysis stage, as seen in Chapter 4. In the particular and frequent case of a binomial indicator, the critical issue is to identify a good whose deprivation really means a status of extreme or at least unquestionable poverty, instead of one whose possession represents obviously a non-poverty status. That's why some goods appearing sometimes in asset poverty like refrigerator, car, and electricity are dubious as poverty indicators.

Regarding the very first requirement, ordinality of the primary indicator, note that there is in multidimensionality a quite subtle issue that does not arise in money-metric poverty, the *non-applicability* issue. The multidimensional approach frequently identifies very good poverty indicators applicable only to a specific socioeconomic subgroup of the statistical units appearing in a given database. Let us think of households as statistical units. It is difficult to conceive of a household as having no income. Now take a multidimensional example. A variable often used as a proxy for farm income is the *ownership of agricultural assets*; another one is the *cultivation technology*. But these variables do not apply to all households, not even to all rural households: they make sense only for farming households. If a specific category is defined as *n.a. (not applicable)*, there is no obvious ordinal relation with the other categories relative to such variables. An alternative proposed by some software, random imputation of *n.a.* considered as missing values, is not really acceptable. Either all households are kept in the analysis, and then such non-universal variables are left out, or the domain of analysis is restricted to a subgroup, e.g., the socioeconomic group of farming households. Similar examples can be found with variables relevant only for specific age groups of women, of children, etc. The most operational approach to such situations, with a view to keep in the analysis all of the important indicators, seems to be a *multilevel poverty analysis*, where at the first level a core set of primary indicators, applicable to all population units, is used for *general poverty measurement* allowing for poverty comparisons within the entire population, followed by a second level with an extended set of indicators specific to some important socioeconomic groups, for *specific poverty* comparisons within these groups.

2.1.1 Multidimensionality of Some Empirical Poverty Vectors

Although it presents a technical challenge for measurement, the income approach to poverty has a great advantage: it is conceptually simple. Income poverty is essentially defined as the deprivation of the capacity to buy goods and services supplied by the market, or for which there is a shadow market price. For measuring this capacity, own-produced goods and services are valued at their market price. Multidimensional poverty, which is conceptually richer, is conversely exposed to an important problem: an important diversity in its measurement, which is primarily a reflection of the diversity of its definition, which is frequently not even explicitly given. This is a handicap for multidimensional poverty analysis when we try to compare different applied research work. Which poverty is a paper talking about?

Multidimensional poverty data are nowadays abundantly collected everywhere and particularly in developing countries. With this book's announced focus on operationalization, we will consider practicable approaches to multidimensional poverty measurement from the perspective of the poverty concept expressed in definition above – namely, poverty with a human face – with ten dimensions. Some empirical cases that have resulted from important consensual efforts can help open our eyes to the measurement constraints, the nature and the reliability of the indicators used, the size of the poverty vector, as well as its conceptual content. After some comments on these empirical vectors, we formalize the poverty concept implemented in each of them. We will see that measurement approaches with different vectors of indicators internalize an implicit weighting of different facets of poverty. Finally, we propose a more refined and operational tool for a quick comparison of the poverty concepts conveyed by different analytical works.

But first we rapidly highlight some technical issues in building poverty indicators.

2.1.1.1 Two Technical Issues: Poverty by Inclusion and Specific Poverty

Poverty by Inclusion

Set inclusion, applied to demographic entities, generates two types of transmission of poverty between statistical units linked by inclusion: exogenous and endogenous poverty.

The most well-known example of *exogenous poverty* is the association of income poverty to each household member if the household is considered as poor, according say to his *per capita* expenditure level. The statistical unit is poor because the demographic unit to which it belongs is poor in some dimension. We easily imagine to which extent this exogeneity can expand the poverty vector when we come to multidimensional poverty: all household poverty characteristics (housing, safe water access, etc.) trickle down to all household members, all community poverty characteristics (unavailability of different services, infrastructures, etc.) trickle down to all households in the community.

Endogenous transmission of poverty goes the other direction: a demographic unit is poor if some of his members are poor at their own level. Some aggregation technique is needed, and the universally known case is the measurement of the poverty incidence (poverty count) at a community level, from household (or individual) poverty. In the multidimensional case, the poverty vector of the demographic unit (community) explodes according to the size of the poverty vector of his members. This raises aggregation difficulties since members of the demographic unit have specific poverty vectors, as appears easily with the case of household/household members. This takes us to the second issue of specific poverty.

2.1.1.2 Specific Poverty

Any concept of multidimensional poverty,[4] e.g., the definition proposed here in our introduction, translates to different poverty characteristics or situations according to whether individuals belong to some age-sex groups: infants, school-age children, working-age adults, 15–49 women, old people, etc. A farming household may be considered as requiring some specific conditions to get out of poverty. We easily see that aggregating individual poverty vectors at the household level is not as straightforward as we would like, due to the heterogeneous demographic structure of households. We raise this issue here because the concept of multidimensional poverty opens the way, with its internal richness, to some complexities in the processing of specific poverty vectors. This situation may suggest the systematization of different poverty types and the recognition that aggregation processes may be much more complex than in the standard money-metric approach.

2.1.2 Poverty Vectors for Local Comparisons

Poverty measurement is frequently needed at the community level (village, city blocks), for managing local development, implementing decentralization policies, fine-targeting of poverty reduction programs, etc. It usually requires a survey of the whole community (a census), frequently initiated by a community questionnaire which takes stock of community assets. This is the case with the community-based monitoring system (CBMS) approach to poverty measurement. Once implemented on a large scale in some parts of a country, it unavoidably generates requests for poverty comparisons between local communities. Consider two poverty vectors built to meet these needs: the Philippine and the Burkina Faso CBMS. The list of indicators provided by each of them is given in Appendix B, *Lists of Indicators of Some Local, National, and International Poverty Measurement Initiatives*.

A comparison of these two lists of indicators suggests the following:

a) the poverty vectors have approximately the same size, 37 and 40 indicators;
b) "education" and "health," thus human capital, dominate clearly in the Burkina Faso CBMS and are more important than in the Philippine case;
c) the Philippine CBMS has an important component, "access to markets," which is missing in Burkina Faso;

---

[4] This issue has already been addressed above in 2.1 from the standpoint of the ordinality requirement.

d) the "income" component is completely different in both systems. The Philippine CBMS tries to measure total income while the Burkina Faso CBMS looks at the ownership of some durable goods and at a specific type of expenditure as a proxy to the level of income;

e) the "education" component in Burkina Faso is richer by incorporating aspects of achievement, success, and persistence in the educational system, which is related to the quality of education, not only to its availability; and

f) the social capital component ("participation/social peace") is much less important in Burkina Faso than in Philippine. It concerns only participation whereas the Philippine CBMS also pays attention to violence in the society.

Thus, the structural analysis of these two lists of indicators shows that there is an implicit weighting of the poverty dimensions in the Philippine and in the Burkina Faso CBMS. Different facets of the poverty dimensions are reflected in the two systems.

2.1.3 Poverty Vectors for National Comparisons

The request for poverty measurement at the national level typically originates from the preparation of Poverty Reduction Strategy (PRS) exercises, which have been implemented in most less-developed countries. Some within-country disaggregation (regions, provinces, urban/rural) is basically mandatory. Appendix B gives the official list of the 24 priority indicators integrated in the monitoring system of the Burkina Faso PRS exercise. Also provided is the standard list of indicators given by an international tool, the Core Welfare Indicators Questionnaire (CWIQ) survey by the World Bank, designed mainly to monitor regularly the progress of developing countries in basic welfare dimensions. It is frequently used, after local customization, as the main source of information to monitor PRS exercises.

We observe that

a. the CWIQ is quantitatively more developed with 41 indicators, but the Burkina Faso PRS basic system covers all ten poverty dimensions, while the CWIQ ignores "participation/social peace";

b. the CWIQ emphasizes "labor/employment" much more than the Burkina Faso PRS system;

c. the "income" component is completely different. The Burkina Faso priority system tries to approximate total agricultural income through the measurement of grain production, while the CWIQ has no money-metric or quantitative income indicator, since it only considers the ownership of durable goods and the perception of change in the household economic situation;

d. the "education" component is also quite different. The Burkina Faso PRS exercise concentrates on the primary level and literacy, while the CWIQ ignores literacy, but considers also the secondary level and insists on accessibility; and

e. in the "health" component, the CWIQ concentrates on the use of infrastructure
   and services (types of care providers), but ignores child mortality and immunization which are present in the Burkina Faso PRS paper.

2.1.4 Poverty Vectors for International Comparisons

Major international initiatives aim to focus and coordinate the efforts of partners
to development, especially those involved in international aid, on specific aspects
of poverty whose eradication should be prioritized. The operationalization of these
initiatives comes out with lists of indicators to assess the progress of each developing
country toward precise targets. These indicators thus allow international comparisons.

In Appendix B, we present the list of indicators of two well-known international
initiatives, the Millennium Development Goals (MDG) indicators and the Multiple
Indicators Cluster Survey (MICS) developed by UNICEF. For the MDG, we con-
centrate on human poverty and thus on the first seven goals, goal #8, "Develop a
global partnership for development," being left out.[5] From the start, it is known that
the UNICEF MICS intends to measure in depth the specific poverty of mothers and
children. In addition, consistency with some MDG indicators is looked for and this
appears in the labeling of indicators, where the appearance of a number refers to the
corresponding MDG indicator. This said, it is still interesting to compare the two
lists of indicators.

We observe that

a) the MICS provides an impressive list of 81 indicators, more than double the
   MDG list of 38 indicators;
b) in both cases, "health" and "education," thus human capital, dominate completely
   with more than 60% of the indicators. This percentage is even higher, 70%, for
   the MICS;
c) "access to markets" is missing in both lists and in addition "access to productive
   assets" is not present in the MICS;
d) "food and nutrition" is relatively much more important in the MICS than in the
   MDG;
e) the "income" component is almost completely absent from the MICS with only
   one indicator, the ownership of a durable good closely linked to "health." In
   contrast, this same component comes in third position in the MDG, where it is
   measured by the classical money-metric indicators;
f) the "education" dimension in MICS includes an important facet absent from the
   MDG, the preschool level, including at-home support for learning; and
g) "participation/social peace" is almost absent from the MDG, while it is important in the MICS with many FGC (female genital cutting) indicators, which we

---

[5] The indicator label includes the numbering specific to MDG.

choose to consider here as a form of domestic violence, instead of classifying it in the health domain.[6]

These two lists of indicators could also be compared with the four previous ones, since by the mechanisms of aggregation and disaggregation they can eventually provide a poverty measure on a same population unit: the country itself, some regions, etc. But it should be obvious that more synthetic tools are required to facilitate and systematize such comparisons, which are important to highlight divergences and convergences in different concepts of multidimensional poverty.

2.2 Tools for Multidimensionality Comparative Analysis

The exercise of the three previous sections demonstrates some empirical facts:

a) applied work aiming at measuring multidimensional poverty usually comes out with a large number of indicators: in our six case studies, this number is around 40 in four cases, and the average number of indicators is 44. Thus, analytical tools like composite indicators or indices should be operational for sets of some dozens of indicators or indices;
b) there is a very large diversity of indicators, even within specific poverty dimensions. In fact, we have seen that allocating the indicators across ten poverty dimensions is not enough for comparing the poverty concepts conveyed by two lists of indicators and to derive the implicit weights given to different facets of poverty. A finer classification tool is definitely needed.

The empirical processes of analyzing many lists of indicators, of which the six of Appendix B are just a sample, have raised the necessity of identifying within each poverty dimension specific subcategories of indicators which can be called "generic indicators." A generic indicator describes a facet of poverty specific to the dimension to which it belongs. How many generic indicators are needed to classify the huge amount of indicators currently used? For the hundreds of indicators we have analyzed, the 45 generic indicators presented in Fig. 2.1 appear both sufficient and relevant.

This poverty matrix structure (PMS) is proposed as a succinct tool for describing explicitly the poverty concept conveyed by a given list of indicators and the underlying weighting associated with the list. A generic indicator (facet of poverty) can be located by its two coordinates, e.g., D2-03 refers to literacy. We do not present and discuss here each of the 45 generic indicators of Fig. 2.1, hoping that their labels are

---

[6] This methodological choice illustrates the fact, which may be obvious from Annex 1.2, that a classification operation cannot be run as an automatism and that some conventions have to be established, a major reason being that the same indicator can sometimes be classified in different poverty dimensions or facets.

	01	02	03	04	05	06	07	08
D1. Income	Income proxy	Ownership of durable goods	Typical expenditures	Perception of economic situation				
D2. Education	Primary enrolment	Secondary enrolment	Literacy	Drop-out rate	IEC resources (Info/Educ to Communic)	Access to school infrastructure services	Education level achieved	Pre-school
D3. Health	Infant/child mortality	Maternal mortality	Morbidity to handicap incidence	Access to health infrastructure services	Specific disease prevention treatment			
D4. Food/Nutrition	Malnutrition	Food security status						
D5. Water/Sanitation	Sources of drinking water	Sanitation facilities						
D6. Employment/labor	Unemployment inactivity	Underemployment	Categories of workers	Child labor	Wage rates			
D7. Housing (environment)	Housing characteristics	Home ownership	Sources of energy	Living environment				
D8. Access to productive assets	Land distribution	Irrigated land	Productive assets (agricultural & others)	Access to credit	Information technology	Production techniques		
D9. Access to markets	Price of basic commodities	Access to market infrastructure	Access to services	Access to roads				
D10. Participation/Social peace	Crime incidence	Domestic violence	Social participation	Participation in election	Access to public meeting infrastructure			

Fig. 2.1 Poverty matrix structure

sufficiently clear. In fact, the application of this PMS to numerous cases is the most practical way to make clear the meaning of each of them and to extend or modify the proposed table.

This tool, the PMS, has been applied to the six previous lists of indicators, an exercise which results in Fig. 2.2.

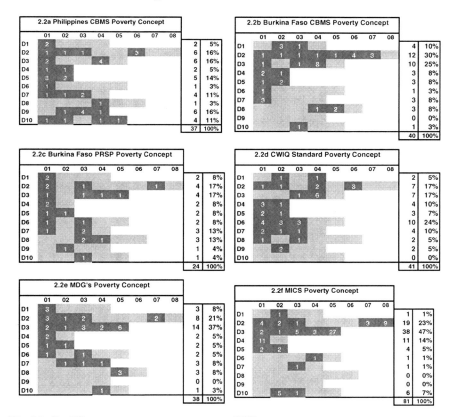

Fig. 2.2 Six different poverty concept structures (PCS)

The poverty concept structure (PCS) of a given list of indicators is built this way from the PMS of Fig. 2.1:

a) the background gray area is always the same: it reproduces the structure of the general PMS of Fig. 2.1;
b) the black cells indicate which facet of poverty is represented in the given list of indicators, with the number of indicators. Thus, we can immediately visualize to which extent the poverty concept conveyed by the list represents the total number of possible facets and even see the implicit weight given to a specific facet;
c) the two columns on the extreme right give the total number and the percentage of indicators in each of the ten dimensions of poverty. It is then easy to

compare immediately, between two poverty concepts, the different implicit relative weights given to the dimensions of poverty D1–D10; and

d) the two extreme bottom-right cells provide the total number of indicators in the list analyzed (100%).

As primitive as it is, and hence obviously open to improvements, the PCS graphical representation can synthesize in one compact and standard format any given list of indicators, whatever its size. It can then facilitate a quick comparative analysis of different poverty concepts. Figure 2.2 for example summarizes in one page the content of 261 indicators and the structure of the six different lists providing them. Coming back to the comments formulated in Sections 2.1.2, 2.1.3, and 2.1.4, it is easy to check how much easier and more precise they can now be done and communicated with reference to Figs. 2.1 and 2.2.

Let us add a few comments to illustrate the ease provided by the PCS tool:

1. the Burkina Faso CBMS poverty concept, coming out of 40 indicators in 9 poverty dimensions, is more deeply rooted in human capital than the Burkina Faso PRSP poverty concept conveyed by a priority list of 24 indicators. This last one is more balanced and covers the 10 poverty dimensions. The facets of "income" are completely different in the two concepts, and the facets of "education" are particularly rich in the CBMS concept.

2. Structurally, the Burkina Faso CBMS poverty concept is closer to the MDG poverty concept, while the Burkina Faso PRSP poverty concept is closer to the standard CWIQ one.

3. The Philippine CBMS poverty concept is closer to the Burkina Faso PRSP poverty concept than to the Burkina Faso CBMS poverty concept.

4. The MICS poverty concept is unique with an implicit weight of 84% on "education," "health," and "malnutrition." Five more poverty dimensions can still be found in such a focused survey.

Figure 2.2 can obviously generate many more such comments.

Chapter 3
Composite Indicator of Poverty

As stated in the introduction, our main objective is to operationalize multidimensional poverty comparisons. After some clarification on this objective and on a first methodological choice in Section 3.1, Section 3.2 presents a quick review of the main methodologies used to build a composite indicator of poverty (CIP). Our second methodological choice takes us to a short presentation of different variants of factorial approaches and to the argument supporting our third methodological choice, the multiple correspondence analysis (MCA) technique (Section 3.3). Finally, Section 3.4 develops the MCA technique and illustrates it with a numerical case study on Vietnam.

3.1 Individual and Population Poverty Comparisons

For discussion, it is important to clarify the terminology regarding the three concepts of *poverty indicator, poverty measure,* and *poverty index.* Let I_{ik} be the value of indicator I_k for the elementary population unit i, called here individual i for simplication.[1] I_{ik} is then a *poverty indicator* value. The value I_{ik} can be transformed as $g_k(I_{ik})$, with the function g_k, to better reflect a poverty concept relative to indicator I_k. This is frequently the case, especially with a quantitative indicator I_k to which is associated a poverty threshold (poverty line) z_k. A basic transformation is simply the censoring of I_k at z_k to get I_k^*. In this case, well-known transformations are $g_k(I_{ki}^*) = (z_k - I_{ik}^*)^\alpha$ or $g_k(I_{ki}^*) = (1 - I_{ik}^*/z_k)^\alpha$. Then, $g_k(I_{ik})$ is called a *poverty measure* value, again defined for individual i. In the particular case where the function g_k is the identity function, the poverty indicator and the poverty measure are the same. Finally, poverty measure values can be aggregated over the units for the whole population U, as $W_k\{g_k(I_{ik}), i = 1, N\}$. W_k is then called a *poverty index* relative to the indicator I_k for the population U. Obviously, this index W_k can be

---

[1] The term "elementary population unit" can refer to individuals and households as well as to villages, regions and countries.

defined on any subpopulation of U consisting of n individuals, $n \geq 1$. For $n = 1$, the poverty index is a poverty measure on each individual.

Poverty indices are required for population comparisons, while poverty indicators and poverty measures are sufficient for comparisons between individuals.

An interesting review in Maasoumi (1999) first distinguishes between the literature addressing the issue of computing a *composite index of poverty* from a multidimensional distribution of poverty indicators on a given population, and the literature aiming at defining a *composite indicator of poverty* on each unit of the given population. The first type of this literature is well represented by Bourguignon and Chakravarty (1999). The first distinction, referring to Sen (1976), is between the identification and the aggregation problems. Any individual who is below the poverty threshold for at least one of the poverty attributes included in the poverty vector is identified as poor. It is thus the union concept of poverty that is used here, in contrast with the intersection concept. The aggregation technique relies on an axiomatic approach to the desired properties of the composite index, largely based on standard axioms enunciated for a univariate poverty index, and on a composite poverty measure referring to a given poverty threshold for each primary indicator. The implicit context is thus a set of quantitative indicators and the resulting index is usually relevant only for that type of indicators. In fact, the composite poverty measure proposed by Bourguignon and Chakravarty is a CES function of the shortfalls (poverty gaps) in each of the primary poverty indicators. Since the direct focus of this approach is on a poverty index, it is called a *one-step* approach to multidimensional poverty indices.

It should be obvious, on the other hand, that solving in a first step the problem of building a numerical composite indicator of poverty opens the way to computing a composite poverty index based on the composite indicator, relying then on the univariate theory of poverty indices. This approach is designated as a *two-step* approach to multidimensional poverty indices, where the focus is mainly on justifying a methodology for the composite indicator, the most critical part of the whole process.

This two-step approach is our first methodological choice.

We are thus also taken away from the multidimensional stochastic dominance theory, extension of the well-known unidimensional one. It can be found in Duclos, Sahn, and Younger (2006). We can see it as another one-step approach, since the focus is on classes of multidimensional poverty indices. This theory releases poverty comparisons from having to make arbitrary choices of poverty lines and poverty indices by looking at the relative position of distribution functions and at identifying regions where a distribution "surface" is over or under another one. This ordinal approach presents the theoretical interest of clarifying necessary and sufficient conditions for the robustness of comparisons. Difficulties remain for the operationalization: since the identification of dominance regions is often uneasy in a two-dimensional case, we can expect difficulties when the number of primary indicators can amount to tens, and when sampling errors must be taken into account in applied work. There is obviously an important trade-off here between the degree of robustness, here placed at a high level, and the power of the dominance tests.

Due to its central role in a two-step approach, the rest of this chapter focuses on the first step, the construction of a composite indicator of poverty (CIP).

3.2   Overview of Methodologies for a Composite Indicator of Poverty (First Step)

In what follows, a *composite indicator of poverty* (CIP) C takes the value $C_i(I_{ik}, k = 1, K)$ for a given elementary population unit U_i.

3.2.1   CIP Based on Inequality Indices: Entropy Concepts, Shorrocks Index

Theil (1967) has first observed that Shannon's entropy $I_n(y)$

$$I_n(y) = \sum_{i=1}^{n} yi \log 2 \frac{1}{yi} = - \sum_{i=1}^{n} yi \log 2 yi$$

where y represents the *income shares* in a population of n units, constitutes a natural measure of income equality, taking the maximal value $\log_2 n$ when every unit has the same income. The corresponding *inequality* measure is then taken as the difference between the maximal entropy (from a uniform distribution) and $I_n(y)$:

$$\log 2n - I_n(y) = \sum_{i=1}^{n} yi \log 2 \left(\frac{yi}{1/n} \right). \tag{3.1}$$

We thus observe that equation 3.1 is the Rényi information gain or divergence measure $I_1(q||p)$,[2] where we take $q = y$ and $p = \{1/n\}$, the uniform distribution. It is called Theil's first inequality index.[3]

The pioneering work of Theil on entropy-based inequality indices has generated a search for larger classes of inequality indices, on the basis of desirable properties defined with respect to redistributions of income in a given population. In particular, the requirement of additively decomposable inequality indices has led to important results by Shorrocks (1980). He proved that the only admissible indices satisfying,

---

[2] The concept of « divergence » between two distributions belongs to information theory. It is not a metric as defined mathematically. The general expression of the Rényi divergence measure, which he calls «information gain », between two distributions q and p is $I_1(q||p) = \sum_{k=1}^{n} q_k \log_2 \frac{q_k}{p_k}$. For details, see Rényi (1966).

[3] To be more precise, Theil and other authors use the natural logarithm in base e instead of base 2; from now on, we will not specify the base.

among others, the decomposable additivity axiom belong to the following class[4]:

$$I_\gamma(y) = \frac{1}{n}\frac{1}{\gamma(\gamma-1)}\sum_{i=1}^{n}\left[\left(\frac{y_i}{1/n}\right)^\gamma - 1\right] \text{ for } \gamma \neq 0.1, \tag{3.2}$$

$$I_\gamma^1(y) = \sum_{i=1}^{n} y_i \log\left(\frac{y_i}{1/n}\right).$$

$$I_\gamma^0(y) = \sum_{i=1}^{n} 1/n \log\left(\frac{1/n}{y_i}\right)$$

Observe that equation 3.2 can be written as

$$I_\gamma(y) = \frac{1}{\gamma(\gamma-1)}\sum_{i=1}^{n} y_i \left[\left(\frac{y_i}{1/n}\right)^{\gamma-1} - 1\right]. \tag{3.2'}$$

Obviously, $I_\gamma^1(y)$ is Theil's first inequality index, and $I_\gamma^0(y)$ is his second inequality index. This γ-class of entropy-based inequality indices is called the class of *Generalized Entropy* indices.

What we highlight here is that this axiomatic development of inequality indices generates a class of divergence measures including, as a particular case, the Rényi's information gain measure $I_1(q||p)$. In fact, the case $\gamma = 1$ corresponds to $I_1(q||p)$ where we take p= {1/n}, and the case $\gamma = 0$ corresponds to $I_1(q||p)$ where we take q = {1/n}. The γ-class of inequality indices is an *asymmetric* measure of divergence between a distribution y and the uniform distribution p = {1/n}.

Maasoumi (1986) relies on these developments of information theory to propose his entropy approach to the composite indicator problem. He looks for a general inter-distributional distance as a basis to derive the composite indicator C from an optimization criterion. Let us observe that the Generalized Entropy index 3.2' generates a divergence measure between *any* two distributions x and y if we substitute a distribution x to the uniform distribution {1/n} appearing as the denominator. This is precisely the divergence measure taken by Maasoumi as the distance between the composite indicator we are looking for, C, and any one of the primary indicators I_k, k = 1, K. We thus have

$$D_\gamma(C, I_k) = \frac{1}{\gamma(\gamma-1)}\sum_{i=1}^{n} C_i \left[\left(\frac{C_i}{I_{ik}}\right)^{\gamma-1} - 1\right] \text{ for } \gamma \neq 0.1 \tag{3.3}$$

and obtain Theil's first and second measures for $\gamma = 1$ and 0 respectively.

---

[4] We write the indices directly in terms of income shares instead of using mean income μ, in order to keep more clearly the link with the theory of distributions.

Maasoumi then proposes to define the optimal indicator as the C that minimizes a *weighted sum of the pairwise divergences*, i.e., the C that minimizes

$$D_\gamma(C, I; \delta) = \sum_{k=1}^{K} \delta_k \left\{ \frac{\sum_{i=1}^{N} C_i \left[\left(\frac{C_i}{I_{ik}} \right)^{\gamma-1} - 1 \right]}{\gamma(\gamma - 1)} \right\} \quad (3.4)$$

where the δ_k are *arbitrary* weights on the divergence component relative to the indicator I_k, $\sum \delta_k = 1$.[5]

By minimizing the divergence $D_\beta(C, I, \delta)$ for the function C, Maasoumi finds the following functional form for the composite indicator:

$$C_i = \left(\sum_{k=1}^{K} \delta_k I_{ik}^{-\gamma} \right)^{-1/\gamma} \quad \gamma \neq 0, -1 \quad (3.5)$$

We recognize here a CES function. For the two specific values $\gamma = 0, -1$, the functional forms are

$$C_i = \prod_{k=1}^{K} I_{ik}^{\delta_k}, \text{ for } \gamma = 0. \quad (3.6)$$

$$C_i = \sum_{k=1}^{K} \delta_k I_{ik}, \text{ for } \gamma = -1. \quad (3.7)$$

Conclusion on the entropy inequality indices approach

1. The whole context of entropy inequality indices, including the associated divergence concept, refers to probability distributions, i.e., to numerical measures taking values in the interval (0.1). Thus, and as can be seen particularly from the divergence measure generated by the Generalized Entropy Index, the natural domain of application for our problem is a set of meaningful numerical indicators, i.e., of quantitative poverty indicators, expressed in terms of "shares," so that the individual value I_{ik} is in the interval (0.1). The money-metric type of poverty indicators, once transformed in individual shares, appears as the domain of validity of a functional form like equation 3.5.
2. There is an important source of indetermination with the parametric nature of the Maasoumi composite indicator. On what basis should we choose the parameter

---

[5] The parametrization used by Maasoumi for the γ-class is slightly different from Shorrocks's one, followed here until now. Maasoumi's parameter γ is Shorrocks's -1. From now on, we will use Maasoumi's γ.

value for the γ-Generalized Entropy indices? A strong point can be made for the
values $\gamma = 1$ and $\gamma = 0$, which provide a simple linear (log-linear) form.[6]

3. If the weighting approach is maintained for the optimization criterion, obviously
   there remains the problem of determining the weights δ_k in a nonarbitrary way.
   There is in fact an optimal system of weights for the functional form (B), as
   Maasoumi (1999) has himself observed: the basic factorial method of principal
   components. This is precisely the type of methods that is reviewed below.

3.2.2 CIP Based on Poverty Structure Analysis: Inertia Concepts, Factorial Approaches

To a K-dimensional poverty vector is associated a K-dimensional distribution. In
some sense, the previous approach looks at the marginal distributions of the primary indicators I_k. A kind of distance between these marginal distributions, the
divergence measure, serves as a basis for identifying a "mean" distribution which
provides the CIP. It is like looking at the multidimensional distribution from outside,
from an external viewpoint. Another viewpoint is to look at the distribution from
inside, trying to identify the numerous associations between the poverty dimensions determining the global form of the poverty "mass" dispersion. It is a search
for a poverty structure, an internal viewpoint. Intuitively, this is what any factorial
technique tries to operationalize, relying on the central concept of inertia which is
in fact a measure of the global dispersion of the distribution. Going through this
structural analysis, we can hope to come out with a CIP summarizing the most
relevant information identified in the distribution.

This structural approach to multidimensional poverty analysis can be seen as
an empirical step to implement the analysis of interconnections between different
freedoms that Sen calls for to assess the effectiveness of development.[7]

Let us consider an example with two numerical indicators, x_1, money income,
and x_2, area of agricultural land. Simply by representing the data in the R^2-space of
individuals (here, households), we could see figures such as Figs. 3.1, 3.2, 3.3, and
3.4.[8]

In Case 1, money income and land area are perfectly correlated. It could be
approximately observed in a highly agricultural country with an easy access to
markets. An obvious way to rank the households with just one number is to use
for each of them their relative position on line Δ. This position, y, is given by the
linear function

$$y = \beta_1 X_1 + \beta_2 X_2 \tag{3.8}$$

---

[6] On this, see Asselin (2002) for a more extensive review of the entropy and information theory
approach.

[7] Sen (1999), p.4

[8] Variables are supposed to be centered.

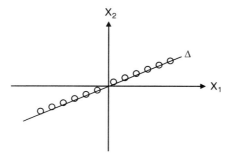

Fig. 3.1 Case 1

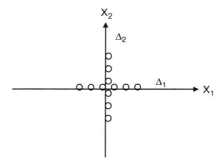

Fig. 3.2 Case 2

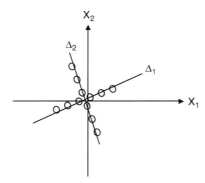

Fig. 3.3 Case 3

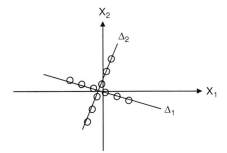

Fig. 3.4 Case 4

where the unit vector $\beta = \begin{pmatrix} \beta_1 \\ \beta_2 \end{pmatrix}$ identifies the support of line Δ, $\beta_1 > 0$, $\beta_2 > 0$.
Equation 3.8 is thus a very relevant CIP. Cases 2, 3, and 4 are clearly situations
where there are two groups of households. Looking further at the two groups of
households on each line, we could discover that on Δ_1 lie urban households whereas
on Δ_2 we find rural households. Lines Δ_1 and Δ_2 would then express two types of
poverty: urban and rural poverty. The extreme situation of Case 2 could plausi-
bly correspond to a country where the rural area is completely disconnected from
markets. In Case 2, using the position on line Δ_1 as a global poverty indicator
would formally be acceptable but would then not allow to discriminate between
rural households. The same is true with line Δ_2 and urban households then being
not discriminated. A better composite indicator should be proposed using both lines.
Cases 3 and 4 are intermediate situations. In Case 3, the line Δ_1 could be eligible as
a global poverty indicator, even if it does not discriminate between rural households.
The vector β has the expected positive signs, and the fact is that rural households
compensate a lower area of land with a higher money income, maybe by selling
their labor force to larger farms. In case 4, the line Δ_2 could be eligible, with a
positive vector β and no discrimination between urban households, these possibly
leaving agricultural production for better opportunities in the labor market. But even
in cases 3 and 4, a deeper analysis could suggest a better composite indicator than
line Δ_1 or Δ_2. Finally, Case 5 shows a situation where the position on line Δ cannot
be taken as a composite indicator of poverty, due to the negative sign of β_2. But it
can be seen that there is more dispersion in x_1 than in x_2 and this fact can eventually
be exploited (Fig. 3.5).

This internal visualization of the multidimensional distribution from the individual (household) viewpoint, i.e., from the line-points of the data matrix X^9 seen in
the R^2-space, has a counterpart from the variable viewpoint, i.e., from the column-
points seen in the R^N-space, where N is the number of individuals in the distribution.
In our case, with $N = 12$ individuals, the two column-vectors determine a plan

---

[9] The convention used here is that in a matrix X, lines correspond to the statistical units (individuals) and columns to the variables (indicators).

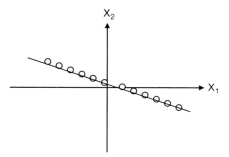

Fig. 3.5 Case 5

in the R^{12}-space, which degenerates in a single line in Cases 1 and 5. Figure 3.6 summarizes Cases 1–5.

Fig. 3.6 Case 1

All these examples suggest that detecting poverty structures, let us say poverty types, through lines like Δ, Δ_1, and Δ_2 can be seen as a promising approach to know more about the real multidimensionality in a given population and to the emergence of a relevant composite indicator of this poverty. This is precisely what a factorial

Fig. 3.7 Case 5

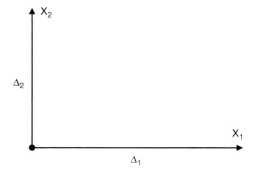

Fig. 3.8 Case 2, 3, 5

approach tries to systematize. Principal component analysis (PCA) is now taken as an example of what can be achieved in that direction (Figs. 3.7 and 3.8).

Essentially, PCA consists in building a sequence of uncorrelated (orthogonal) and normalized linear combinations of input variables (K primary indicators), exhausting the whole variability of the set of input variables, named "total variance" and defined as the trace of their covariance matrix, thus the sum of the K variances. These uncorrelated linear combinations, in fact the lines Δ above and their related unitary vectors β, are latent variables called "components." The optimality in the process comes from the fact that the first component looked for has a maximal variance λ_1, the basic idea being to visualize the whole set of data in reduced spaces capturing most of the relevant information.

Let X(N,K) be the data matrix giving the distribution of the K numerical, centered, primary poverty indicators, K < N. From now on, let W be the normalized (unitary) K-dimensional vector[10] previously identified as β, and let $\Sigma = X'X$ be the covariance matrix. The problem of estimating the first component consists in finding a linear combination XW such that $W'\Sigma W$ is maximal under the constraint $W'W = 1$. With λ as the Lagrange multiplier, the problem consists in solving the equation

$$(\Sigma - \lambda I)W = 0 \tag{3.9}$$

where I is the unit (K,K) matrix. There are different ways of solving equation 3.9, a frequent one being an iterative method.[11] The vector W is called an eigen or characteristic vector, and the value λ an eigen or characteristic value. The line whose support is given by W is called a factorial axis, and the word "factor" is also taken to be the same as "component." The K elements of W are called "factor-score coefficients."

All subsequent components α have decreasing variances λ_α whose sum is the total variance of the K indicators. This total variance is also named the *total inertia* of the distribution of the K indicators. The stepwise reduction process just described corresponds geometrically to a change in the Cartesian axis system (translation and rotation) of the K-dimension euclidean space R^K. It is neutral regarding the orientation of the factorial axis. The whole process relies on analyzing the structure of the covariance matrix of the K initial variables.

The first component F_1 is an interesting candidate for the composite indicator of poverty C, but it must satisfy obvious consistency conditions relative to the signs of the K elements of W. C has the following expression for the population unit i:

$$C_i = \sum_{k=1}^{K} W^{1,k} I_i^{*k}. \tag{3.10}$$

---

[10] W is a (K.1) column-vector.

[11] See Anderson (1958).

The I^{*k} are the standardized primary indicators, i.e., the columns of the data matrix X after standardization. The factor score coefficients $W^{1,k}$ must all be positive (negative) to interpret the first component as a decreasing (increasing) poverty indicator, depending on whether the primary indicators increase (decrease) when people become wealthier. At the end of the process, it comes out that the $W^{\alpha,k}$ are in fact the usual multiple regression coefficients between the component F_α and the standardized primary indicators. Built this way, the first component can be described *as the best regressed latent variable on the K primary poverty indicators.* No other explained variable is more informative, in the sense of explained variance.

3.2.3 The Fuzzy Subset Approach[12]

The fuzzy subset approach is motivated by the artificial dichotomization between the poor and the non-poor, which is determined by a poverty line whose definition is rarely uncontroversial. Let x be a welfare indicator, e.g., total expenditure per capita, which we want to use as a poverty indicator. The starting idea is then to transform x in x' = 1 − F(x), where F(x) is the distribution function of x. x', taking its values in [0.1), is then interpreted as a degree of poverty and the function $1 - F(x)$ is called a membership function. Clearly this definition can be applied also to any categorical discrete ordinal indicator, which is then recoded as a numerical indicator. In this categorical case, Betti et al. (2006) use instead the definition

$$x' = \{1 - F(x)/1 - F(x_1)\} \tag{3.11}$$

where x_1 is the smallest value taken by the indicator. The poorest individuals then take the value 1, and the richest, the value 0.

Suppose now there are K indicators with transformed values x'^k according to equation 3.11, and the value $x'^{k,1}$ for individual i. The composite indicator C is then defined as the weighted average:

$$C_i = \frac{\sum_{k=1}^{K} Wkx'k, i}{\sum_{k=1}^{K} wk} \tag{3.12}$$

where w_k is an indicator weight defined a priori from the average $\overline{x'k}$ of x'^k:

$$wk = \ln \frac{1}{x'k}. \tag{3.13}$$

---

[12] We follow here essentially Betti et al. (2006), focusing on the basic framework of the fuzzy approach.

It must be observed that, according to equation 3.11, $\overline{x'k}$ tends to be smaller with smaller frequencies of the most deprived ones (lower values of $x_1'^k$). In fact, for a dichotomous indicator, it gives $\overline{x'k} = \frac{N_1^k}{N}$, where N_1^k is the number of deprived individuals. Then the weight given to indicator k is larger with a smaller number of deprived people. "Thus deprivations which affect only a small proportion of the population, and hence are likely to be considered more critical, get larger weights; while those affecting large proportions, hence likely to be regarded as less critical, get smaller weights".[13]

We retain from the basic fuzzy approach that

a) it is immediately applicable to categorical ordinal indicators;
b) an important preliminary step before aggregation consists in a numerical rescaling of each primary indicator, based on marginal distributions; and
c) indicator weights are defined a priori from the marginal distributions allowing for greater importance given to less frequent deprivations.

At the end of this overview of methodologies for defining a composite indicator of poverty, our second methodological choice is to explore deeper the factorial approach, essentially since it seems a priori more promising, with its internal viewpoint, to articulate our understanding of multidimensionality, while offering at first sight an interesting proposal for a composite indicator. But some variants of the factorial techniques still need to be discussed.

3.3 Factorial Techniques

3.3.1 *Factor Analysis (FA)*[14] *and Principal Component Analysis (PCA)*

As seen above (Section 2.2.2), PCA is a factorial technique searching for a small set of independent *linear combinations of the K primary indicators*, called "components," to catch a maximal portion of the total variance of the distribution. When all possible components have been extracted, the whole variance is explained. The first component, accounting for the largest portion of the variance, is an interesting CIP candidate if some consistency conditions are met. This is the approach used by Filmer and Pritchett (1998) for their household asset index.

Factor analysis (FA) is the reverse way of exploring multidimensionality. It tries to identify *K linear combinations of m < K latent (nonobservable) variables*, called factors or communalities, able to predict the K observed indicators with as small an error as possible. More precisely, the predictive model to be estimated is[15]

---

[13] loc. cit.

[14] A specific technique not to be confounded with Factorial Analysis, which is a generic term.

[15] See Anderson (1958), Section 14.7.

$$I = \Lambda f + U \tag{3.14}$$

where I is the vector of the K primary indicators,[16] Λ is a (K,m)-matrix of *factor loadings*, f is an m-component vector of nonobservable factor scores and U is a K-vector of error. A difficult decision has to be made on the number m of factors to retain in the model. Different estimation techniques can be used, including a principal component approach. Clearly this modeling factorial technique does not respond directly to our research objective to get a CIP. But the m latent factors can in fact be expressed as linear combinations of the K primary indicators through equation[17] 3.15 linking factor-score coefficients and factor loadings:

$$W = \Sigma^{-1}\Lambda \tag{3.15}$$

where W is the (K,m) matrix of the *factor-score coefficients* as defined above with PCA and Σ^{-1} is the inverse covariance matrix[18] of the K primary indicators. Once the matrix W is obtained through equation 3.15, as in PCA, the first factor is an interesting candidate for a CIP, again if consistency conditions hold with the first factor-score coefficients. This is in fact the way Sahn and Stifel (2000) proceed to build a household asset index from data sets provided by the Demographic and Health Surveys (DHS), taking m = 1 in the model, i.e., only one factor.

In comparison with PCA, it should be noted here that "in PCA, multicollinearity is not a problem because there is no need to invert a matrix. For most forms of FA and for estimation of factor scores in any form of FA, singularity or extreme multicollinearity is a problem."[19]

In addition to being theoretically developed for numerical variables as PCA, for the objective of defining a CIP, the FA approach appears to us as an unnecessary detour with possible technical difficulties.

3.3.2 Multiple Correspondence Analysis (MCA) and PCA

Interesting as it is, the PCA technique has some limitations:

a) the whole technique has been developed for a set of quantitative variables, measured in the same units. The optimal sampling properties for parameter estimation depend on the multivariate normal distribution and do not any more exist with categorical variables[20];

---

[16] We suppose here that the K indicators are standardized.

[17] See Tabachnick and Fidell (2001), Chapter 13, *Principal Components and Factor Analysis*.

[18] Here a correlation matrix since the indicators are supposed already standardized.

[19] Tabachnick and Fidell (2001), p. 589.

[20] See, among others, Kolenikov and Angeles (2004) for a similar critique of using PCA with discrete data. The authors ignore MCA as a possible solution. They use a parametric approach based

b) the operationalization of the composite indicator, for population units not involved in the sample used for estimation, is not very appealing since weights are applicable to *standardized* primary indicators. Particularly, standardization adds some ambiguity in a dynamic analysis where the base-year weights are kept constant, as we think they should.

Since concepts of multidimensional poverty are frequently measured with categorical ordinal indicators, for which PCA is not a priori an optimal approach, looking for a similar but more appropriate factorial technique is justified. Here comes naturally into the picture multiple correspondence analysis (MCA), designed in the 1960s and 1970s[21] to improve the PCA approach when the latter loses its parametric estimation optimal properties and to provide more powerful description tools of the hidden structure in a set of categorical variables.

The most important technical difference between PCA and MCA is the use of the χ^2 metric (chi-square), instead of the usual Euclidean metric used in PCA, to measure distances between two lines or two columns of the data matrix being analyzed. This χ^2 metric has been introduced into the area of factorial analysis in the years 1960–1970 by the French school of statistics led by J.-P. Benzécri, and then appeared as factorial techniques specifically designed for categorical variables "Correspondence Analysis" (CA) and its extension "Multiple Correspondence Analysis" (MCA).

From now on, we will assume that the K primary indicators are categorical ordinals, the indicator I_k having J_k categories. This is a very general setting, applicable to any mix of quantitative and categorical poverty indicators, since a quantitative variable can always be redefined in terms of a finite number of categories. Let us associate with each primary indicator I_k the set of J_k binary variable 0/1, each corresponding to a category of the indicator. We introduce the following notation:

1. X(N,J): the matrix of N observations on the K indicators decomposed into J_k binary variables, where $J = \sum\limits_{k=1}^{K} J_k$ is the total number of categories. X is named the *indicatrix matrix*.
2. N_j: the absolute frequency of category j, i.e., the sum of column j of X;
3. N': the sum of the elements of matrix X, i.e., N × K;
4. $f_j = \frac{N_j}{N'}$: the relative frequency of category j $f_j^i = \frac{X(i,j)}{X(i)}$, where X($i$) is the sum of line i of the matrix X. The set $f_j^i = \left\{ f_j^i, j = 1, J \right\}$ is named the profile of observation i.

---

on the multivariate normal distribution and the estimation of a polychoric correlation coefficient matrix.

[21] The French school of data analysis led by Benzécri has been particularly creative and influential in the development of correspondence analysis.

MCA is a PCA process applied to the indicatrix matrix X, i.e., to the set of the J binary variables in the R^N space, transformed into profiles, but with the χ^2 metric on row/column profiles, instead of the usual Euclidean metric.

The χ^2 metric is in fact a special case of the Mahalanobis metric developed in the 1930s and used in Generalized Canonical Analysis. It takes here the following form, for the distance between two observed profiles i and i' in the R^J space:

$$d^2\left(f_J^i, f_J^{i'}\right) = \sum_{j=1}^{J} \left(\frac{1}{f_j}\right)\left(f_j^i - f_j^{i'}\right)^2. \qquad (3.16)$$

The only difference with the Euclidean metric lies in the term $\left(\frac{1}{f_j}\right)$, by which low-frequency categories receive a higher weight in the computation of distance.

The χ^2 metric has two important properties not possessed by the Euclidean metric[22]: the distributional equivalence property and the duality property. The χ^2 metric is directly linked to statistics used in very old statistical tests like the Pearson χ^2-test of the theoretical distribution of a given empirical distribution and the Pearson χ^2-test of the independence of two categorical variables presented in a two-way frequency table.

The distributional equivalence property means that the distance between two lines (individuals, households, etc.) of the profile matrix remains invariant if two identical columns (poverty variable) are merged, or if we add to the data matrix a column identical to another one. And symmetrically, for modifying lines and keeping invariant the distance between columns. Concretely, it means that the factorial analysis run with the χ^2 metric, as with MCA, is quite robust (stable, invariant), to the way a set of categorical variables, as poverty indicators, is built: extending a set of indicators with closely correlated additional indicators, defining categories within a same indicator, etc. PCA, with the Euclidean metric, is sensitive to such transformations. This theoretical property is empirically observed and illustrated in references given in the preceding footnote.

The duality property is explicitly presented with the duality equations 3.18a and 3.18b. These equations are also referred to in the literature as "transition" or "barycentric" equations.[23] This duality property is the theoretical basis (see the literature just referred to) allowing the simultaneous representation, in the same factorial plane, of the lines (individuals, households), often aggregated in socioeconomic groups, and of the columns (poverty attributes). This simultaneous representation, unique to MCA, is a very powerful exploration tool for the identifi-

---

[22] That these properties are specific to the χ^2 metric can be found in Benzécri J.P. and F. Benzécri (1980), pp. 37–40, Greenacre M. and J. Blasius (1994), p. 35, and Lebart L., A. Morineau and M. Piron (1990), p. 74.

[23] The duality equations can be found in Benzécri J.P. and F. Benzécri (1980), pp. 80–90, Lebart L., A. Morineau and M. Piron (1990), pp. 75–79, and Greenacre M. and J. Blasius (1994), p. 14.

cation of poverty determinants, associated with poverty types. In fact, this property, much more than the distributional equivalence one, is the main advantage of MCA for applying factorial concepts and methods to multidimensional poverty analysis.

To sum up, due to using the χ^2 metric, the difference between MCA and PCA shows up particularly in two properties which seem highly relevant for the poverty meaning of the numerical results.

Property #1 (marginalization preference)

Factorial scores produced by MCA overweight the smaller categories within each primary indicator. In fact, we have

$$W_{j_k}^{\alpha,k} = \frac{N}{N_{j_k}^k} \text{ Covariance } \left(F_\alpha^*, I_{j_k}^k\right) \tag{3.17}$$

where

$W_{j_k}^{\alpha,k}$ = the score of category j_k on the factorial axis α(non – normalised)

$I_{j_k}^k$ = the binary variable 0/1 taking the value 1 when the population unit has the category j_k.

F_α^* = the normalized score on the factorial axis α

$N_{j_k}^k$ = the frequency of the category j_k of indicator k

Thus, in the case of a binomial indicator, the marginal category will receive a higher weight, since the covariance is the same for both categories.

In terms of poverty, if we think of (extreme) poverty in a given society as being more relative than absolute and characterized by social marginalization, i.e., by the belonging to a minority group within the population, the group of people characterized by a poverty category j_k, then this category will receive more weight in the computation of a composite indicator of poverty. If we interpret the factorial weights (regression weights) as expressing the social choice in poverty reduction, then these highly weighted poverty attributes represent those which this society tries to eliminate in priority. As noticed above (Section 3.2.3), this higher weight given to a smaller number of deprived people is looked for by the indicator weighting system defined a priori with the fuzzy approach.

Property #2 (reciprocal bi-additivity or duality)

The way it is defined, MCA can be applied on the indicatrix-matrix either to the row-profiles (observations) or to the column-profiles (categories), so that it has the following remarkable and unique duality property:

$$F_\alpha^i = \frac{\sum_{k=1}^{K} \sum_{j_k=1}^{J_k} \frac{W_{jk}^{\alpha,k}}{\sqrt{\lambda_\alpha}} I_{i,jk}^k}{K} \tag{3.18a}$$

where

K = number of categorical indicators

J_k = number of categories for indicator k

$W_{jk}^{\alpha,k}$ = the score of category j_k on the factorial axis α(non – normalised)

I_{i,j_k}^{k} = the binary variable 0/1 taking the value 1 when the unit i has the category j_k.

F_{α}^{i} = the score (non - normalized) of observation i on the factorial axis α

and reciprocally

$$W_{jk}^{\alpha,k} = \frac{\displaystyle\sum_{i=1}^{N_{jk}} \frac{F_{\alpha}^{i}}{\sqrt{\lambda_{\alpha}}}}{N_{jk}^{k}}. \tag{3.18b}$$

Let us assume, for example, that the first factorial axis meets the consistency conditions to be considered as a poverty axis[24] and that we can take as the composite indicator of poverty $C_i = F_1^i$. Then the duality relationships stipulate

Equation 3.18a: the composite poverty score of a population unit is the simple average of the factorial weights (standardized) of the K poverty categories to which it belongs.

Equation 3.18b: the weight of a given poverty category is the simple average of the composite poverty scores (standardized) of the population units belonging to the corresponding poverty group.

We feel that these two properties, especially equation 3.18b for the reciprocal bi-additivity, are quite relevant for the poverty meaning of the numerical results coming out of this specific factorial analysis, MCA.[25] With the simultaneous graphical representation of population units and poverty attributes, MCA appears as an analytic tool particularly efficient for the study of multidimensional poverty represented in a set of categorical ordinal indicators.

It must also be observed that by breaking down each indicator I_k in as many variables, J_k, as there are categories, MCA allows for *non-linearity* in the categorical weights, contrary to a PCA which would be run on a numerical coding 1 to J_k of the indicator I_k , as some researchers could be tempted to do.

Having looked at some variants of factorial analysis, FA, PCA, and MCA, our third methodological choice is to go on with MCA, due essentially to its particular convenience for categorical variables, its remarkable duality properties and its operationality. This is why we explore more attentively in the following section a research strategy that is relevant in applying MCA to the problem of measuring multidimensional poverty.

---

[24] We come back to these consistency conditions in Section 3.4 below.

[25] A complete description of MCA can be found in Lebart et al. (2000) or Greenacre and Blasius (1994).

3.4 MCA Technique Applied to Multidimensional Poverty Measurement

Since MCA consists basically in exploring the internal structure of a covariance matrix while producing at the same time an additive decreasing disaggregation of the total variance (inertia) of the matrix, the rationale for using such a technique in the context of multidimensional poverty consists in searching the real multidimensionality of poverty reflected in a set of poverty indicators more or less correlated. And the specific by-product of such a search is a significant composite indicator of multidimensional poverty, as we will now see.

3.4.1 A Fundamental Consistency Requirement

We now consider more closely the conditions under which the factorial approach, and especially the MCA variant, can generate a truly relevant composite indicator of multidimensional poverty. We could have here a full axiomatic formulation so that the objective of poverty comparison is satisfactorily met. But the axiomatic requirements can be largely simplified with a two-step approach. If the first step has provided a relevant composite indicator of poverty, the axiomatic requirements for the second step, regarding the computation of aggregated poverty indices, can rely on standard requirements now generally accepted in the case of unidimensional poverty measurement, especially for the well-known case of money-metric poverty. For the first step of constructing a composite indicator C from K ordinal categorical indicators I_k, there is at least the following requirement:

Monotonicity axiom $(M)^{26}$

The composite indicator of poverty must be monotonically increasing in each of the primary indicators I_k.

The axiom just means that if a population unit i improves its situation for a given primary indicator I_k, then its composite poverty value C_i increases: its poverty level decreases.

Let us see what it means to take the first factorial component F_1 as the composite indicator of poverty C. From equation 3.18a above, its expression would be

$$C_i = F_1^i = \frac{\sum_{k=1}^{K} \sum_{jk=1}^{Jk} \frac{W_{jk}^{1,k}}{\sqrt{\lambda_1}} I_{i,jk}^k}{K}.$$

(3.19a)

---

[26] We assume that the sign of the composite indicator is selected in such a way that a larger value means less poverty or, equivalently, a welfare improvement, and that the ordering relation A < B between two categories A and B of the same indicator means that B is preferable to A.

To simplify, let us write $W^{*\alpha.k} = \frac{W^{\alpha.k}}{\sqrt{\lambda_\alpha}}$ for the normalized category-score on the factorial axis α. Then we have

$$C_i = \frac{\sum_{k=1}^{K} \sum_{j_k=1}^{J_k} W_{jk}^{*1.k} I_{i.j_k}^{k}}{K}. \tag{3.19b}$$

The monotonicity axiom translates into two requirements:

> *M1: First Axis Ordering Consistency (FAOC-I)* for an indicator I_k
> For an indicator I_k for which the ordering relation between categories is noted $<_k$ the ordering relation $<_w$ of the weights $W_{j_k}^{*1.k}$ must be equivalent to either $<_k$ or to $>_k$.
> M2: *Global First Axis Ordering Consistency (FAOC-G)*
> For all indicators I_k, the FAOC-I condition is fulfilled with the same orientation: the ordering relation $<_w$ is equivalent to either $<_k$ for all indicators or to $>_k$ for all.

If and only if the monotonicity axiom is satisfied can $C = F_1$ be taken as a composite indicator of poverty, after eventually changing the sign of F_1 when $<_w$ is equivalent to $>_k$ for all indicators. But then the reciprocal bi-additivity property of MCA gives a very interesting consistency result for C_i. Due to equation 3.18b which says that the weight of an indicator category, $W_{j_k}^{1.k}$, is given by the average composite poverty score of the population group of size N_{j_k} having the category (attribute) j_k, we can state the following property of C:

Composite Poverty Ordering Consistency (CPOC)

With $C = F_1$ satisfying the monotonicity axiom (M), for a given indicator I_k, let the population group P_{j_1} have a category j_1 of I_k inferior to the category j_2 possessed by the group P_{j2}. Then the group P_{j_1} is also poorer than P_{j2} relative to the composite poverty.

In other words, the population ordering for a primary indicator I_k is preserved with the composite indicator. This is a remarkable consistency property specific to MCA, due to the dual structure of the analysis.

Clearly, there is no guarantee that MCA run on the K primary indicators will come out with the FAOC property, and then using the first factorial component as the composite indicator of poverty would be inconsistent and not acceptable. In fact, everything depends on the structure of the covariance matrix X'X.[27]

There are two ways of overcoming this unpredictable difficulty: minor adjustments to the set of the K primary indicators, or exploiting more than one factorial axis.

---

[27] We use X for the matrix of centered variables.

3.4.2 Positive Rescaling of the K Primary Indicators[28]

As seen above, due to the duality relationship equation 3.18b, the categorical weight $W_{jk}^{*1,k} = \frac{W_{jk}^{1,k}}{\sqrt{\lambda_1}}$ appearing in the CIP equation 3.19b has a strong meaning in terms of multidimensional poverty: it is the average multidimensional poverty level of the group of individuals having the category j_k of the primary indicator I_k. But the numerical value of $W_{jk}^{*1,k}$, either negative or positive since by construction the average is zero, is irrelevant inasmuch as the numerical scaling of I_k remains unchanged relative to the distances between categories. Developing this idea, it is possible to improve the meaning of the categorical weights by rescaling I_k with the gap between the worst-off individuals, $j_k = 1$, and any better-off group, $j_k = 1$. We are thus led to rescale the indicator I_k, on the factorial axis α, here supposed to satisfy the consistency requirements, with the following categorical weights:

$$W_{jk}^{+\alpha,k} = \frac{W_{jk}^{\alpha,k} - W_1^{\alpha,k}}{\sqrt{\lambda_\alpha}}. \tag{3.20}$$

Thus, the most deprived category for I_k always has a weight equal to zero, and the weight given to any superior category j_k, strictly positive, represents the gain in *total* poverty reduction, as measured on axis α, when an individual can get out of the most deprived status in the primary indicator I_k by accessing the status $j_k, k > 1$. Under the hypothesis that the first factorial axis satisfies the FAOC condition, the definition of equation 3.19b of the CIP is now transformed as

$$C_i = \frac{\sum_{k=1}^{K} \sum_{jk=1}^{J_k} W_{jk}^{+1,k} I_{i,jk}^k}{K}, \quad C_i \geq 0. \tag{3.21}$$

From this point of view, MCA appears as a technique of rescaling numerically, in a meaningful way, a set of categorical ordinal indicators and of providing at the same time the rationale for a consistent aggregation of the rescaled indicators.

3.4.3 Adjustments to the Set of the K Primary Indicators

It should be noted that a binomial indicator always meets the FAOC-I requirement. In the case in which a multinomial indicator does not satisfy this requirement, regrouping some categories can sometimes achieve the FAOC-I. If this operation does not succeed, a more radical solution is to eliminate the indicator. Obviously,

---

[28] This section assumes that the factorial axis referred to, usually the first axis, meets the FAOC-G condition, with the orientation chosen such that welfare increases (poverty decreases) from left (negative side) to right. A simple adaptation of this will be made below in a more general case.

if the primary indicators have been carefully selected, defined and tested, this is a high price to pay for satisfying a technical condition. Although we do not in general favor the elimination of indicators, the option does become more acceptable when the number of indicators K is large and there appears to be some duplication in a specific domain (or dimension) of poverty.

If all indicators satisfy FAOC-I but FAOC-G is not met, it means that relative to the first factorial axis there are two subsets of indicators with opposite ordering on this axis, thus negatively correlated. Two such disjoint subsets of indicators will always appear with K binomial indicators, this being in particular the case when applying MCA to asset poverty, where the indicator for each asset is usually binomial: ownership or not. In this last case, there is no consistency problem if one of the two subsets is the empty subset $\varnothing$, which is not unusual. Let us assume that both subsets are not empty. It means that the multivariate measurement of poverty cannot be shrunk into a unidimensional poverty measurement restricted to the first factorial axis, and that in spite of existing correlations, the poverty concept reflected in the K chosen indicators is really deeply multidimensional. If we stick to the first factorial axis, the only way to get out of this inconsistency would be to eliminate one of the two subsets of indicators, which does not seem a priori acceptable: the information loss would then be too important. We need a more appropriate research strategy going beyond the first factorial axis.

3.4.4 A Research Strategy Using More than the First Factorial Axis

We need some additional tools to design a research strategy that will not consider only the first factorial axis. Let L be the number of factorial axes, determined by the rank of the matrix X. We have $L \leq J - K$, where J is the total number of categories for the K indicators.

$$\text{Let } \Delta_l^k = \frac{\sum_{j_k=1}^{J_k} N_{j_k}^k W_{k,j_k,l}^2}{N} \tag{3.22}$$

be the *discrimination measure* of indicator I_k on the factorial axis l. It is in fact the variance of the distribution of the categorical weights on axis l, since the average weight is always 0.

We know from the theory of MCA that

$$\lambda_l = \frac{\sum_{k=1}^{K} \Delta_l^k}{K}, \tag{3.23}$$

i.e., the eigenvalue of axis l, is the average of the discrimination measures of the K indicators.

It follows from the basic factorial equation

$$\text{Total Inertia} = I_{tot} = \sum_{l=1}^{L} \lambda_l \qquad (3.24)$$

that we have the equation 3.25 below:

3.4.4.1 Total Inertia Decomposition

$$I_{tot} = \frac{\displaystyle\sum_{l=1}^{L}\sum_{k=1}^{K}\sum_{j_k=1}^{J_k} N_{j_k}^{k} W_{k.j_k.l}^{2}}{K \times N} = \frac{\displaystyle\sum_{l=1}^{L}\sum_{k=1}^{K} \Delta_l^{k}}{K}. \qquad (3.25)$$

In the case of MCA, $I_{tot} = \frac{J}{K} - 1$, i.e., it is the average number of categories per indicator minus 1.[29] If all indicators are binomial, total inertia is precisely 1. It is also shown that the contribution of indicator I_k to total inertia is $J_k - 1$.

Let us denote $\kappa = \{1, 2, \ldots, K\}$ as the set of integers from 1 to K.

We will now generalize the previous approach to the composite indicator of poverty.

First observe that there is an obvious one–one correspondence between the categorical coefficients appearing in the linear expression of the L possible factorial components and the categorical contributions to the disaggregated total inertia, as shown in matrices A and B. The general term of matrix B is the square of the matrix A general term. The usual approach restricted to consider only the first factorial axis to pick up from A the J coefficients of the composite indicator, conditional on the FAOC-G requirement, is based on the fact that in matrix B the first line has a maximal sum in the inertia decomposition. Equation 18a is then the functional frame of the composite indicator, as proposed by the factorial theory. But there is no specific reason why a maximal inertia criterion, conditional to ordering (poverty) consistency as revealed in matrix A, should be restricted to the first line of matrix B. A more efficient approach can be looked for, and this is the idea explored to generalize the usual factorial approach to the CIP (Figs. 3.9 and 3.10).

	1	...	j_1	...	j_1	1	...	j_k	...	J_k	1	...	j_K	...	J_K
1															
:															
l								$W_{jk}^{l.k}$							
:															
L															

Fig. 3.9 Matrix A categorical coefficients in factorial components: Equation (3.18a)

For each factorial axis l, we can look for two *subsets* of indicators, each subset satisfying the axis ordering consistency condition (AOC) in one of the two axis

---

[29] See Lebart et al. (2000) p.120.

	1	...	j_1	...	J_1	1	...	j_k	...	J_k	1	...	j_K	...	J_K
1															
:															
l							$W_{k,jk,l}^2$								
:															
L															

Fig. 3.10 Matrix B categorical contributions in total inertia disagregation: Equation (3.25)

orientations, i.e., both requirements AOC-I and AOC-G, which now no more refer only to the first axis. The worst situation occurs when, for a given axis l, no indicator meets AOC-I; both subsets are then the empty subset $\emptyset$. Among these AOC subsets, we retain the one whose sum of discrimination measures is maximal. We will then consider that there is a *poverty type* specific to axis l if and only if the *sum of discrimination measures* of this AOC subset represents the larger part of the total discriminating power of axis l, i.e., is larger than 50% of $K \times \lambda_l$. Axis l will then be named a *poverty axis* and the sum of discrimination measures of this AOC subset is identified as the *poverty-relevant inertia* of axis l. To each factorial axis l, we can thus associate a unique subset of the K indicators, whose indices are a *subset κ_l* of κ.

Poverty Type Set of Axis l

The Poverty Type Set of the factorial axis l, $\{I_k\}_{k\in\kappa_l}$, is the most discriminating subset of AOC indicators satisfying $2 \times \sum\limits_{k\in\kappa l} \Delta_l^k > K\lambda_l$.

It should be clear that the set $\{I_k\}_{k\in\kappa_l}$ can be empty, which means that the factorial axis l does not represent any poverty type set.

It should also be clear that the poverty type sets from different axes are not necessarily disjoint: the same indicator can belong to many of them. The potential intersection between these sets can be eliminated by a sequential process starting with the first axis and continuing with the others as ordered by MCA, since the discriminating power of each axis is decreasing. The way to eliminate these intersections, while trying to retain at each step the maximal inertia, is naturally coming out of the total inertia decomposition (3.25): at each step, we keep a given indicator k into the poverty type set where its discrimination measure is larger. We refer to this sequential process as to *the algorithmic identification of independent poverty types*, more simply the *poverty types algorithm*. Let then $\kappa_l^* \subseteq \kappa_l$ be the subset of indicator indices at step $L^* \geq 1$ in the sequential process.

Normally, to ensure that the process retains a maximal proportion of I_{tot} in the disjoint poverty sets, the algorithm must be pursued until $L^* = L$. We then have built a complete sequence of poverty type sets.

3.4.4.2 Complete Sequence of Poverty Type Sets

The sequence of disjoint subsets of indicators $\{I_k\}_{k\in\kappa_l^*}$ resulting from the application of the poverty types algorithm until $L^* = L$, is called a complete sequence of poverty type sets. The number d of non-empty subsets is the number of independent poverty types provided by the set of the K primary indicators.

Two cases are then possible: all K indicators belong to the sequence, i.e., $\bigcup_{l=1}^{L} \kappa_l^* = \kappa$, or some indicators are not retained in the process. In this last case, they could simply be eliminated from the search of a composite indicator: in a simultaneous factorial analysis of all K indicators, they do not meet the minimal consistency requirement on any factorial axis. But again, we cannot necessarily assume that these rejected indicators are not good. A less radical approach would be to process them separately as a second set of indicators and to build with them a second composite indicator.[30] With two numerical CIP, any of the reviewed aggregation techniques well fitted to quantitative indicators could be used, including PCA.

The poverty types algorithm can rapidly become quite demanding with a large number K of primary indicators, let us say $K \geq 10$, which is not unusual in applied multidimensional poverty analysis. As an example, with 10 indicators having on average 3 categories, the process could involve the analysis of $L = 20$ factorial axis. Even if all well-known software allows such an analysis with some tedious work for the analyst, to facilitate the operationalization, it seems admissible, even if not optimal, to introduce the possibility of interrupting the algorithm when some kind of ideal situation is met, that is, as soon as all K indicators appear in a sequence of disjoint poverty type sets. This leads us to the following definition:

3.4.4.3 Minimal and Admissible Sequences of Poverty Type Sets

A *minimal sequence of poverty type sets* is obtained when the poverty types algorithm is interrupted at the smallest value L* ≤ L for which either $\bigcup_{l=1}^{L^*} \kappa_l^* = \kappa$, i.e., all indicators are included in the sequence of disjoint poverty sets, or L* = L.

Here also, the number d of non-empty subsets is the number of independent poverty types provided by the set of the K primary indicators.

It should be stressed that this definition allows, in particular, for stopping the process to the first factorial axis if the FAOC condition is achieved. To our knowledge, this has been the usual practice until now, unfortunately at the expense of frequently giving up a subset of the primary indicators or of merging relevant categories, which means an information loss.

If a minimal sequence of poverty type sets is reached for a small $L^* < L$, e.g., for $L^* = 1$ (first axis), there can still be an important loss of information with some indicators having a very low discriminating power. In that case, important improvements can be obtained by considering additional axes beyond L^*, without necessarily going until $L^* = L$. It is clear that beyond L^*, all K indicators remain in the disjoint sequence of poverty sets, but some indicators could be associated to a poverty set and axis l in which their discrimination measure is higher. It then seems better to extend the algorithm until some criterion is met. One possible criterion is to stop the process when the sum of the L^* eigenvalues represent at least 50% of

---

[30] This means a rerun of the first factorial analysis without these indicators.

the total inertia, I_{tot}, given by $I_{tot} = \frac{J}{K} - 1$. That type of minimal sequence can then be called an *admissible sequence of poverty type sets*. Each axis that appears in the sequence then has an inertia (eigenvalue) larger than the average inertia per factorial axis, $1/K$. This application of the algorithm obviously requires analyzing less than half of the total number of factorial axes, possibly much less depending on the inertia captured by the first axes. When a minimal sequence exists, especially when it occurs immediately at $L^* = 1$, our proposal would thus be to pursue the algorithm until an admissible sequence has been reached.

We can now derive, from equation 3.21, a generalized definition of the composite indicator of poverty, which can be applied when the first factorial axis does not meet the FAOC-G requirement.

3.4.4.4 Generalized Definition of the Composite Indicator of Poverty

Let a complete or admissible sequence of complete poverty type sets be obtained, which is always possible with the poverty dimensions algorithm. Then the value C_i of the composite indicator of poverty for the population unit i is given by

$$
C_i = \frac{\sum_{l=1}^{L^*} \sum_{k \in \kappa_l^*} \sum_{jk=1}^{J_k} W_{jk}^{+l.k} I_{i.jk}^k}{K}. \tag{3.26}
$$

Definition of equation 3.21 is the special case where $L^* = 1$: all K indicators belong to the poverty type subset of the first factorial axis. This is the case where the multivariate measurement of poverty can be logically reduced to one aggregate poverty type, due to the structure of the correlation matrix: all K indicators are positively correlated. In the general case, there is more than one poverty type, in fact one for each poverty type set; the way to aggregate them is suggested by the structure of equation 3.19a and the fundamental equation of decomposition of the total inertia 3.23: instead of picking up the J_k weights attributed to the indicator I_k only from the set of weights provided by the first factorial axis, it takes them from the axis which define the poverty type subset to which it belongs with a maximal variance. The positive rescaling of the indicators (Section 3.4.2) is done only for the poverty type set, with the orientation of the axis chosen consequently from left (poorer) to right (less poor).

Coming back to matrices A and B above, this algorithmic approach to the CIP means that we move simultaneously in the whole matrices A and B, A to identify any existing poverty ordering consistency, B to keep the most relevant ones according to the discrimination measure, and, avoiding any overlapping, this optimization process is translated into a CIP according to the duality frame 3.18a.

Deliberately we did not use the term poverty *dimension* set in place of poverty *type* set. A poverty dimension is identified a priori as a subset of indicators relative to the same domain of basic needs or basic welfare. It is an a priori concept. A poverty type is a statistical concept defined from the multivariate distribution of the whole set of indicators in a given population. A poverty type can, and will usually be, poverty multidimensional. It is a concept that helps exploring, reducing, and clarifying the meaning of multidimensional poverty in a given population, according to a behavioral specificity of that population and/or to specific poverty reduction policies. Numerous poverty dimensions can thus shrink into just one poverty type, or some types, which obviously should simplify the analysis. This is what we try to achieve by the proposed generalized construction of the composite indicator of poverty.

It should be noted that the two very relevant properties of MCA, the marginalization preference equation 3.17 and the reciprocal bi-additivity, especially equation 3.18b, are valid in each of the L^* axes involved in the generalized definition and thus keep their meaning, in the relevant poverty type I, for the interpretation of the categorical weights of the κ_I^* indicators defining this type. Moreover, the composite poverty ordering consistency remains valid for each identified poverty axis, with obvious adaptation.

The whole generalization approach must be viewed as an effort to highlight the multidimensional poverty structure hidden in the K-variate measurement of poverty, and at the same time to integrate into the composite indicator of poverty the maximum amount of information from the full information contained in the K primary indicators, as measured by the total inertia.

3.5 MCA: A Numerical Illustration

To illustrate the MCA technique described in Section 3.4, we use a household data set provided by the poverty observatory experimented in Vietnam in 2002 for monitoring the National Programme for Hunger Eradication, Poverty Reduction and Job Creation. The household survey was run in 4,000 households drawn from 20 communes, following the CBMS methodology developed in Vietnam by the Vietnam Socio-Economic Development Centre in partnership with MOLISA.[31]

Thirteen nonmonetary poverty indicators have been aggregated into a composite indicator. These indicators come from the areas of education (schooling, literacy), health (sickness events, sick days), housing conditions (type of house, toilet, and electricity), and household equipment (bicycle/motorcycle, radio/TV). Education and health indicators are broken down according to gender. These indicators are presented in Table 3.1, which provides the main numerical results coming out of the MCA computation.

The two columns "Factorial scores" give the values $W_{jk}^{\alpha,k}$ and the columns show the values Δ_I^k defined in equation 3.22.

---

[31] MOLISA: Ministry of Labour, Invalides and Social Affairs.

Table 3.1 Vietnam MOLISA poverty observatory; MCA results

		Factorial score		Discrimination measures	
INDICATOR	Category	axis # 1	axis # 2	axis # 1	axis # 2
Male child. 6–15 not	Yes	−1,109	−0,056	0,07	0,00
going to school	No	0,059	0,003		
Female child. 6–15	Yes	−1,166	0,132	0,09	0,00
not going to school	No	0,074	−0,008		
Hld with illiterate	Yes	−2,04	0,222	0,27	0,00
male adults	No	0,134	−0,014		
Hld with illiterate	Yes	−1,371	0,267	0,29	0,01
female adults	No	0,211	−0,041		
Sickness events	no sickness	0,03	0,518	0,00	0,61
male per cap.	0–1/2	−0,071	−0,734		
	1/2 to 1	−0,065	−1,049		
	103>=1	−0,051	−1,596		
Sickness events	no sickness	0,025	0,628	0,00	0,60
female per cap.	0–1/2	−0,146	−0,54		
	1/2 to 1	0,021	−0,832		
	103>=1	0,019	−1,335		
Hld with radio or tv	With radio or tv	0,37	−0,021	0,43	0,00
	Without radio and tv	−1,153	0,067		
Hld with bicycle or motocycle	With bicycle/moto	0,265	−0,031	0,44	0,01
	Without bicycle/moto	−1,671	0,198		
Type of housing	Multi-storey permanent	1,063	0,38	0,40	0,01
	One-storey permanent	0,577	−0,037		
	Semi-permanent	0,08	0,013		
	Temporary	−1,125	−0,084		
	Not having owned house	−1,948	−0,035		
Type of toilet	Flush toilet septic tank	0,841	0,088	0,40	0,01
	Double vault compost latrine	0,584	−0,045		
	On fish ponds	0,236	0,186		
	Simple toilet/pit latrine	−0,482	0,016		
	On river, canal	−0,505	−0,122		
	Not having owned toilet	−0,905	−0,187		
Hld with electricity	Hld with electricity	0,284	−0,03	0,49	0,01
	Hld without electricity	−1,761	0,185		

Table 3.1 (continued)

INDICATOR	Category	Factorial score		Discrimination measures	
		axis # 1	axis # 2	axis # 1	axis # 2
Number of sick days male per cap.	No sick days	0,053	0,445	0,01	0,57
	Less than 5 days	−0,046	−1,255		
	More than 5 days	−0,216	−1,305		
Number of sick days female per cap.	No sick days	0,045	0,528	0,00	0,56
	Less than 5 days	−0,121	−0,956		
	More than 5 days	−0,076	−1,122		
	average = eigenvalue			0,22	0,18

These results are summarized in Graphs 3.1, 3.2, 3.3, and 3.4.

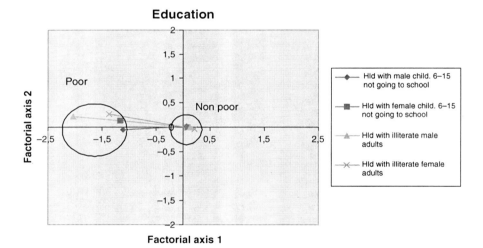

Graph 3.1 Factorial scores (categories), first two axes, education

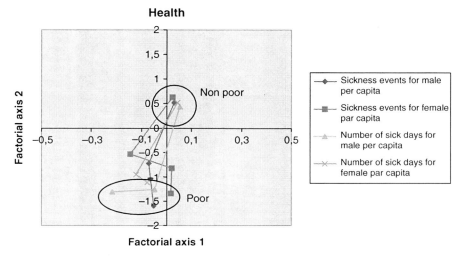

Graph 3.2 Factorial scores (categories), first two axes, health

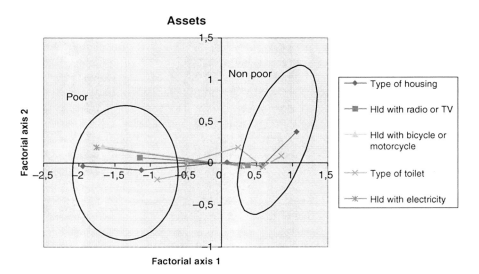

Graph 3.3 Factorial scores (categories), first two axes, household assets

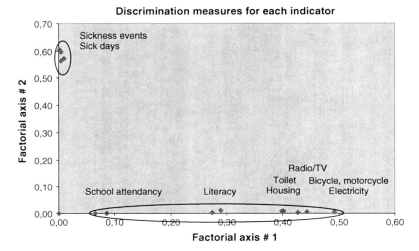

Graph 3.4 Discrimination measures, first two axes

From Graphs 3.1 and 3.3 we see that the subsets of the four education indicators and the five household assets indicator meet the FAOC-I consistency requirement, and since the orientation is the same, altogether these nine indicators are globally consistent. But first-axis consistency problems appear with the health indicators. In fact, three of these four indicators are not consistent with the first axis, as can be seen from Graph 3.2. Only "number of sick days for male per capita" is FAOC-I and could be kept in a composite indicator with the nine others since it is globally consistent with them. Thus, considering only the first factorial axis, three health indicators should be eliminated from the composite indicator.

But we observe immediately from Graph 3.2 that these three health indicators are consistent relative to the second axis (as well as the fourth one). In fact, the four health indicators have a high discrimination power on the second axis, and almost no power relative to the first axis. Graph 3.2 illustrates very clearly this observation: education and asset indicator discriminate highly on axis #1 and very little on axis #2, with the reverse situation for health indicators. This is precisely the case where, to avoid an important loss of information, the poverty types algorithm of Section 3.4.4 can be expected to be more efficient in the construction of a composite indicator by translating numerically what is immediately revealed graphically. Computations are presented in Table 3.2.

The 13 indicators are listed in lines, with their discrimination measures on all factorial axes as columns. Here we limit the table to the first three axes since the algorithm, version "admissible sequence," stops at axis #2. The algorithm has been pursued until factorial axis #8, where 50% of the total inertia 2 (39/13 −1) is reached, without providing any additional poverty set beyond axis #2.

The first step identifies, on axis # 1, only one subset of indicators satisfying the AOC condition, the 10 indicators colored[32] in dark gray in the relevant column. This identification requires going back to Graphs 3.1, 3.2, and 3.3 or to Table 3.1. The other three indicators (health) are not consistent. Then we check if the inertia explained by these 10 indicators, 2.886, is at least 50% of the first axis total inertia, which is 1.448. We thus accept axis #1 as describing a poverty type, the poverty type set being the 10 consistent indicators.

The second step, relative to axis #2, identifies a first subset of five consistent indicators, dark gray colored: the four health indicators plus the male school attendance indicator.[33] Their discriminating power is 2.339. A second subset, light gray colored, consistent in the direction opposite to the first subset, includes five indicators with a discriminating power of 0.028. The dark gray subset has more inertia than the required 50% of 1.192 and can thus be accepted as a poverty type subset of indicators; it is completely dominated by the four health indicators. Then arises the elimination of overlapping between the poverty type subsets of axes #1 and #2. "Hld with male child. 6–15 not going to school" is kept in axis #1 where its discriminating power 0.066 is much higher than the 0.000 on axis #2. "Number of sick days for male per capita" is kept in the poverty type subset of axis #2 with a discriminating power of 0.572 instead of 0.010 on axis # 1. The two overlapping indicators are now labeled in white color on the axis where they are eliminated.

We then have two nonoverlapping poverty type subsets, one with nine indicators, another with four, covering the whole set of the 13 indicators. According to the minimal sequence algorithm, we can stop here. Just for curiosity, in Table 3.2 we present the third axis. As can be seen, there are two subsets of AOC indicators, but none of them can reach the requested inertia value 0.749. A similar situation is met for all subsequent axes until axis #8, where at least 50% of the total inertia is explained, and thus an admissible sequence is achieved. Only the first two axes provide poverty sets.

There is a large information gain by using the poverty types algorithm:

- with 13 indicators and 39 categories, the total inertia is $(39/13) -1 = 2$;
- with reference to equation 3.25, "Total Inertia Decomposition," and Table 3.2, the inertia relative to the 10 indicators consistent on axis #1 is $2.886/13 = 0.222$, 11.1% of total inertia;
- the inertia collected by the 13 indicators coming out of the first two axes is $(2.876 + 2.339)/13 = 0.401$, 20.0% of total inertia, i.e., 81% more than with only the first axis. But the most important fact is that all 13 primary indicators appear in the composite indicator.

---

[32] As a convention, the dark gray color identifies the left to right (bottom-up) axis orientation, and the light gray color shows the reverse orientation.

[33] Its very low discrimination measure is 0.000169.

Table 3.2 Poverty types algorithm, minimal sequence

Indicators	Discrimination measures Dimension (factorial axis)		
	1	2	3
Hld with male child. 6–15 not going to school	0.066	0.000	0.047
Hld with female child. 6–15 not going to school	0.087	0.001	0.039
Hld with illiterate male adults	0.274	0.003	0.022
Hld with illiterate female adults	0.289	0.011	0.027
Sickness events for male per capita	0.002	0.605	0.271
Sickness events for female per capita	0.003	0.598	0.342
Hld with radio or TV	0.427	0.001	0.030
Hld with bicycle or motorcycle	0.443	0.006	0.007
Type of housing	0.399	0.008	0.020
Type of toilet rec	0.401	0.009	0.058
Hld with electricity	0.492	0.005	0.001
Number of sick days for male per capita	0.010	0.572	0.220
Number of sick days for female per capita	0.004	0.564	0.416
13*50% eigenvalue	**1.448**	**1.192**	**0.749**
Before eliminating intersections	2.886	2.339	0.135
		0.028	0.038
After eliminating intersections- 3 axis	2.876	2.339	

Table 3.3 summarizes the computation of the final rescaled weights appearing in the generalized CIP formula 3.26 above.

Table 3.3 Final categorical weights

INDICATOR	Category	Factorial score		Rescaled weights° 1000		Final weight
		Axis # 1	Axis # 2	Axis # 1	Axis # 2	
Male child. 6–15 not going to school	Yes	−1.109	−0.056	0		0
	No	0.059	0.003	2475		2475
Female child. 6–15 not going to school	Yes	−1.166	0.132	0		0
	No	0.074	−0.008	2627		2627
Hld with illiterate male adults	Yes	−2.04	0.222	0		0
	No	0.134	−0.014	4606		4606
Hld with illiterate female adults	Yes	−1.371	0.267	0		0
	No	0.211	−0.041	3352		3352
Sickness events male per cap.	No sickness	0.03	0.518		4936	4936
	0–1/2	−0.071	−0.734		2013	2013
	1/2–1	−0.065	−1.049		1277	1277
	I03>=1	−0.051	−1.596		0	0

Table 3.3 (continued)

INDICATOR	Category	Factorial score		Rescaled weights × 1000		Final weight
		Axis # 1	Axis # 2	Axis # 1	Axis # 2	
Sickness events female per cap.	No sickness	0.025	0.628		4584	4584
	0–1/2	−0.146	−0.54		1856	1856
	1/2 to 1	0.021	−0.832		1175	1175
	l03>=1	0.019	−1.335		0	0
Hld with radio or TV	With radio or TV	0.37	−0.021	3227		3227
	Without radio and TV	−1.153	0.067	0		0
Hld with bicycle or motorcycle	With bicycle/moto	0.265	−0.031	4102		4102
	Without bicycle/moto	−1.671	0.198	0		0
Type of housing	Multi-storey permanent	1.063	0.38	6379		6379
	One-storey permanent	0.577	−0.037	5350		5350
	Semi-permanent	0.08	0.013	4297		4297
	Temporary	−1.125	−0.084	1744		1744
	Not having owned house	−1.948	−0.035	0		0
Type of toilet	Flush toilet septic tank	0.841	0.088	3699		3699
	Double-vault compost latrine	0.584	−0.045	3155		3155
	On fish ponds	0.236	0.186	2417		2417
	Simple toilet/pit latrine	−0.482	0.016	896		896
	On river, canal	−0.505	−0.122	847		847
	Not having owned toilet	−0.905	−0.187	0		0
Hld with electricity	Hld with electricity	0.284	−0.03	4333		4333
	Hld without electricity	−1.761	0.185	0		0
Number of sick days male per cap.	No sick days	0.053	0.445		4086	4086
	Less than 5 days	−0.046	−1.255		117	117
	More than 5 days	−0.216	−1.305		0	0
Number of sick days female per cap.	No sick days	0.045	0.528		3853	3853
	Less than 5 days	−0.121	−0.956		388	388
	More than 5 days	−0.076	−1.122		0	0
	eigenvalue			0.22	0.18	

Chapter 4
Multidimensional Poverty and Inequality Analysis

According to our two-step approach to multidimensional poverty indices, we come out of the first step with a composite indicator of poverty (CIP) that is positive and whose increase is interpreted as a better basic welfare. This CIP then has the technical characteristics of an "income" indicator, and any money-metric technique developed for poverty and inequality analysis can in principle be applied to this CIP. Such applications are not developed here and are left to case studies presented in Part II.

Nevertheless, multidimensional poverty analysis can be enriched by the factorial technique proposed in Section 3. This fact is illustrated in Section 4.1. Some issues specific to multidimensionality still need to be addressed, among others poverty lines. This is done in Section 4.2.

4.1 CIP Policy-Oriented Analysis: Poverty Groups, Sectoral Poverty Reduction Efficiency

4.1.1 Poverty Groups Identification and Targeting

Factorial planes offer a strong graphical analytic potential. Here, the main interest is with MCA factorial planes relative to the representation of indicators (columns of the data matrix) due to the duality equation 3.18b. Category coordinates in these planes correspond to the average factorial score of the statistical units belonging to these categories. Thus, *for an axis recognized as representing a poverty type*, the categorical coordinate corresponds essentially to the average of this multidimensional poverty type, for those being in the specific category. In these same planes, it is possible to position additional points corresponding to different socioeconomic groups, and then to quickly identify which groups are particularly poor or non-poor, for given poverty types. Consistent with equation 3.18b, these socioeconomic groups are represented by their average score on each factorial axis. Such representations can obviously suggest which groups in the population should be targeted with specific sectoral poverty reduction policies.

L.-M. Asselin, *Analysis of Multidimensional Poverty,*
Economic Studies in Inequality, Social Exclusion and Well-Being 7,
DOI 10.1007/978-1-4419-0843-8_4, © Springer Science+Business Media, LLC 2009

There are many factorial axes, and there thus remains the problem of choosing which factorial planes should be used. The usual practice is to represent the first two or three axes since the captured inertia decreases with the sequential numbering of these axes. But according to Section 3.4.4 above, only the factorial axes recognized as poverty axes are relevant for poverty analysis, i.e., for representing a poverty type. And then the poverty-relevant inertia of these poverty axes (see Section 3.4.4) naturally becomes the ranking criterion for determining the most relevant factorial planes to be represented for targeting analysis.

For our numerical example, factorial axes #1 and #2 are the two poverty axes identified by the poverty type algorithm. Graph 4.1 represents some socioeconomic groups in the corresponding plane.

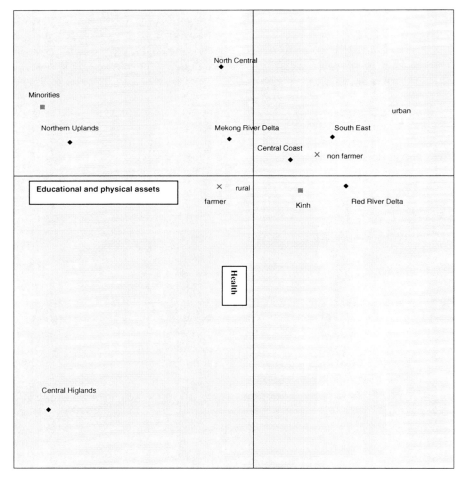

Graph 4.1 Socioeconomic groups in the poverty plane

The first important difference of Graph 4.1 with respect to a standard factorial plane is that axes have names. They are identified by the poverty type that each of them represents. To avoid graphical congestion and illegibility, categorical points are not represented, as they have already been represented in Graphs 3.1, 3.2, and 3.3 above. These graphs could in fact be superimposed, or more simply looked at simultaneously.

At first glance it can be observed[1] that

a) poverty in education and physical assets is found mainly in mountainous areas, Northern Uplands and Central Highlands, and among minorities. Urban areas in general, more specifically the Red River Delta (Hanoi region) and the South East (Ho Chi Minh City region), escape this type of poverty as well as farmers;

b) poor health concentrates again in Central Highlands and seems to be much less among minorities than among the Kinh. This poverty type concentrates also in rural areas.

This type of analysis shows how important it is to integrate in household surveys an extended set of socioeconomic characteristics which can be judged a priori as poverty related and could be used eventually as targeting instruments.

4.1.2 Sectoral Policies Comparative Efficiency

The previous graphical analysis helps to identify poverty groups according to poverty types, but a finer analysis is required to pinpoint in which poverty dimensions and subdimensions, policies and programs can be more efficient to tackle poverty.[2] Two tools are proposed: the poverty reduction unitary gain (PRUG) diagram and the poverty elimination efficiency diagrams (PEE and PSEE).

4.1.2.1 The Poverty Reduction Unitary Gain (PRUG) Diagram

Primary poverty indicators represent a subset of poverty dimensions and subdimensions according to the Poverty Matrix Structure proposed in Fig. 2.1. Indicator categories correspond to different states of poverty in each subdimension. The CIP, as built with MCA, is an aggregate measuring the total poverty of a given popula-

---

[1] Note that the sample of communes from which data have been collected has not been drawn randomly, but by judgment sampling. The poverty observatory was in an experimental phase, and data are used here just for illustrative purposes of the methodology. Comments should not be taken as applying necessarily to the whole of Vietnam.

[2] For expositional purposes, from now on it is assumed that all K primary indicators are pure poverty indicators as defined in Section 2.1. Adjustments required with extended poverty indicators are mentioned below in Section 4.2.1.

tion unit, say a household. In fact, as a positively increasing variable, it measures the total basic welfare level, the qualifier «basic» meaning that, with the poverty focus, only basic capabilities and functioning are represented in the K indicators. The categorical weight of a given poverty state j_k in the subdimension (indicator) k measures the marginal gain in total basic welfare if a household moves from the extreme poverty state in this indicator ($j_k = 1$) to the poverty state j_k. These unitary gains in total basic welfare are called here «poverty reduction unitary gains» and can be represented in diagrams like Graphs I.4, for quick and easy retrieval of the most efficient among these unitary gains, within subdimensions and across dimensions. The numerical example is always the same as above.

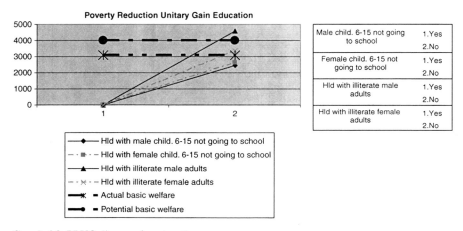

Graph 4.2 PRUG diagram for education

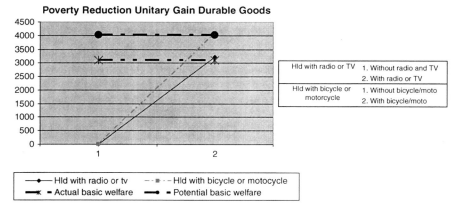

Graph 4.3 PRUG diagram for durable goods

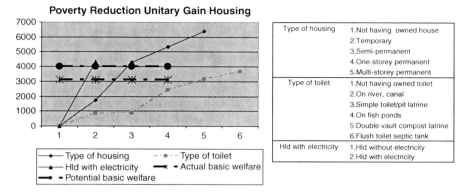

Graph 4.4 PRUG diagram for housing

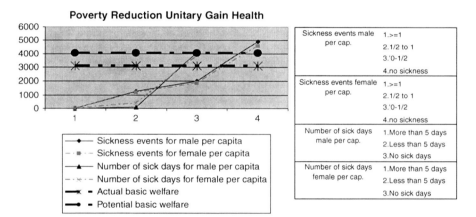

Graph 4.5 PRUG diagram for health

The interpretation of Graphs 4.2, 4.3, 4.4, and 4.5 calls for some remarks.

a) The PRUGs are distribution independent ex post.[3]
b) Consistency (individual, global, and composite, Section 3.4.1) in the categorical weights is immediately revealed by the non-decreasing behavior of each specific indicator line.
c) Highest welfare changes when passing from a specific poverty state j_k to the closest improved state $j_k + 1$ are given by the steepest slopes of lines between two states. For example, it can be observed here that

   – in «education,» *male illiteracy* elimination has the dominating PRUG;

---

[3] Ex post meaning, from the policy standpoint, *once factorial computations have been completed.*

- in «durable goods,» *transportation (bicycle/motorcycle)* offers a higher gain than *radio/TV;*
- in «housing,» the highest PRUG is with *electricity*, followed by moving from *temporary* to *semi-permanent* house;
- in «health,» the elimination of *s days* calls for a higher attention.

Across these four dimensions, *male illiteracy* elimination keeps a slight advantage over access to *electricity*, closely followed by the other poverty reduction steps identified above.

d) There are two additional lines in all Graphs 4.2, 4.3, 4.4, and 4.5 – the *actual basic welfare* line and the *potential basic welfare* line.

The first one is the arithmetical mean of the CIP in the population, something analogous to the mean household income, at the time of the survey. But it is also, obviously, the average value of all PRUGs appearing in Graphs I.4, i.e., the average of all unitary gains needed to come from an initial value of zero basic welfare to the level of basic welfare presently achieved. From (3.26), its value $\overline{C}$ is given by

$$\overline{C} = \frac{\sum\limits_{i=1}^{N} C_i}{N} = \frac{\sum\limits_{i=1}^{N}\sum\limits_{l=1}^{L*}\sum\limits_{k\in\kappa_l^*}\sum\limits_{j_k=1}^{J_k} W_{j_k}^{+l,k} I_{i,j_k}^k}{NK} = \frac{\sum\limits_{l=1}^{L*}\sum\limits_{k\in\kappa_l^*}\sum\limits_{j_k=1}^{J_k} W_{j_k}^{+l,k} N_{i_k}^k}{NK}. \qquad (4.1)$$

In our case its value is 3101.

The second one is the mean CIP which would be attained if poverty was totally eliminated in each of the K subdimensions (primary indicators). If we refer here to the definition given above, Section 2.1, of a pure categorical poverty indicator, the *potential basic welfare* $\overline{C}^{\max}$ is the arithmetical mean of the K maximal weights $W_{J_k}^{+l,k}$ in the K primary indicators. From (4.1), it is given by

$$\overline{C}^{\max} = \frac{\sum\limits_{l=1}^{L*}\sum\limits_{k\in\kappa_l^*}\sum\limits_{j_k=1}^{J_k} W_{J_k}^{+l,k} N_{i_k}^k}{NK} = \frac{\sum\limits_{l=1}^{L*}\sum\limits_{k\in\kappa_l^*} W_{J_k}^{+l,k} \sum\limits_{j_k=1}^{J_k} N_{i_k}^k}{NK} = \frac{\sum\limits_{l=1}^{L*}\sum\limits_{k\in\kappa_l^*} W_{J_k}^{+l,k}}{K}. \qquad (4.2)$$

In our example, it takes the value of 4020.

These two additional lines, at the same positions in all PRUG diagrams, facilitate the comparisons of PRUGs within and across poverty dimensions.

The two values $\overline{C}$ and $\overline{C}^{\max}$ provide an important estimate. The potential basic welfare increase if poverty is completely eliminated is given by the

$$Poverty\ Elimination\ Basic\ Welfare\ Gain(PEBWG) = \frac{\overline{C}^{\max}}{\overline{C}} - 1.$$

In our case, *PEBWG* takes the value 29.6%.

4.1.2.2 The Poverty Elimination Efficiency (PEE) Diagram

The first question any policy analyst will raise is whether *PEBWG* is additively decomposable across all still existing poverty states. From (4.1) and (4.2), the answer is obviously yes. The contributed value resulting from the elimination of the poverty state j_k is given by

$$Contribution \ of \ poverty \ state \ j_k = \frac{N_{i_k}^k \times \left(W_{J_k}^{+l,k} - W_{j_k}^{+l,k} \right)}{N K \overline{C}} \tag{4.3}$$

Obviously, the contribution of category J_k is zero, since it is, for indicator k, the first non-poverty state.

The sum of all these contributions, whose number is $J = \sum_{k=1}^{K} J_k$, with J-K strictly positive values, gives the *PEBWG*. These contributions can thus be seen as a measure of the potential efficiency of a policy or program aiming to eliminate the concerned state of poverty. Obviously, contrary to the previous PRUG, this measure of poverty elimination efficiency (PEE) is *distribution dependent*. Added across the different poverty states of a given subdimension (indicator), it gives the gain achieved by eradicating that subdimension of poverty in the given population. To facilitate a comparative analysis of all the different possible poverty elimination operations, the poverty elimination efficiency (PEE) diagram is built, first in a cumulative way across a same indicator, to provide the efficiency relative to each subdimension of poverty.

These PEE diagrams are presented in Graphs 4.6, 4.7, 4.8, and 4.9 for our numerical case. Since the contribution of category J_k is zero, as noticed above, the last line segment, in each of these diagrams, is always a flat line, so that in case of a binary indicator, the whole cumulative line is horizontal. Its level corresponds to the gain obtained by the elimination of the only poverty state, j_1.

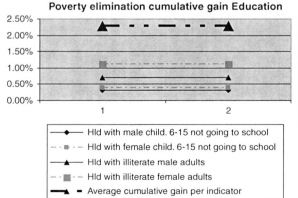

Graph 4.6 PEE diagram for education

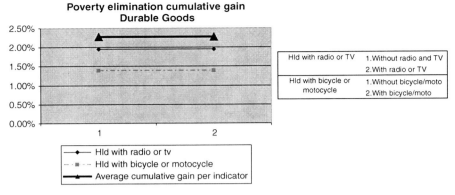

Graph 4.7 PEE diagram for durable goods

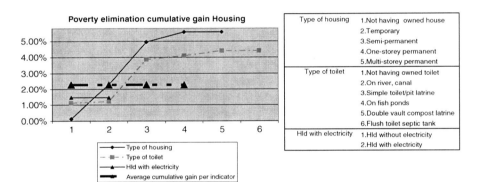

Graph 4.8 PEE diagram for housing

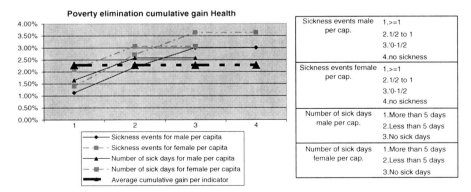

Graph 4.9 PEE diagram for health

As explained above, in case of binary indicators, the cumulative line is always flat.

As explained above, the last segment of the cumulative line is always flat, since the last state is a non-poverty state. Also, Graphs 4.8 and 4.9 illustrate the non-linearity property mentioned at the end of Section 3.3.2.

As can be seen in Graphs 4.6, 4.7, 4.8, and 4.9,

a) within each of the four poverty dimensions, the most efficient poverty elimination policy is
   - in education, with female illiteracy elimination. We have seen above that the highest PRUG is with male illiteracy, but here we see that the distribution effect renders female illiteracy elimination more rewarding, even with a smaller PRUG;
   - for durables, with access to radio or TV, again even if its PRUG is less than for bicycle or motorcycle;
   - for housing, with improving the type of housing;
   - for health, with eliminating sickness events for females, but challenged by eliminating sick days for women.

b) in each graph, a horizontal line has been drawn always at the same level, identi-fied as the «average cumulative gain per indicator.» The level of this line is given by $\frac{PEBWG}{K}$, the Poverty Elimination Basic Welfare Gain divided by the number of indicators (subdimensions). Here it takes the value $29.6\%/13 = 2.28\%$. Looking globally across all poverty dimensions, i.e., across all four graphs representing here the efficiency of the thirteen subdimensions, it is immediately observed that eliminating poverty in the type of housing, with an efficiency close to 5.5%, dominates any other subdimension specific policy.

4.1.2.3 The Poverty State Elimination Efficiency (PSEE) Diagram

The last representation of additive efficiency, in a cumulative way for each subdi-mension of poverty elimination, gives quickly a comprehensive overview of which sectoral policies appear as more productive for reducing the total poverty in the given population. But this type of analysis can be criticized on at least two points. First, it is in some sense unfair since, as seen in Section 3.4.4, the total contribu-tion of a given indicator (subdimension) I_k to the total multidimensional inertia is determined by its number of categories J_k[4]; second, the preceding analysis calls for some fine-tuning at the level of the multiple poverty states to try to identify which one, within each subdimension and across all of them, it is more efficient to eliminate. A noncumulative presentation of the efficiency relative to each poverty state elimination is thus needed. This is done in Graphs 4.10, 4.11, 4.12, and 4.13, named «poverty state elimination efficiency» (PSEE) diagrams. They are in fact the direct representation of the additive contributions defined in equation (4.3) above.

---

[4] The relation of efficiency with J_k is not absolute. See for example in Graph 4.8 where «Type of housing», with 5 categories, is more efficient than «Type of toilet» with 6 categories.

In our numerical example, the aggregate potential efficiency is 29.6%. With J-K poverty states, here $39 - 13 = 26$, the average potential efficiency per poverty state is thus 1.14%. The horizontal axis is situated precisely at that level of the vertical axis to facilitate the analysis.

From Graphs 4.10, 4.11, 4.12, and 4.13, it is quickly seen that

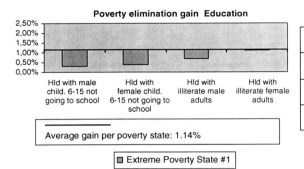

Graph 4.10 PSEE diagram for education

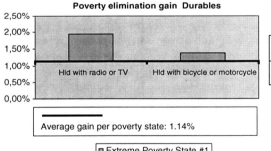

Graph 4.11 PSEE diagram for durable goods

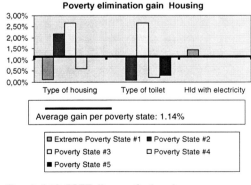

Graph 4.12 PSEE diagram for housing

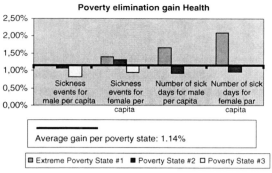

Graph 4.13 PSEE diagram for health

a) in the case of education, only female illiteracy elimination offers the average gain of all poverty states;

b) highest efficiency appears again in the dimension of housing, but quite curiously, we find in this same poverty dimension the lowest efficient poverty states. Thus policy makers have to pay attention here to which poverty states deserve a priority. It appears from Graph 1.6c that the most efficient policies would be in eliminating semi-permanent type of housing and having households replacing simple toilets or pit latrines with a flush toilet;

c) the health dimension offers its highest potential efficiency in fighting against diseases causing a large number of s days for women, with a level close to what has just been observed for some housing characteristics.

Globally, from Graphs 4.6, 4.7, 4.8, 4.9, 4.10, 4.11, 4.12, and 4.13, a persistent policy result emerges: more efficiency in reducing total multidimensional poverty is to be expected by eliminating female rather than male poverty in the specific dimensions of education and health.

4.2 Multidimensional Poverty Lines, Indices, Inequality, Dynamic Analysis

One of the reasons for adopting the two-step approach to multidimensional poverty indices is, once the first step of building a CIP is completed, to exploit most, if not all, of the poverty analysis techniques developed since decades in the money-metric unidimensional field. These techniques depend in general on the determination of a poverty line. Even if not absolutely required to take stock of the analytic advantages of having at our disposal a CIP, as seen in Section 4.1, this issue of multidimensional poverty lines is the main focus here, with some complementary issues relative to poverty indices, inequality, and dynamic analysis.

4.2.1 Multidimensional Poverty Lines

4.2.1.1 Union-Poverty

A prerequisite before trying to identify a poverty line for the CIP is to have a clear concept of how we define "poor" in a multidimensional context. In the literature the discussion is on «intersection poverty» versus «union poverty»: a population unit is «intersection-poor» if it is poor in *all* K primary indicators and «union-poor» if it is poor in *at least one* of the K primary indicators. We adopt here the concept of *union poverty*, assuming that all K indicators include real and unacceptable poverty states, at least as their respective lowest category identified by $j_k = 1$. This concept of union poverty is the position taken by Bourguignon and Chakravarty (1999). This definition requires that there be a specific poverty threshold for each primary indicator I_k,. In the discrete case, when a category $\bar{j}_k$ is set as the first non-poverty state, all population units *strictly below* $\bar{j}_k$ are then considered as poor in I_k. Note that the qualifier «strictly» is extremely important in the discrete variable case; this also implies that we should have $1 < \bar{j}_k \leq J_k$. In the case of I_k being a *pure categorical poverty indicator* (as defined in Section 2.1), we have $\bar{j}_k = J_k$. It should be highlighted that these definitions of multidimensional poverty are completely independent of any recoding of the primary indicators and do not require any CIP.

The numerical value of the specific poverty threshold, for the recoded indicator I_k^+ as it appears in expression (3.26) of the CIP, is given by

$$\bar{W}_k = W_{\bar{j}_k}^{+l,k}. \tag{4.4}$$

With this definition of multidimensional poverty, it is immediately seen that

a) the multidimensional poverty count can be easily computed without any reference to the CIP;
b) a lower bound of the poverty count is given by the simple frequency distribution of the K primary indicators: it is the highest value of all specific poverty rates.

Table 4.1 gives the specific poverty thresholds retained in our numerical example. The way for fixing any threshold $\bar{W}_k$ should be as consensual and participative as possible. We see that the highest specific poverty rate is 52.1% for the indicator «Type of toilet.» The «union» multidimensional poverty rate could not be lower and is in fact 80.1%. It is the percentage of households poor in at least one of the 13 poverty indicators. The union poverty rate is quite sensitive to a small change in specific poverty thresholds. For example, if here the threshold for «Type of toilet» is taken as « Simple toilet/pit latrine» instead of «On fish ponds,» the union poverty rate falls from 80.1 to 72.7%.[5] Empirically, the multidimensional union headcount seems to increase with the number of primary indicators K, which is not surprising

---

[5] These percentages are household rates.

Table 4.1 Poverty thresholds and specific poverty rates

Indicator	Category	Weight threshold	Distribution %	Poverty rate (%)
Male child. 6–15 not going to school	Yes	0	5.1	5.1
	No	2475	94.9	
Female child. 6–15 not going to school	Yes	0	6.0	6.0
	No	2627	94.0	
Hld with illiterate male adults	Yes	0	6.3	6.3
	No	4606	93.7	
Hld with illiterate female adults	Yes	0	13.5	13.5
	No	3352	86.5	
Sickness events male per cap.	No sickness	4936	68.0	
	0–1/2	2013	11.2	
	1/2–1	1277	11.6	20.8
	103≥1	0	9.2	
Sickness events female per cap.	No sickness	4584	58.4	
	0–1/2	1856	13.8	
	1/2–1	1175	15.4	27.8
	103≥1	0	12.4	
Hld with radio or TV	With radio or TV	3227	75.7	
	Without radio and TV	0	24.3	24.3
Hld with bicycle or motorcycle	With bicycle/moto	4102	86.4	
	Without bicycle/moto	0	13.6	13.6
Type of housing	Multi-storey permanent	6379	4.2	
	One-storey permanent	5350	24.4	
	Semi-permanent	4297	51.7	
	Temporary	1744	18.9	19.7
	Not having owned house	0	0.8	
Type of toilet	Flush toilet septic tank	3699	17.7	
	Double vault compost latrine	3155	23.1	
	On fish ponds	2417	7.1	
	Simple toilet/pit latrine	896	38.6	52.1
	On river, canal	847	1.2	
	Not having owned toilet	0	12.2	
Hld with electricity	Hld with electricity	4333	86.1	
	Hld without electricity	0	13.9	13.9
Number of sick days male per cap.	No sick days	4086	74.3	
	Less than 5 days	117	9.4	
	More than 5 days	0	16.3	16.3

Table 4.1 (Continued)

Indicator	Category	Weight threshold	Distribution %	Poverty rate (%)
Number of sick days female per cap.	No sick days	3853	66.7	
	Less than 5 days	388	11.2	
	More than 5 days	0	22.1	22.1
	Average poverty threshold	**2755**		

and is irrelevant for poverty comparisons. It is not surprising in the sense that if many dimensions of poverty are measured simultaneously, and if the extended concept of poverty *adds* really something to the standard money-metric one, it can reasonably be expected that more poverty will be observed.

Interesting poverty comparisons across space, socioeconomic groups, and time can already be done with the union poverty headcount, but if the objective is to go deeper as in the money-metric case, an important issue arises: is it possible to operationalize the concept of multidimensional union poverty through some kind of poverty line for the CIP?

4.2.1.2 The Multidimensional CIP Absolute Poverty Line

According to the definitions given in Section 2.1 of pure and extended poverty indicators, two cases are considered. First, all K primary indicators are pure; second, some indicators are extended poverty indicators.

Case 1: all K primary indicators are pure poverty indicators.

Let us define the *CIP absolute poverty line*

$$\overline{C} = \frac{\sum_{k=1}^{K} \overline{W}_k}{K}.$$ (4.5)

$\overline{C}$ is the CIP value of a population unit who just meets the K thresholds required to be non-poor. In our numerical example, which is not a case 1 type, the absolute poverty has the value 2755 as it appears in Table 4.1.

In case 1, we know that

$$\overline{C} = \frac{\sum_{k=1}^{K} W_{J_k}^{+l.k}}{K}.$$ (4.6)

It is immediately seen that in case 1, a population unit U_i is poor if and only if

$$C_i < \overline{C}.$$ (4.7)

If Ui is poor, by definition it is poor for at least one indicator I_k, thus its value is necessarily strictly below the maximal weight of I_k and equation 4.7 is true. If equation 4.7 is true, Ui is obviously poor for at least one value k. Thus, in case 1, the absolute poverty line (equation 4.6) fully operationalizes the union-poverty definition. It must again be emphasized that the *strictly smaller* sign in equation 4.7 is required.

Case 2: some of the K primary indicators are extended poverty indicators.

In this case, for at least one value of k, we have

$$\overline{W}_k < W_{J_k}^{+l.k}. \tag{4.8}$$

This is the case met in the numerical example where 6 of the 13 primary indicators are extended poverty indicators.

This means that with the absolute poverty line in equation 4.5, condition 4.7, while still being a sufficient condition for being poor, is no more a necessary condition. A poor unit can compensate a specific poverty status by a superior status in an extended indicator. The strict operationalization of the concept of union-poverty is no more provided by equation 4.5. There are two options open to the analyst.

The first one is to censor the extended recoded indicator I_k by replacing any categorical weight strictly superior to the threshold with the poverty threshold $\overline{W}_k$. Pure indicators are in fact like already censored indicators. Then, in the generalized definition (equation 3.26) of the CIP, the positively recoded primary indicators are replaced by the censored primary indicators I_k^*. With this modification to the definition of the CIP, case 1 is in fact obtained, and equation 4.7 is again a necessary and sufficient condition to be union-poor.[6]

It should be noticed that the way the CIP absolute poverty line is defined here, with the «censoring before» CIP, is equivalent, in terms of absolute poverty shortfalls, to the way Bourguignon and Chakravarty (1999) build their «aggregator function of the shortfalls» in view of defining their class of multidimensional poverty indices with numerical indicators.[7]

The second option, in case 2, consists in accepting a compensating mechanism between primary indicators and then to take as the definition of poverty condition 33: a population unit is poor if its CIP is strictly below the CIP absolute poverty line. Obviously, this definition is no more equivalent to the concept of union-poverty: some population units can be union-poor while having $C_i \geq \overline{C}$. We will then name this poverty definition «compensated poverty,» and the derived multidimensional indices as «compensated poverty indices.» In the same way, the absolute poverty line will be called a «compensated absolute poverty line.» To respond to

---

[6] In this case, the sectoral policies efficiency tools proposed in Section 4.1.2 above should be restricted to the censored poverty indicators.

[7] Their parameters β and B are here taken with the admissible values 1.

the terminology used above, this second option will sometimes be referred to as the «censoring after» approach, since the standard construction of poverty indices will rest on censoring the CIP at the absolute poverty line.

The two options can generate very different poverty indices. In the numerical example, it has already been seen that the union-poverty rate is 80.1%. The compensated poverty rate is 27.9%.

Is there any rationale for taking the second option? We think so. Behind the whole technology used here for recoding numerically a set of K categorical indicators lies the covariance matrix. Poverty indicators are correlated and the whole algorithm for identifying poverty types on different axis tries to throw some light on this complexity. Also, the fundamental duality relationships 18a and 18b in Section 3.3.2, especially 18b, mean that once a population unit escapes poverty and reaches a higher welfare status in a given dimension of poverty, it is in a much better position for eliminating residual poverty in other dimensions. In some way, the compensated poverty approach reflects a more dynamic view of poverty, in the sense that it acknowledges the existence of forces interacting in the fight against poverty. It could also reflect the idea that a given poverty status is possibly felt less acute when it soaks in an affluent environment enjoyed by the afflicted population unit.

Obviously the more there are extended poverty indicators and the more each of them is extended beyond the specific poverty threshold, the more compensation is possible and the farther is the whole measurement system from the pure concept of union-poverty. This *compensating power of the absolute poverty line* can be measured. For the union-poor poverty units, taking into account the K indicator distributions, it suffices to measure the total poverty gap which needs to be compensated (A), to measure in the same fashion the total welfare gap beyond the specific thresholds (B), and to form the ratio (B)/(A). This provides a measure of how far from the union-poverty concept is the compensated-poverty concept underlying the compensated-poverty indices, if the second option is chosen in case 2.

This very simple computation is illustrated in Table 4.2 for the numerical case considered here. The *compensating power* of the absolute poverty line 2755 takes here the value 137.8%. Thus, there is enough welfare among the 80.1% union-poor households to compensate for all the poverty. It explains why the compensated poverty rate is 27.9%. All poverty is not compensated simply because of mismatching poverty and welfare status at the household level. The compensating power is obviously 0% for a pure absolute poverty line and can take any finite positive value. In Part II, for the Vietnam case study based on another set of indicators, the compensating power is only 21.0%.

To summarize, a unique CIP poverty line is defined in view of operationalizing the union-poverty concept, the *CIP absolute poverty line*. According to the nature of the K primary poverty indicators and to the methodological choice done in case 2, this poverty line conveys a pure or a compensated-poverty concept, and in this last case, a measure of the gap with the pure concept is available, the compensating power. Obviously, since the CIP is positive, any other type of CIP poverty line can be used, like quintiles and relative poverty lines (50% of the median). But the absolute

Table 4.2 Compensating power of the absolute poverty line 2755

Indicator	Category	Weight / threshold	Distribution absolute	Compensation needed	Compensation available
Male child. 6–15 not going to school	Yes	0	200	494935	
	No	2475	2957		
Female child. 6–15 not going to school	Yes	0	236	620025	
	No	2627	2921		
Hld with illiterate male adults	Yes	0	247	1137711	
	No	4606	2910		
Hld with illiterate female adults	Yes	0	531	1779822	
	No	3352	2626		
Sickness events male per cap.	No sickness	4936	1958		5724155
	0–1/2	2013	379		
	1/2–1	1277	456	335405	
	I03≥1	0	364	732661	
Sickness events female per cap.	No sickness	4584	1603		4371905
	0–1/2	1856	458		
	1/2–1	1175	607	413872	
	I03≥1	0	489	907759	
Hld with radio or TV	With radio or TV	3227	2201		
	Without radio and TV	0	956	3084845	
Hld with bicycle or motorcycle	With bicycle/moto	4102	2622		
	Without bicycle/moto	0	535	2194495	
Type of housing	Multi-storey permanent	6379	71		147872
	One-storey permanent	5350	683		719205
	Semi-permanent	4297	1627		
	Temporary	1744	745	1902037	
	Not having owned house	0	31	133200	
Type of toilet	Flush toilet septic tank	3699	372		476841
	Double vault compost latrine	3155	536		395202
	On fish ponds	2417	196		
	Simple toilet/pit latrine	896	1523	2316860	
	On river, canal	847	49	76929	
	Not having owned toilet	0	481	1162803	

Table 4.3 (Continued)

Indicator	Category	Weight threshold	Distribution absolute	Compensation needed	Compensation available
Hld with electricity	Hld with electricity	4333	2610		
	Hld without electricity	0	547	2370043	
Number of sick days male per cap.	No sick days	4086	2179		8649689
	Less than 5 days	117	335		
	More than 5 days	0	643	75072	
Number of sick days female per cap.	No sick days	3853	1900		6583879
	Less than 5 days	388	385		
	More than 5 days	0	872	338002	
	Average poverty threshold	2755		20076475	27068749
	Compensating power	134.8%			

poverty line and its compensating power provide a firm reference for assessing the poverty concept attached to the chosen poverty line, which is essential for policy purposes.

4.2.2 Multidimensional Poverty Indices, Inequality, Dynamic Analysis

Once the first of the two-step approach to multidimensional poverty indices is completed, a CIP is available, and with the MCA methodology, this CIP is positive (≥ 0). In Section 4.2.1, a poverty line is defined, the CIP absolute poverty line. Technically, all the components are present to access the rich world of poverty analysis tools developed for the unidimensional money-metric poverty analysis: well-known FGT indices, stochastic dominance, etc. The same can be said for the inequality analysis and its most usual tools and indices: Lorentz curve, Gini index, etc. The most important point when computing all these indices is to be clear about the conveyed poverty concept, pure or compensated poverty, with precise reference to the poverty vector involved and the specific poverty thresholds.

Wonderful software is available for this purpose of univariate CIP-based analysis, among them DAD[8] that is specifically dedicated to poverty and inequality analysis. Whatever the software used, it should be checked if computations are done with strict inequality signs, an important issue in the discrete case, as repeatedly noticed before. An interesting point here is that with the CIP there is no more a concern with price adjustments across space and time. Categorical weights remain the same

---

[8] See Duclos and Araar (2006).

across space and time. For a dynamic analysis with two or more points across time, the best practice seems to be the computation of categorical weights in the base-year, and the use of the same weights in the subsequent periods. The rationale is the same as for keeping constant basket weights when computing a consumption price index.

Chapter 5
Conclusion

Multidimensional poverty is a complex concept. It is important to explore its philosophical and ethical roots (Section 1 and Appendix A), because methodological choices at crucial steps of measurement rely on *values*. The first concrete form of the concept is a vector of K primary indicators, K > 1, with a different structure for each application. The poverty vector structure is described in Section 2 through the notions of poverty dimension and subdimension, poverty type, pure and extended indicator, and poverty by inclusion with endogenous and exogenous transmission. Tools like the Poverty Concept Structure are designed to visualize and compare these conceptual structures and highlight implicit weighting at the very beginning of the measurement operation. These tools are applied to real and well-known poverty vectors (Section 2.3 and Appendix B).

The ultimate goal is to develop multidimensional poverty indices in a rational, consistent, and meaningful way. Section 3 first reviews different approaches, the very first distinction being between one- and two-step approaches. With a deliberate choice of a two-step approach, the focus is on the construction of a composite indicator of poverty (CIP). The methodological classification then relies on entropy and inequality measurement, inertia, and poverty structure analysis. The fuzzy subset approach is viewed as a positive numerical recoding of the primary indicators. The retained poverty structure analysis runs into the vast methodological area of factorial analysis, described in Section 3.3. The central structure falling under close scrutiny is the K-indicator covariance matrix. Due mainly to the type of indicators met in multidimensional poverty, multiple correspondence analysis (MCA) is identified as the most relevant factorial technique and is extensively described in Section 3.4. A fundamental consistency requirement, Axis Ordering Consistency, is formulated and described. Relevance and optimality of MCA is connected to the duality properties of 18a and 18b. A numerical algorithm is proposed to explore the poverty structure beyond the first factorial axis, in view of avoiding the unfortunate rejection of very good poverty indicators on the sole basis of their inconsistency with other indicators relative to the first axis. The proposed algorithm tries to systematize evidence coming out of graphical displays provided by factorial techniques and thus becomes the tool for identifying poverty types. At the end of the process, MCA emerges as an appropriate technique for achieving a meaningful positive recoding of ordinal

L.-M. Asselin, *Analysis of Multidimensional Poverty,*   73
Economic Studies in Inequality, Social Exclusion and Well-Being 7,
DOI 10.1007/978-1-4419-0843-8_5, © Springer Science+Business Media, LLC 2009

categorical indicators and providing at the same time a positive composite indicator of poverty (CIP). A numerical example illustrates these computation techniques.

Equipped with these tools, before proceeding to poverty indices, specific policy analysis can be performed: identification of poverty groups and the relative efficiency of sectoral poverty reduction policies (Section 4.1). Different types of diagrams (PRUG, PEE and PSEE) summarize the different efficiency concepts. Finally, in Section 4.2, the *absolute multidimensional poverty line* is defined and analyzed with reference to the concepts of pure union-poverty and compensated poverty. Standard money-metric technology can then be transposed to the CIP with its associated poverty line to generate multidimensional poverty and inequality indices. This is the second step of our proposed methodology.

This book is on multidimensional poverty *measurement*. Even if some statistical analysis tools are proposed in Section 4, deep analysis is still required from analysts from all horizons of social sciences and even of other sciences like human biology. The paths to multidimensional poverty eradication are complex and still quite obscure, and very much culture dependent. A patient exploration of these paths cannot emerge without a vast amount of observations transformed in reliable and relevant measurements. We hope this book will modestly contribute to that exploration.

Part II
Case Studies

This second part presents two case studies using partially or fully the methodology developed in the first part. The first one is a static analysis realized in Senegal by Jean-Bosco Ki (coordinator), Salimata Faye, and Bocar Faye. It considers 21 indicators measured in 2000–2001. The second one has been realized by Louis-Marie Asselin and Vu Tuan Anh. It is a dynamic analysis of poverty in Vietnam during the period 1993–2002. Both case studies are based on large household surveys implemented by the different national statistical offices.

The two poverty concepts of these case studies are not identical. Using the tools developed in Section 1-2.3, a quick comparison of these poverty concepts is provided by the tables below showing their Poverty Concept Structure, referring to the Poverty Matrix Structure proposed in Fig. II.1 and reproduced here.

In both cases, the dimension «D2.Education» is the dominating dimension, largely ahead (38%) in the Vietnam case. The second rank is taken by «D7.Housing (environment)» for the Senegal study, while this D7 comes third in the Vietnam case, after «D5.Water/Sanitation». The Senegal study embraces eight of our ten dimensions of poverty and the Vietnam case five dimensions (Table II.1).

Regarding the poverty types algorithm (I-3.4.4), the Senegal study stops at a minimal sequence obtained with the sole first factorial axis, while the Vietnam study identifies three poverty types through an admissible sequence obtained with the first four factorial axes. The main reasons why the first case study does not use the full methodology of Part I is that it has been completed before 2005, before the poverty types algorithm was first presented at a conference of the UNDP Poverty Centre in Brasilia, August 2005. At that time, the usual practice, with factorial methods, was to restrain the CIP computation at the sole first factorial axis. Nevertheless, this research working paper has contributed, like some others achieved through the IDRC PEP network, to develop the application of MCA to the analysis of multidimensional poverty. The main author of this book owes a lot to this work realized by many researchers from the developing world, as a technical adviser and a regular discussant of the papers produced by this group of researchers. These papers provide a deep insight on the poverty in many sub-Saharan African countries, illustrating at the same time the analytic potential of the factorial methodology, more specifically MCA, for the analysis of multidimensional poverty.

	01	02	03	04	05	06	07	08
D1. Income	Income proxy	Ownership of durable goods	Typical expenditures	Perception of economic situation				
D2. Education	Primary enrolment	Secondary enrolment	Literacy	Drop-out rate	IEC resources (Info/Educ to Communic)	Access to school infrastructure services	Education level achieved	Pre-school
D3. Health	Infant/child mortality	Maternal mortality	Morbidity to handicap incidence	Access to health infrastructure services	Specific disease prevention treatment			
D4. Food/Nutrition	Malnutrition	Food security status						
D5. Water/Sanitation	Sources of drinking water	Sanitation facilities						
D6. Employment/labor	Unemployment inactivity	Underemployment	Categories of workers	Child labor	Wage rates			
D7. Housing (environment)	Housing characteristics	Home ownership	Sources of energy	Living environment				
D8. Access to productive assets	Land distribution	Irrigated land	Productive assets (agricultural & others)	Access to credit	Information technology	Production techniques		
D9. Access to markets	Price of basic commodities	Access to market infrastructure	Access to services	Access to roads				
D10. Participation/Social peace	Crime incidence	Domestic violence	Social participation	Participation in election	Access to public meeting infrastructure			

Fig. II.1 Poverty matrix structure

Table II.1 The three poverty concept structures

Senegal case study Poverty Concept										
	01	02	03	04	05	06	07	08		
D1		3							3	14%
D2	1		1		2	2			6	29%
D3				1					1	5%
D4		1							1	5%
D5	2	1							3	14%
D6									0	0%
D7	2		3						5	24%
D8									0	0%
D9		1		1					2	10%
D10									0	0%
									21	100%

Vietnam case study Poverty Concept										
	01	02	03	04	05	06	07	08		
D1									0	0%
D2	1		1		1				3	38%
D3			1						1	13%
D4									0	0%
D5	1	1							2	25%
D6		1							1	13%
D7	1								1	13%
D8									0	0%
D9									0	0%
D10									0	0%
									8	100%

Chapter 6
Case Study # 1 Multidimensional Poverty in Senegal: A Nonmonetary Basic Needs Approach

Jean Bosco Ki, Salimata Faye, and Bocar Faye

Abstract An appreciation of poverty that is as complete as possible constitutes an essential step in the analysis of the causes of poverty and in the formulation of policies to combat it. The monetary approach is not sufficient to capture the multiple aspects of poverty: a multidimensional analysis is also needed. The main objective of this research is therefore to construct a composite indicator of poverty using a basic needs approach. The analysis shows that the most widespread forms of poverty in Senegal are related to the vulnerability of human existence and to the lack of infrastructures, elements of comfort, and equipment. We estimate the incidence of multidimensional poverty to reach 60%, compared to 48.5% for monetary poverty. Rural areas are particularly affected by nonmonetary poverty whereas urban areas are affected more by monetary poverty in spite of the existence of human capital and basic infrastructures. The two types of poverty are quite strongly and positively correlated.

Keywords Multidimensional poverty · Composite indicator of poverty · Composite index · Basic needs approach · Nonmonetary poverty · Multiple correspondence analysis
JEL Classification: I31 · I32

Résumé

L'approche monétaire n'est pas suffisante pour cerner les aspects multiples de la pauvreté. Une analyse multidimensionnelle est nécessaire pour établir une mesure exhaustive de ce phénomène, tant du point de vue de ses causes que des politiques de lutte contre la pauvreté. C'est l'objectif principal de cette recherche qui a permis de construire un indicateur composite de la pauvreté à partir des besoins de base. L'analyse de cet indicateur montre que les formes de pauvreté les plus répandues au Sénégal sont liées à la vulnérabilité de l'existence humaine, au manque d'infrastructures, et au manque d'éléments de confort et d'équipement. L'incidence de la pauvreté multidimensionnelle vaut 60% contre 48.5% pour la pauvreté monétaire. La zone rurale est particulièrement touchée par la pauvreté non monétaire tandis que la zone urbaine est plus beaucoup plus affectée par la pauvreté monétaire malgré l'existence du capital humain et d'infrastructures de base. Cependant il faut noter que les deux types de pauvreté demeurent positivement corrélés.

Mots-clefs: Pauvreté multidimensionnelle, Indicateur composite, Indice composite, Besoins de base, Pauvreté non monétaire, Analyse des Correspondances Multiples.

Numéros JEL: I31, I32

List of Acronyms

ACG/GCA	Generalized Canonical Analysis
ACM/MCA	Multiple Correspondence Analysis
ACP/PCA	Principal Component Analysis
CFA	Communauté Financière Africaine
COPA/OCFA	Ordinal Consistency on the First Axis
CRDI/IDRC	International Development Research Center
CREA/AERC	Applied Economic Research Center
DPS	National Statistic Office
DR	District of Census
DSRP/PRSP	Poverty Reduction Strategy Paper
ESAM	Senegalese Households survey
FAOC	First Axis Ordinal Consistency
FGT	Foster, Greer and Thorbecke
CIP	Composite indicator of poverty
MIMAP	Micro Impacts of Macroeconomic and Adjustment Policies
MDG	Millennium Development Objectives
PEP	Poverty and Economic Policies
GDP	Gross Domestic Product
UNDP	United Nations Development Program
QUID	Unified Questionnaire on Development Indicators
PRS	Poverty Reduction Strategy
GER	Gross Enrollment Ratio
NER	Net Enrollment Ratio
UEMOA	Union Economique et Monétaire Ouest Africaine

6.1 Introduction

Poverty being a multidimensional phenomenon, the monetary approach is not always sufficient to capture the multiple aspects poverty involves, and whose consequences compromise the ability of populations affected by this phenomenon to lead decent and happy lives. For, even though an individual may have the wherewithal necessary to satisfy his needs, some other goods and infrastructures must also be available and accessible in the locality where he lives. Otherwise he may have no choice but to consume undrinkable water, for instance, even though he has the means to pay for the services of the water company located near his residence area. Or, he may have the financial means to acquire an education, but end up being unable to attend school for lack of educational facilities in the proximity. Or again, he may die through a minor illness before arriving at the hospital, simply because the latter is far from his residence area. These situations actually constitute other forms through which poverty manifests itself. They illustrate the fact that poverty is not solely monetary, but presents itself as a multidimensional phenomenon. It is therefore important for researchers to take this fact into account in their effort to achieve a better understanding and measurement of poverty. Hence the research interest in a multidimensional approach to poverty analysis, so as to be able to identify the poor and their concerns better, for the design and inplementation of appropriate strategies likely to help fight against poverty efficiently.

Very few studies have addressed the multidimensional aspect of poverty by using composite indicators in the case of Senegal. On the other hand, several nonmonetary poverty studies have been realized in that country, based on a one-dimensional approach, which consists of analyzing each dimension of poverty separately. The present study mainly aims to construct a composite indicator of poverty (CIP) that may help provide an aggreagte welfare measure embodying several dimensions. The construction of such a composite indicator will also permit to study the links between monetary and nonmonetary poverty, and to work out a multidimensional poverty index in order to evaluate its incidence.

In addition to the above introduction, the remainder of this study is organized into five sections. A brief presentation of Senegal will be followed by a review of the literature, a discussion of the methodology used, a presentation of the results, and finally, the conclusion and recommendations of the study.

6.2 Senegal, A Country affected by Poverty, However with Significant Initiatives in Progress

Senegal is located in the far western region of the African continent bordering the Atlantic Ocean, and spreads over an area of 196,000 km^2. Its population was estimated at 10,500,000 inhabitants in 2004, with a growth rate of 2.7%. The Gross Enrollment Ratio (GER) in primary school is 80%.[1] The country is endowed with very few natural resources, but it has a long coastline whose strong potentialities for fishing are already overexploited. Fishing remains one of the most important export sectors, followed by phosphates and groundnuts.

On the macroeconomic level, the country witnessed an average growth rate of 4.3% over the 1996–2001 period, which reached 6.5% in 2003. Inflation is controlled and contained below a 3% ceiling (the inflation rate was 2.3% in 2003) in accordance with the convergence criteria prescribed by the Economic and Monetary

---

[1] The GER was 79.9% in 2004/Ministry of Education.

Union of West Africa (UEMOA) currency area, of which Senegal is a member. However, Senegal is still a heavily indebted country (its debt service/exports ratio being 74.3%).

Senegal's first household survey (ESAM I)[2] was carried out over the 1994–1995 period, and the incidence of monetary poverty was estimated to be around 57.9%.[3] This incidence dropped to 48.5%[4] in 2000–2001, according to ESAM II results. Among the Government future economic policy orientations, the fight against poverty takes center stage. Poverty reduction is also very much at the fore of the millenium development objectives (MDO). To fight efficiently against poverty, the Government has drawn up a poverty reduction strategy paper (PRSP) in order to determine the policies, programmes and projects (PPP) to be implemented. The PRSP has identified and centered on three main priority areas : (i) wealth creation; (ii) capacity building and the promotion of basic social services; and (iii) improvement in the living conditions of vulnerable groups. These priorities constitute the major challenges the poverty reduction strategy (PRS) must take up. Consequently, research in the area of poverty analysis has positioned itself as the foundation on which the success of this vast program has to be based to increase the likelihood of achieving its objectives. The following section presents a brief review of the existing literature on the measurement of poverty.

6.3 Review of the Literature

The literature on poverty measures distinguishes between two approaches: the monetary approach supported by welfarists or utilitarians, and the nonmonetary approach supported by the non-welfarists.

6.3.1 The Monetary Approach

This utilitarian approach places the conceptualization of welfare in the utility space (Ravallion, 1994) whose satisfaction determines the level of welfare. But since utility is not directly observable, resources (i.e., income and expenditures) have been used to measure welfare.

The utilitarian approach thus arises out of an essentially unidimensional welfare concept which is reduced to a simple lack of financial resources necessary for the attainment of a minimum quality of life. In terms of economic policy, it recommends the reduction of poverty by increasing labor productivity by way of interventions of a general nature.

---

[2] Direction de la Prévision et de la Statistique (DPS), 1994/1995.

[3] Poverty thresholds estimates by the DFS amount to 787 CFA francs per day for the city of Dakar, 429 CFA francs for other cities, and, 281 CFA francs for the rural area.

[4] The poverty incidence of 53.9% given in the PRSP in 2001 comes from estimates of expenditure vectors that were available in the first ESAM II results.

6.3.2 *The Nonmonetary Approach*

The nonmonetary approach corresponds to the nonutilitarian view. It places welfare in the space of freedoms and accomplishments. A distinction is made between the approach by way of capacities,[5] and the approach through basic needs. The former emphasizes the concept of " functionings " and maintains that the individual must be adequately fed, have an education, be in good health, participate in community life, be free, appear in public without shame, etc. The approach through basic needs generally integrates the fundamental variables taken into consideration by the capacities approach, but adds to it other variables such as access to basic social services, including water, energy, education, health, food, housing, infrastructures, etc.

The empirical application of this approach has been hindered for a long time by the problems invoved in aggregating all the above deprivations. From the economic policy standpoint, the nonmonetary approach usually proposes targeted interventions which have the advantage of reducing the selection bias in favor of the poor relative to general kinds of interventions. In the case of Senegal, very few studies have tackled multidimensional poverty with the use of composite indicators. Studies carried out by the United Nations Development Program (UNDP) may only be considered as preliminary attempts to apply this concept.

The present study proposes an evaluation of nonmonetary poverty using the multidimensional approach, which permits the construction of a composite indicator aggregating welfare deficits through variables affecting human existence. The study uses the following methodology:

6.4 Methodology

6.4.1 *Methodological Choices*

In the context of this study, we adopt a nonmonetary approach based on basic needs, in which the latter place the welfare concept in the accomplishments space, unlike the monetary approach that gives priority to the space of resources. The main variables taken into account by this approach are education, nutrition, health, hygiene, sanitation, drinking water, the environment, housing, infrastructures, longevity, communications, access to energy, possession of consumer durables, and goods of comfort. We also resort to a technique that allows to aggregate different nonmonetary poverty dimensions in order to have an overall view of the latter and therefore, to facilitate the monitoring of their overall evolution. Several approaches such as the entropy approach[6] and the inertia approach,[7] in particular, may help take up this challenge.

---

[5] Mostly developed by Amartya Sen.

[6] See details in Appendices.

[7] See details in Appendices, and Louis-Marie Asselin (2002), « Pauvreté multidimensionnelle, théorie ».

The entropy approach is derived from dynamic mechanics. It is often used in statistical information theory from which Massoumi (1986) has developed an optimal composite indicator (OCI) that minimizes a weighted sum of divergences taken two by two at a time. The main limits of this approach reside in the choice of parameters and weights used in the composite indicator functional form.[8]

As concerns the inertia approach, it stems from the field of static mechanics. It is mainly based on multidimensional analytical techniques, often known as factorial analyses. One may find in the works of Meulman (1992),[9] Bry (1996),[10] Volle (1993),[11] and Escofier and Pagès (1990) a complete methodology of these techniques among which we may only mention the main ones, such as the following: Principal component analysis (PCA), generalized canonical analysis (GCA), and multiple correspondence analysis (MCA).[12] The other multidimensional analytical techniques originate in the development of the latter. The inertia approach is based on these various techniques, and it proposes a methodology that may help construct a composite indicator with the least possible arbitrariness in the definition of its functional form. It also allows to make an optimal choice of the pertinent dimensions of poverty while brushing redundant information aside. A complete development of this approach may be found in the work entitled, Pauvreté multidimensionnelle, by Louis-Marie Asselin (2002).

In this study, the methodology we use for the construction of the composite indicator of poverty (CIP) will be based on the inertia approach with the help of multidimensional analyses. The choice of these techniques may be explained above all by the fact that, they help eliminate arbitrariness as much as possible in the calculation of a composite indicator. The factorial analysis technique most suitable to the present study is multiple correspondence analysis (see Appendices), since the study uses categorical variables that can be codified in binary form by means of (0 or 1).

6.4.2 Functional Form of the Composite Indicator of Poverty (CIP)

The construction of the CIP is based on the inertia approach which aims to define a composite indicator for each given population unit, using multidimensional analytical techniques. Among these tools, the most adapted to our case study is multiple correspondence analysis (MCA) (see Sections 3.3.2 and 3.4).

The CIP functional form is defined as follows: Let's consider i the index of a given household, and C_i its CIP value. According to Section 3.4.1, equation 19b, the CIP functional form is

---

[8] See details in Appendices.

[9] Louis-Marie Asselin (2002), Pauvreté multidimensionnelle, IMG.

[10] Xavier Bry (1996), Analyses factorielles simples.

[11] Michelle Volle (1993), Analyse des données, Paris 1993.

[12] See details in Appendices.

$$Ci = \frac{\sum\limits_{k=1}^{K} \sum\limits_{j_k=1}^{J_k} W_{j_k}^k I_{j_k}^k}{K},$$

where K = number of indicator categories; J_k = number of indicator k categories; $W_{j_k}^k$ = the category-weight (standardized score on the first axis, $\frac{score}{\sqrt{\lambda_1}}$) of category j_k, λ_1 being the first eigen value.

$I_{j_k}^k$ = the binary variable 0/1, which takes on the value of 1 when the unit has category j_k.

The weights given by MCA correspond to the standardized scores on the first factorial axis. The CIP value for any household m simply corresponds to the mean of standardized scores of categorical variables. The weight of a category is the mean of standardized scores of population units belonging to that category.

When all the variable modalities are transformed into binary indicators codified by means of 0 or 1, giving a total of P binary indicators, the CIP for a given household i, can also be written as

$$ICP_i = \frac{1}{K}(W_1 I_{i1} + W_2 I_{i2} + \ldots + W_P I_{iP}),$$

W_p = the weight (score of the first standardized axis, $\frac{score}{\sqrt{\lambda_1}}$) of category p, λ_1 being the first eigen value.

$I_{p.}$ $_{p=1\ \text{à}\ P}$: binary indicator 0/1, which takes on the value of 1 when the household has modality p, and 0 otherwise.

6.4.3 Data Sources

The main data sources used in the study are drawn from the QUID (Questionnaire Unifié sur les Indicateurs de Développement) survey and ESAM II. The QUID survey constitutes the first phase of ESAM II during which only nonmonetary indicators were measured. Data on monetary indicators were gathered during the second phase. The additional data used in this study originate in national accounts and other reports related to poverty.

6.5 Presentation of the Results

6.5.1 Multiple Correspondence Analysis of Nonmonetary Poverty Dimensions

In the context of this study, we have carried out a preliminary MCA to visualize the multidimensional aspects of poverty which take into account all nonmonetary

Table 6.1 Preliminary list of 37 variables for the composite indicator of poverty[13]

Variables	Variables
Education	Energy
Primary schooling rate	Type of lighting
Secondary schooling rate	Electricity
Literacy rate	Fuel
Access to primary school	Communications
Access to secondary school	Television
Health	Radio/radio-cassette player
Access to health services	Access to public transport
Consultation of health services	Goods of comfort, equipment, and other assets
Rate of assistance to childbirth	Car or truck
Morbidity	Motorcycle
Prenatal care	Bicycle
Drinking water	Refrigerator/freezer
Source of drinking water	Stove
Access to water in less than 30 minutes	Iron
Nutrition	Sewing machine
Food problems	Mattress/bed
Access to the food market	Watch or alarm clock
	Plots of land, building
Housing and sanitation	Other land
Nature of roof	Cattle
Nature walls	Sheep/goats
Housing occupancy status	
Type of toilet	

dimensions of poverty (see Table 6.1). This first MCA also constitutes the basis for constructing the CIP.

The histogram of MCA eigen values (see Appendices) highlights the unhooking of the first factorial axis. The latter explains 10.29% of the total inertia of the variable cluster, whereas the other axes show a low explanatory power (each with less than 3% of the inertia explained). This distinction of the first axis underscores the particular phenomenon of poverty. MCA analysis will mainly center on this axis which describes poverty. Examination of the first simplified factorial plane (see Table 6.2) shows that variables which determine a poverty state lie on the left-hand side of the plane and those indicating a state of wealth on the right-hand side.

The MCA first factorial axis generally opposes two household categories: poor households and non-poor households. As to the second axis, it introduces a differentiation within each class. In the case of the well-to-do, it makes a distinction between very rich households and rich households. Similarly, it generally distinguishes poor hoseholds from very poor households within the class of the poor.

Overall, the poor have very limited access to education, health, sanitation, drinking water, housing, energy, means of communication, transport, food, goods of

[13] The malnutrition indicator of children less than 5 has not been taken into account owing to the fact that the QUID survey collected data on this indicator only on a quarter of all the households surveyed, given the problems encountered in measuring and weighing children less than 5 years old.

Table 6.2 Summary of the first plane derived from multiple correspondence analysis[14]

Factor 2 (vertical axis): 2.89% inertia	
Lack of comfort (television, refrigerator, car, radio, watch/alarm clock, iron for pressing clothes, stove)	Access to educational, health infrastructures, and to public transport
	Hygienic toilets
No consultation in case of illness	Roof and walls solid, mattress/bed
Household with all members illiterate	Without plots of land, without cattle, nor goats
No child educated or partly educated	Drinking water
Limited access to educational, health	Births assisted during delivery
infrastructures or to public transport and water	Seldom experience food problems
Non-modern lighting or fuel used	Fuel, electricity, charcoal
Unhygienic toilets	Lighting with power generating units, candles
Undrinkable water	No member sick, all members sick
Housing in non-solid material	
Food problems	
No access to electricity	
POVERTY	WEALTH
Very limited access to infrastructures (education, health, water, public transport, market)	Comfort (car, television, radio, watch/alarm clock, refrigerator, sewing machine, stove, electric iron)
No assistance during childbirth	Solid housing
No child with primary school education	Household members all literate
Some of the members literate	Schooling for all children
Lighting non-modern	Good access to secondary school
Undrinkable water	Hygienic toilets
	Modern lighting, fuel
	Never experience food problems
	Factor 1 (horizontal axis): 10.29% inertia

Source: MCA with SPAD using the QUID 2001 data.

comfort, and durables. The very limited access to education is due to the remoteness of primary and secondary schools, a low literacy rate, and low primary and secondary schooling rates. Households often spend more than an hour to reach school infrastructures. As regards the areas of health, sanitation, and potable water, MCA shows that the poor do not consult health service personnel very often in case of illness, are not very often assisted by qualified personnel, notably during chilbirth. Moreover, medical infrastructures are quite remote from the poor who, in some cases, spend more than an hour to reach them. Furthermore, the poor do not use hygienic toilets, and do not have access to drinking water whose sources of supply – most often drill holes – are not located in the vicinity of their residence areas. During the QUID survey, these households stated that they were always or at times confronted with food problems; and they are often located far from food markets.

In the area of housing, the poor have no access to secure accommodations although, most often, they have ownership of their houses. Their housing is characterized by banco (i.e., mud), sheet metal or straw walls, and thatched or straw

---

[14] See the complete plane in Appendices.

roofs. These materials show very little resistance to natural disasters. In the area of energy, wood is most often used as fuel. As to lighting, poor housholds most often use kerosene storm lamps.

Relative to means of communication, the poor do not have access to television and to radio, and they often travel by bicycle in rural areas. They lack means of comfort such as cooking stoves, irons, refrigerators, freezers, beds, mattresses, and alarm clocks.

On the multidimensional level, it is useful to note that in this group of poor households, we find a category of non-poor households[15] when we consider variables such as ownership of cattle, poultry, and land. On the other hand, when other aspects of poverty such as education, health, drinking water, housing, sanitation, energy, communications, comfort, and nutrition are taken into account, these households become very disadvantaged. This brings out an interesting characteristic in the multidimensional approach to poverty, which requires taking into account several criteria before considering a household as being poor.

Unlike poor households, well-to-do households are the ones who have access to education, health, sanitation, drinking water, secure accommodations, energy, means of communication and transport, food, and goods of comfort.

In the area of education, most of these households are literate, and provide education to all their children, in addition to access to educational infrastructures. They benefit from an acceptable access to health services, are assisted during chilbirth, and consume drinking water. They never experience food problems and dwell in secure accommodations whose walls and roofs are built with solid materials. They use hygienic toilets with flushes connected to sewers, to a cesspool, or they may be ventilated. They use modern energy sources (electricity, gas) for lighting, cooking, and household appliances. They have access to means of communication (television, radio), and public and private transport (public transport, private cars, etc.). Concerning goods of comfort, they are the most equipped with refrigerators, cooking stoves, irons, beds/mattresses, etc. It should be noted that the majority of these housholds do not have ownership of their houses, and neither do they hold assets such as land or cattle.

6.5.2 Construction of the Composite Indicator of Poverty (CIP)

6.5.2.1 Selection of Variables for the Construction of the CIP

Multiple correspondence analysis has provided the basic elements for selecting the variables used in the construction of the CIP. The main criterion to consider here is the first axis ordinal consistency (FAOC) on the Factorial Axis which generally expresses a welfare state. This property is a necessary condition for the CIP to effect an ordering of households in accordance with their level of welfare. It consists, for a given primary indicator, of ensuring that the latter's ordinal welfare structure is

---

[15] These refer to certain ethnic groups such as the " peuhls ".

respected by the ordinal structure of the coordinates (scores) of its modalities on the first axis. Other second order criteria deal with discrimination measures, the spreading over on the first axis, the high frequency of non-responses or the very low frequencies of some of the modalities. The variables finally selected are presented in Table 6.3.

Table 6.3 Final list of 21 variables and 44 modalities for the CIP

Variables	Modalities
Education	
Primary schooling rate	Households providing no education to any child
	Households providing education to some children
	Households providing education to all children
Literacy rate	Illiterate households
	Households in which some members are literate
	Households in which all members are literate
Access to a primary school in less than 30 minutes	Lees than 30 minutes, more than 30 minutes
Access to a secondary school in less than 30 minutes	Less than 30 minutes, more than 30 minutes
Health	
Access to health services in less than 30 minutes	Less than 30 minutes, more than 30 minutes
Drinking water	
Source of water used for drinking	Drinking water, undrinkable water
Access to drinking water in less than 15 minutes	Less than 15 minutes, more than 15 minutes
Nutrition	
Access to food market	Less than 30 minutes, more than 30 minutes
Food problems	Never had a food problem, experience food problems
Housing and sanitation	
Nature of the roof	Roof solid (concrete, cement, slate, zinc), thatched roof, and others
Nature of walls	Cement bricks, banco bricks, and wood
Type of toilets	Toilets hygienic, toilets unhygienic
Energy	
Electricity in the household	Yes, no
Fuel	Modern fuel, non-modern fuel
Type of lighting	Modern lighting source, non-modern lighting source
Communications	
Television	Yes, no
Radio/radio-cassette player	Yes, no
Access to public transport in less than 15 minutes	Less than 15 minutes, more than 15 minutes
Goods of comfort	
Possession of refrigerator/freezer	Yes, no
Possession of mattress/bed	Yes, no
Possession of watch/alarm clock	Yes, no

6.5.2.2 A Final MCA on the CIP Variables

A final MCA run on the 21 variables retained for the construction of the CIP has resulted in a considerable increase in the explanatory power of the first axis, which has risen from 10.29 to 30.94%. The explanatory power of the second axis has also increased from 2.89 to 7.94%. In the new factorial plane, welfare moves from left to right. In this plane, all variables have the ordinal consistency on the first axis (OCFA) property owing to which a net separation of the poor from the rich takes place, for they are opposed on the first factorial axis which describes real welfare states (Fig. 6.1).

The following paragraph provides the scores of different indicators used as weights for the CIP.

6.5.2.3 Weights of the CIP

Relative to the CIP functional form which may be written as $ICP_i = \frac{1}{K}(W_1 I_{i1} + W_2 I_{i2} + \ldots + W_P I_{iP})$, where all variable modalities have been transformed into binary indicators encoded with either 0 or 1, the weights $W_{p, \quad p=1 \, à \, P}$ correspond to standardized scores $\left(\frac{score}{\sqrt{\lambda_1}}, \lambda_1 \text{ being the first eigen value}\right)$ on the first factorial axis. These scores are presented in Table 6.4, in addition to the contributions of variables to the construction of the axis, and square cosines of modalities.

Modalities with positive scores increase welfare, while those with negative scores reduce it. The largest positive scores are observed to be associated with goods and services of comfort whose access is limited to a certain number of well-to-do households. The richer the households are, the more access they have to these goods and services which include, possessing a refrigerator, a television, using a modern source of lighting and fuel, access to electricity, and the acquisition of literacy by all household members.

Modalities associated with the largest negative scores on the first axis are the most accessible goods and services. The poorest the households are, the less they possess such goods. This is a situation in which households lack beds/mattresses to sleep on, the roofs and walls of their houses are built with nonresistant materials, they have no access to drinking water or to hygienic toilets, a situation in which illiteracy prevails with no access to primary schools.

The way in which weights are determined here confers to the MCA an interesting property which aims to separate the poor from the rich as much as possible. The attribution of significant weights to scarce or luxury goods indicates an increase in welfare, on the one hand, and of higher weights to the most accessible goods to a decrease in welfare, on the other hand, expresses the logic of the MCA pocedure which aims at a better identification of poor populations. According to this method, a household with access to several luxury goods will tend to have a high living standard, which can be said to correspond to actual fact. Moreover, a household will be all the poorer because it has less or no access to the basic goods accessible to the majority of the population.

As shown in Table 6.5, the variables that have contributed the most to the construction of the first axis involve the energy area, and more specifically, access to

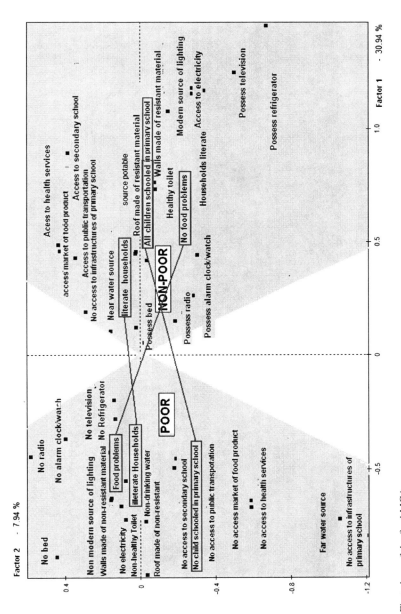

Fig. 6.1 First plane of the final MCA
Source: Calculated with SPAD using the QUID 2001/DPS survey data.

Table 6.4 Scores, contributions and square cosines of the final MCA

Variables/modalities	Scores on the first axis	Contribution/ discrimination	Cosines squared	Distance to the center	Frequencies
Refrigerator/freezer		5.7			
Refrigerator/freezer	1.46	4.8	0.41	5.21	0.16
No refrigerator/freezer	−0.28	0.9	0.41	0.19	0.84
Television		7.4			
Possess television	1.25	5.6	0.53	2.92	0.25
No television	−0.42	1.9	0.52	0.34	0.75
Mattress/bed		0.6			
Possess mattress/bed	0.05	0	0.04	0.06	0.94
No mattress/bed	−0.88	0.6	0.05	17.00	0.06
Radio		0.9			
Radio	0.15	0.2	0.07	0.33	0.75
No radio	−0.44	0.7	0.06	3.06	0.25
Watch/alarm clock		1.4			
Watch/alarm clock	0.26	0.6	0.09	0.72	0.58
No watch/alarm clock	−0.36	0.8	0.09	1.40	0.42
Electricity		10.4			
Electricity	1.18	6.8	0.74	1.87	0.35
No electricity	−0.62	3.6	0.72	0.53	0.65
Food problems		1.2			
Never had food problems	0.44	0.9	0.09	2.23	0.31
Experience food problems	−0.2	0.4	0.09	0.45	0.69
Nature of roof		6.2			
Roof solid	0.46	2	0.45	0.47	0.68
Roof non-solid	−0.96	4.2	0.44	2.11	0.32
Nature of walls		8.2			
Cement bricks	0.74	4	0.59	0.92	0.52
Banco (mud) walls	−0.79	4.2	0.58	1.08	0.48
Drinking water		4.6			
Drinking water	0.45	1.8	0.33	0.61	0.62
Undrinkable water	−0.73	2.8	0.33	1.63	0.38
Type of toilets		7.7			
Toilets hygienic	0.77	4	0.57	1.05	0.49
Toilets unhygienic	−0.72	3.7	0.54	0.95	0.51
Fuel for cooking		8.3			
Fuel modern	1.08	5.5	0.60	1.95	0.34
Fuel non-modern	−0.55	2.8	0.59	0.51	0.66
Type of lighting		10.3			
Source of lighting modern	1.16	6.7	0.74	1.81	0.36
Source of lighting non-modern	−0.63	3.6	0.72	0.55	0.64

Table 6.4 (Continued)

Variables/modalities	Scores on the first axis	Contribution/ discrimination	Cosines squared	Distance to the center	Frequencies
Access to water		1			
Less than 15 minutes	0.1	0.1	0.07	0.14	0.87
More than 15 minutes	−0.72	0.9	0.07	7.00	0.13
Access to food market		4.1			
– Less than 30 minutes	0.46	1.7	0.29	0.72	0.58
– More than 30 minutes	−0.64	2.4	0.29	1.39	0.42
Access to public transport		3.3			
– Less than 15 minutes	0.43	1.5	0.24	0.78	0.56
– More than 15 minutes	−0.55	1.9	0.24	1.29	0.44
Access to primary school		2.1			
– Less than 30 minutes	0.19	0.4	0.15	0.24	0.81
– More than 30 minutes	−0.79	1.7	0.15	4.24	0.19
Access to secondary school		5.7			
– Less than 30 minutes	0.9	3.8	0.42	1.95	0.34
– More than 30 minutes	−0.45	1.9	0.39	0.51	0.66
Access to health services		4.6			
– Less than 30 minutes	0.49	1.9	0.33	0.73	0.58
– More than 30 minutes	−0.66	2.6	0.32	1.38	0.42
Primary net rate of schooling		1.8			
No child attending school	−0.49	1	0.16	1.52	0.40
Some children attending school	−0.13	0	0.00	3.46	0.22
All children attending school	0.42	0.7	0.11	1.64	0.38
Literacy rate		4.3			
All illiterate	−0.66	1.9	0.20	2.22	0.31
Some literate	0.12	0.1	0.02	0.76	0.57
All literate	1.17	2.3	0.19	7.38	0.12

Source: Calculations with SPAD using the QUID 2001/DPS survey data.

electricity, the type of lighting, and the fuel used for cooking. Next in line follow the nature of walls, the type of toilets, television, the nature of the roof, the refrigerator, access to secondary school, access to drinking water, access to health services, and the literacy rate.

The variables which contributed the least to the formation of the first axis are the possession of a bed, a mattress, a radio or an alarm clock, and food problems.

6.5.2.4 Sensitivity Analysis for the CIP

The objective here is to underline the fact that the CIP orders households in accordance with their levels of welfare. Table 6.6 clearly shows that the percentage of households with no access to basic needs strictly dereases from the first to the last

Table 6.5 Discrimination measures and contributions to the construction of the first axis

Variables	Discrimination measures	Contributions (%)	Variables	Discrimination measures	Contributions (%)
Electricity	0.750	10.4	Literacy rate	0.312	4.3
Type of lighting	0.747	10.4	Access to food markets	0.296	4.1
Cooking fuel	0.601	8.3	Access to public transport	0.239	3.3
Nature of walls	0.593	8.2	Access to primary school	0.15	2.1
Type of toilets	0.558	7.7	Net enrollment ratio at the primary level	0.125	1.7
Television	0.536	7.4	Watch/alarm clock	0.098	1.4
Nature of roof	0.448	6.2	Food problems	0.089	1.2
Refrigerator/ freezer	0.411	5.7	Access to water	0.075	1.0
Access to secondary school	0.411	5.7	Radio	0.066	0.9
Drinking water	0.334	4.6	Mattress/bed	0.047	0.7
Access to health services	0.329	4.6	Total	7.215	100

Source: Calculations with SPSS using QUID 2001/DPS survey data.

CIP quintile. For instance, the percentage of households with no access to television amounts to 99.7 in the first quintile, 99.2 in the second quintile, 93.6 in the third quintile, 62.9 in the fourth quintile, and 17.2 in the last quintile. The same trends are found again in the case of other aspects such as education, health, drinking water, nutrition, housing, sanitation, energy, communications, and comfort goods.

The CIP is a welfare indicator which ranks households according to their non-monetary welfare levels. Since all households are not affected by the same type of multidimensional poverty, the following paragraph summarizes nonmonetary poverty typology.

6.5.3 Typology of Nonmonetary Poverty

Figure 6.2 permits to distinguish three types of nonmonetary poverty: a poverty indicative of the vulnerabilty of human existence (inadequacy of human capital, and unpleasant living conditions), poverty from the standpoint of infrastructures, and poverty in terms of household comfort.

The vulnerabilty of human existence is the most perceptible form of poverty. It is the form of poverty that characterizes a poor person at first glance. It is attributable

Table 6.6 Percentage of households with no access to basic needs according to CIP quintile

Dimensions of nonmonetary poverty	CIP quintiles				
	1	2	3	4	5
Do not possess television	99.7	99.2	93.6	62.9	17.2
Do not possess mattress/bed	14.1	8.4	3.5	1.5	0.3
Do not possess radio	37.2	33.2	23.8	20.7	8.3
Do not possess watch/alarm clock	58.2	51.8	43.8	38.6	16.3
Do not have access to electricity	99.7	99.5	95	31.7	0.1
Experiencing food problems	83.1	78.7	71.3	65.8	46.2
Non-solid roof	87.1	54.5	18.4	0.5	0
Non-solid walls	98	83.7	48.4	8.8	0.9
Undrinkable water	78	59.6	36.5	14.3	1.7
Unhygienic toilets	96.9	83.7	58	16.4	1.5
Non-modern fuel	99.8	98.3	86.3	39.2	6.7
Non-modern lighting	99.9	98.4	93.7	30	0.1
Water source at more than 15 minutes	30.6	14.7	8.4	6.9	1.9
Food market at more than 30 minutes	87.4	57.8	31.8	26.4	5.6
Public transport at more than 15 minutes	88.6	52.8	37.1	28	12.1
Primary school at more than 30 minutes	54.4	17.5	10.7	11.6	1.3
Secondary school at more than 30 minutes	99.5	92.7	72.9	50.5	15.1
Health service at more than 30 minutes	92.9	58.1	30	23.8	5.6
Households with no child attending primary school	63.6	46.9	40.8	27.7	12.4
Illiterate households	62.1	44.4	28.2	17.2	3.5
Do not possess refrigerator/freezer	100	100	99.3	87.1	33.4

Source: From the QUID 2001/DPS survey data.

to the housing conditions of the poor: banco (mud) walls, thatched roof, absence of drinking water, toilets, electricity, television, the use of wood as fuel, and of a storm oil lamp for lighting.

In addition to these difficult conditions, parents and children alike are not educated, do not visit health services, and do not eat their fill. These vulnerable households do not have at their disposal the minimum capacities which could help improve their living conditions, and their possibilities of choice are very limited.

Beyond the vulnerability of human existence, one will find poverty in terms of infrastructures, and poverty in terms of household equipment and comfort. The first manifests itself through poor access to infrastructures such as schools and health services, sources of drinking water, food markets etc. This form of poverty exceeds the possiblities of a household. It is rather directly linked to the policies and capacity of the State to equitably porvide the basic infrastructures necessary for improving the living conditions of their populations. The third and last form of poverty manifests itself through the under-equipment of households in terms of durable and comfort goods such as refrigerators, televisions, radios, alarm clocks, and beds.

Since we have just covered the different types of multidimensional poverty, the following paragraphs will help appreciate the ranking of urban and rural areas, regions and socioeconomic groups relative to the CIP.

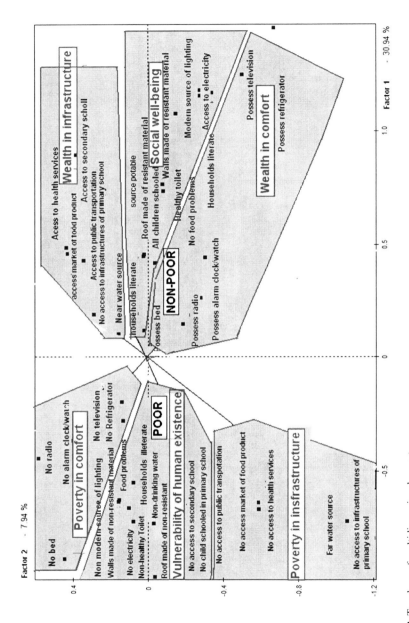

Fig. 6.2 Typology of multidimensional poverty
Source: Calculations with SPAD using QUID 2001/DPS data.

6.5.4 CIPs Characteristic of the Household Head

6.5.4.1 CIP and Residence Area

For a given category, the CIP corresponds to the mean of standardized scores on the first axis for individuals possessing this category. The following graph gives the position of urban and rural areas relative to the CIP. Welfare moves from left to right. The farther left the category is located, the more it is linked to poverty, and the farther right it is, the more it indicates a position of wealth.

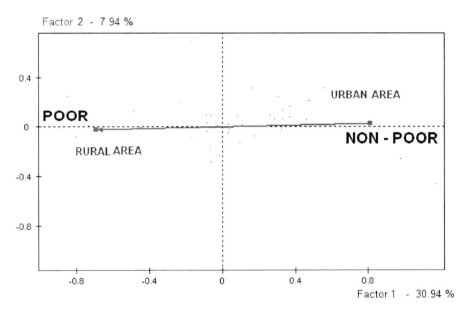

Graph 6.1 CIP and residence area
Source: Calculations using the QUID 2001/DPS survey data.

The welfare axis (the horizontal axis) directly associates the rural area with poverty and the urban area with wealth. Overall, it shows that household living standards are distinctly better in the urban area than in the rural area. The CIP is equal to -0.69 for the rural area and 0.81 for the urban area. Of the three forms of nonmonetary poverty identified above, the rural area is the most affected by all of them.

6.5.4.2 CIP and Regions

The following graph presents the regions in the first factorial plane.

The poverty axis isolates the most urbanized regions, namely, Dakar and Thiès, and shows that in general, households residing in these localities enjoy a higher well-being than those in other regions. Regions with low living standards are

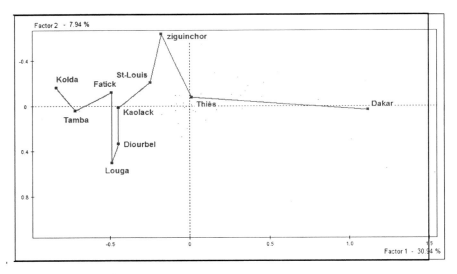

Graph 6.2 CIP and regions
Source: Calculations using the QUID 2001/DPS survey data.

those of Kolda and Tambacounda. As to other regions, their living standards range between these two extremes. The regions of Ziguinchor, Louga et Diourbel are positioned significantly further apart from the first axis. The Ziguinchor region is not only affected by the vulnerabily of human existence, but it seems particularly affected by the lack of comfort and household equipment. Concerning the regions of Louga and Diourbel, the lack of infrastructures sets them apart from the other regions. The regional CIP values are presented in the Appendices.

6.5.4.3 CIP and Household Head Gender

The following factorial graph shows that the CIP is higher for women household heads (0.37) than for men household heads (−0.10). This means that overall, households managed by a woman have a higher level of welfare than those managed by a man.

6.5.4.4 CIP and the Household Head Activities

The CIP very clearly distinguishes two categories of activities: agriculture broadly defined, and nonagricultural activities (administration, industry, commerce, construction, services, and others). In the factorial graph, the welfare axis associates

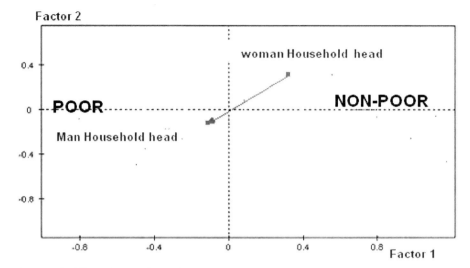

Graph 6.3 CIP and household head sex
Source: Calculations using the QUID 2001/DPS survey data.

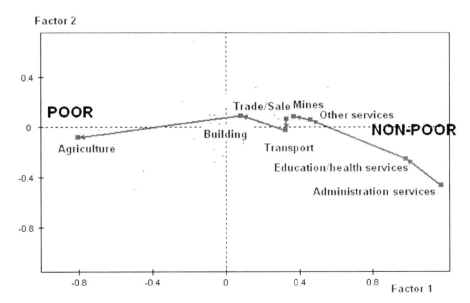

Graph 6.4 CIP and household head activities
Source: Calculations using the QUID 2001/DPS survey data.

agriculture with poverty, and other activities with wealth, implying that the welfare level of households whose head carries out an agricultural activity is lower than that of households managed by a head engaged in other activities.

6.5.4.5 CIP and Household Head Matrimonial Status

The following graph shows that polygamy is associated with poverty, whereas monogamists, divorced, widowers, and singles are positioned on the wealth side.

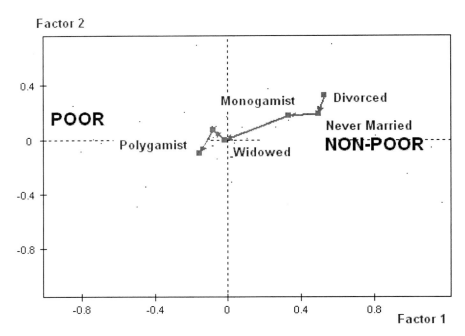

Graph 6.5 CIP and household head matrimonial status
Source: Calculations using the QUID 2001/DPS survey data.

6.5.4.6 CIP and Household Size

On the following graph, the welfare axis shows that the living standard of households falls with their size, meaning that the bigger the household size, the higher the household level of poverty also is.

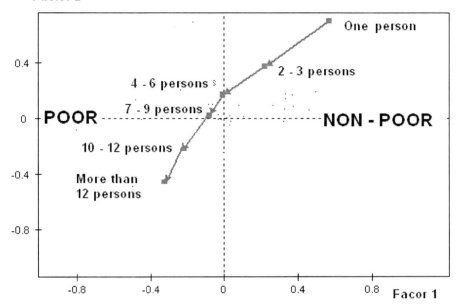

Graph 6.6 CIP and household size
Source: calculations using the QUID 2001/DPS survey data.

6.5.5 Incidence of Multidimensional Poverty

6.5.5.1 Classification of Households

By ranking households in increasing order of CIP values (see Appendices), the histogram of index nodes shows a disconnection between the first and second node, thus indicating the pertinence of grouping households into two classes. Classification results are given in Table 6.7.

Table 6.7 Proportion of classes

	Minimum	Maximum	%
Poor	−1.03	0.1172	61
Non-poor	0.1178	1.11	39
Total	−1.03	1.11	100

Source: Calculations using the QUID 2001/DPS survey data.

6.5.5.2 Class Characteristics

As the Table 6.8 indicates, poor households are the ones that actually do not have access to basic needs. This class of poor persons mostly brings together households with no access to modern energy, health, education, secure housing, the media,

Table 6.8 Characteristics of the poor class

Active variables	Modalities	% of the class in the modality	% of the modality within the class	Total frequency of the modality
Access to electricity	No access to electricity	92	98	65
Type of lighting	Non-modern source of lighting	92	97	64
Fuel	Non-modern	87	94	66
Nature of walls	Banco (mud) bricks	96	76	48
Type of toilets	Unhygienic	94	78	51
Television	No television	80	97	74
Nature of roof	Non-solid roof	100	53	32
Refrigerator/freezer	No refrigera-tor/freezer	72	100	84
Access to secondary school	More than 30 minutes	80	87	66
Drinking water	Non-potable source	92	57	38
Access to health services	More than 30 minutes	86	59	42
Access to food markets	More than 30 minutes	85	58	42
Access to public transport	More than 15 minutes	82	59	44
Literacy	Illiterate households	88	45	31
Schooling at the primary level	Household with no child attending school	82	39	29
Access to primary school	More than 30 minutes	87	27	19
Possession of alarm clock/watch	No alarm clock/watch	75	51	42
Food problems	Experience food problems	68	77	69
Access to source of drinking water	More than 15 minutes	86	18	12
Possession of radio	No radio	78	31	25
Possession of bed/mattresss	No bed/mattress	93	8	6
Illustrative variables				
Residence area	Rural	93	82	54
Main activity	Agriculture	95	50	32
Region	Kolda	94	11	7
Region	Tamba	89	8	6
Region	Kaolack	82	13	10
Region	Fatick	87	9	6
Sex	Male	64	86	81
Region	Diourbel	80	14	11
Matrimonial status	Polygamous	67	32	29
Household size	More than 9 persons	64	40	38

Table 6.8 (Continued)

Active variables	Modalities	% of the class in the modality	% of the modality within the class	Total frequency of the modality
Matrimonial status	Monogamous	62	56	56
Household size	Between 6 and 9 persons	61	39	39
Main activity	Construction	60	3	3
Main activity	Transport	48	2	3

Source: Calculations using the QUID 2001/DPS survey data.

drinking water, nutrition, basic infrastructures, and elements of comfort. These households for the most part reside in the rural area (82%), and agriculture is their main activity. This class is also characteristic of large and polygamous families. Households managed by men in this class predominate those managed by women. It should be noted that no household in this class owns a refrigerator, and all the households of this class live under a roof built with non-solid material.

Concerning the rich class, it gathers together households that have a satisfacory access to basic needs. The characteristics of this class are summarized in the following Table 6.9.

Table 6.9 Characteristics of the non-poor class

Active variables	Modalities	% of the class in the in the modality	% of the modality within the class	Total frequency in the modality
Electricity in the household	Electricity	97	86	35
Type of lighting	Modern source of lighting	96	87	36
Fuel	Modern fuel	90	78	34
Nature of walls	Cement bricks	72	95	52
Type of toilets	Hygienic toilets	74	91	48
Television	Television	94	61	25
Nature of the roof	Solid roof	57	100	68
Refrigerator/freezer	Refrigerator/freezer	99	41	16
Access to secondary school	Less than 30 minutes	77	66	34
Access to drinking water	Potable source	58	92	62
Access to health services	Less than 30 minutes	57	85	58
Access to food markets	Les than 30 minutes	56	83	58
Access to public transport	Less than 15 minutes	56	79	56
Literacy	All households literate	88	27	12

Table 6.9 (Continued)

Active variables	Modalities	% of the class in the in the modality	% of the modality within the class	Total frequency in the modality
Access to primary school	Less than 30 minutes	45	93	80
Possession of alarm clock/watch	Watch	49	73	58
Food problems	No food problems ever	56	44	31
Schooling at the primary level	Households schooling all the children	56	40	28
Possession of radio	Radio	45	86	75
Access to source of drinking water	Lees than 15 minutes	43	95	87
Possession of bed/ mattress	Bed/mattress	41	99	94
Literacy	Households with some literate members	43	63	57
Illustrative variables				
Residence area	Urban	76	90	46
Region	Dakar	92	60	26
Main activity	Administration	92	7	3
Main activity	Education/health	83	6	3
Sex	Female	54	26	19
Main activity	Services and others	59	15	10
Main activity	Commerce/sale	53	18	13
Matrimonial status	Divorced	64	4	2
Matrimonial status	Single	60	5	3
Household size	Between 1 and 5 persons	45	28	24
Matrimonial status	Monogamous	38	54	56
Region	Thiès	36	12	13
Region	Ziguinchor	24	3	5
Region	St Louis	26	7	11

Source: Calculation using the QUID 2001/DPS survey data.

This class of the non-poor is characterized by access to electricity, secure housing, drinking water, health, education, nutrition, the media, household appliances, and goods of comfort. The majority of these households live in urban areas (90%), and they are engaged in administrative, trade, and service activities. They are not very numerous, and the household manager in this class is often monogamous, single, or divorced.

6.5.5.3 Multidimensional Poverty Thresholds

Firstly, and as an illustration, we may consider the intermediate value separating the poor class and the non-poor class as a threshold below which a household may be considered as being poor. This value may be approximated by

[Maximum CIP value in the poor class] × [Poor class weight]

+minimum CIP value in the rich class] × [Rich class weight].

With a maximum of 0.1172 for the poor class, and a minimum value of 0.1178 for the non-poor class, we obtain an intermediate value of 0.1174.

From this value, we can calculate the FGT[16] indices for $\alpha = 0$ corresponding to the incidence of poverty.

A poverty threshold can also be defined from the partial thresholds determined for each basic indicator used in the construction of CIP. By considering a household of reference with access to basic needs, its CIP which will define a multidimensional poverty threshold, can be calculated.

In the case of this study, we have 19 binary variables and 2 variables (primary education and literacy) with 3 modalities. If we assume that our household of reference is not poor in all dimensions, the result would be almost the same, as if we had chosen an intersection from partial poverty thresholds.

Let's assume that a household is not poor in all the 19 (binary) dimensions, that all its children attend school, and all household members are literate; this household will have the greatest CIP value, which is equal to 1.11. For another household that is destitute in all dimensions, the minimum CIP value will be −1.03. To determine our threshold, we have considered a household of reference with access to a subgroup of basic goods and services. Most of the partial thresholds considered come from the PRSP drawn up for Senegal. This household has the following characteristics (Table 6.10):

Table 6.10 Characteristics of the household of reference

Goods to which it has access	Goods to which it has no access
1 – All its children attend school	14 – No television
2 – It has access to primary school in less than 30 minutes	15 – No watch/alarm clock
3 – It has access to health services in less than 30 minutes	16 – Non-modern cooking fuel
	17 – Food market more than 30 minutes away
4 – It consumes drinking water	18 – No refrigerator/freezer
5 – Its source of water is less than 15 minutes away	19 – May not have access to electricity produced by SENELEC, but uses modern energy
6 – It does not have food problems	20 – Public transport more than 15 minutes away
7 – Some of its members are literate	21 – Secondary school more than 30 minutes away
8 – It uses modern energy (electricity, sun, gas)	
9 – It has a radio	
10 – A roof built with resistant material	
11 – Walls built with resistant material	
12 – It has a mattress/bed	CIP value of household of reference (threshold) = 0.088
13 – Hygienic toilets	

[16] Foster, Greer, and Thorbecke (1984).

With these characteristics, the household of reference has a CIP score of 0.088. This threshold is close to the one obtained by ranking households in increasing order (0.1174). The incidences obtained are presented in the following paragraph.

6.5.5.4 Monetary and Multidimensional Poverty According to Household Head Characteristics

The incidence of poverty with households classified in increasing order corresponds to the weight of the poor class which is equal to 61%. With a household of reference, we have an incidence close to 60% against an incidence of 48.5% for monetary poverty.

On the monetary as well as nonmonetary level, the rural area remains the most affected as compared to the urban area, though multidimensional poverty is more pronounced in the rural area, however. The least poor regions are the most urbanized, such as the cities of Dakar, Thiès, and Saint-Louis. The poorest cities are those of Kolda, Tambacounda, and Fatick. The status of regional poverty on the multidimensional level is similar to the one observed on the monetary level. In effect, the rank correlation of regions according to both types of poverty is equal to 0.73 (Table 6.11).

Table 6.11 Multidimensional and Monetary Poverty According to Household Head Characteristics

Variables	Modalities	Incidence of multidimensional poverty/ Classification (1)	Incidence of multidimensional poverty/ household of reference (2)	Incidence /monetary poverty (3)[17]	Deviations (1)–(3)	Deviations (2)–(3)
Area	Urban	23.9	22.3	37.6	−14	−15
	Rural	93.1	92.3	64.9	28.2	27.4
Total		61.2	60	48.5	12.7	11.5
Region	Dakar	8.6	7.4	33.6	−25	−26.2
	Ziguinchor	75.8	74.3	67.1	8.7	7.2
	Diourbel	80.9	80.2	61.5	19.4	18.7
	St Louis	74.3	72.9	41.2	33.1	31.7
	Tamba	89.5	88.6	56.2	33.3	32.4
	Kaolack	81.7	80.4	65.3	16.4	15.1
	Thiès	64.6	62.5	48.6	16	13.9
	Louga	80.4	79.4	36.2	44.2	43.2
	Fatick	87.7	86.9	46.3	41.4	40.6
	Kolda	94	93.8	66.5	27.5	27.3
Total		61.2	60	48.5	12.7	11.5
Sex	Male	64.7	63.6	51.2	13.5	12.4
	Female	46.4	45.1	37.1	9.3	8
Total		61.2	60	48.5	12.7	11.5

---

[17] The monetary results are drawn from the ESAM II Report on poverty produced by the DPS, and entitled " La pauvreté au Sénégal : de la dévaluation de 1994 à 2001–2002 "

Table 6.11 (Continued)

Variables	Modalities	Incidence of multidimensional poverty/ Classification (1)	Incidence of multidimensional poverty/ household of reference (2)	Incidence /monetary poverty (3)[17]	Deviations (1)–(3)	Deviations (2)–(3)
Size	1 person	34.9	34.6	3.3	31.6	31.3
	2 to 3	51.5	50.2	8.7	42.8	41.5
	4 to 6	62.7	61.8	32.7	30	29.1
	7 to 9	64.7	63.1	53.5	11.2	9.6
	10 to 12	63.5	61.9	60.4	3.1	1.5
	More than 12	59.8	59	69.4	−9.6	−10.4
Total		61.2	60	48.5	12.7	11.5
Matrimonial status	Monogamous	62.3	61.2	47	15.3	14.2
	Polygamous	66.8	65.4	56	10.8	9.4
	Single	39.4	39.4	28.2	11.2	11.2
	Widower	48.9	47	41.9	7	5.1
	Divorced	35.7	35	38.2	−2.5	−3.2
	Other	55.5	55.5	–	–	–
Total		61.2	60	48.5	12.7	11.5
Main activity	Agriculture	95.2	95	72.2	23	22.8
	Mines, quarries	45.3	43.1	36.6	8.7	6.5
	Construction	59.3	58.1	52.9	6.4	5.2
	Transport	48	46.1	37.3	10.7	8.8
	Commerce/sales	47.6	46	33.7	13.9	12.3
	Services	41	39.7	34.2	6.8	5.5
	Education/health	16.9	16.9	15.3	1.6	1.6
	Administration	8.7	7.8	8.6	0.1	−0.8
	Others	50.7	48.7	44.1	6.6	4.6
Total		61.2	60	48.5	12.7	11.5

Source: l4ESAM II/DPS Report on monetary poverty and calculations using the QUID 2001/DPS survey data.

For both concepts of poverty, households managed by a woman are less poor than those managed by a man. Both monetary and nonmonetary poverty increase with household size. It should be noted that multidimensional poverty does not increase with household size indefinitely. Relative to the matrimonial status of the household head, polygamists are poorer than monogamists, singles, widowers, and divorcees. Relative to activity, on the monetary as well as on the nonmonetary level, farmers remain the poorest.

6.5.6 Divergence and Convergence of Multidimensional and Monetary Poverty by Region

With a rank correlation of 0.5 between regions according to the two measures, over-all convergence is average. As indicated in Map 6.1, convergence is perfect in the areas of Dakar and Saint-Louis which keep the same ranks relative to the two mea-

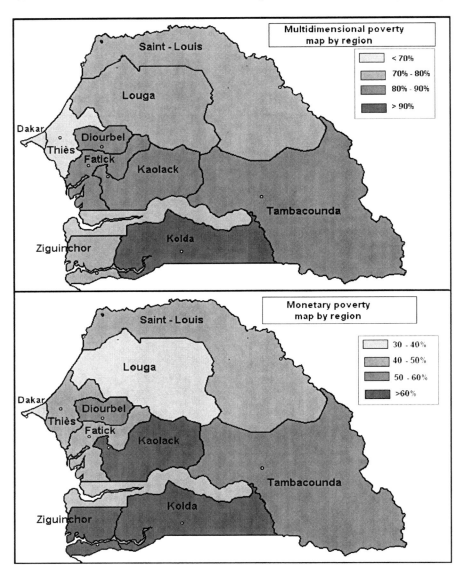

Map 6.1 Mapping of multidimensional and monetary poverty
Source: ESAM II/DPS Report on monetary poverty, and calculations by the authors for
multidimensional poverty.

sures. It is also very strong in the regions of Kolda, Tambacounda, and Diourbel. It is
average for the regions of Thiès, Louga, and Fatick. There exists a strong divergence
for the region of Ziguinchor which is less poor on the multidimensional level, but
very poor on the monetary level. This is probably due to the good position it holds
on the educational level, since it registers the highest rates of access to education

among the regions in Senegal each year. But this situation is not accompanied by an unlimited access to monetary resources owing to market imperfections, notably, in the labor market.

6.5.7 Link between Monetary and Nonmonetary Poverty

In general, this amounts to looking for the correlations between monetary and non-monetary poverty and, in particular, to find out whether those who are poor at the nonmonetary level, are also poor on the monetary level. The following graph, which positions the quintiles of expenditure per head and per adult equivalent relative to the composite poverty index, detects a positive relationship between the two indicators

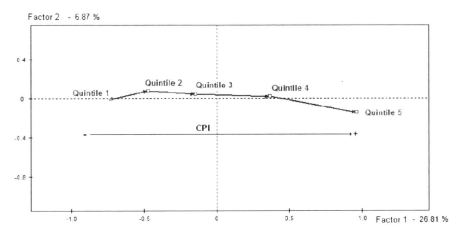

Graph 6.7 CIP and quintiles of expenditure per adult equivalent
Source: Calculations using the QUID and ESAM II 2001/DPS survey data.

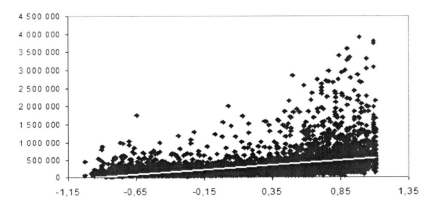

Graph 6.8 Expenditure per adult equivalent as a function of the CIP
Source: Calculations using the QUID and ESAM II 2001/DPS survey data.

of welfare measurement. The first quintiles position themselves toward the lowest CIP values, and the last quintiles toward the highest CIP values.

The graph below, which presents expenditure per head as a function of the CIP, shows a cluster of points revealing a positive correlation between the two indicators. These results confirm the link established in the preceding factorial graph.

The correlation coefficient between the CIP and expenditure per head and per adult equivalent is equal to 0.47.[18] The nonparametric correlation coefficient between housholds ranks according to the CIP and expenditure per head is 0.60. These results show that there exists a positive link between monetary and nonmonetary poverty. This means that when a poor person is destitute on the nonmonetary level, he is also more likely to be poor on the monetary level. The results of a nonparametric regression establishing the link between the CIP and expenditure per head corroborate the results arrived at earlier.

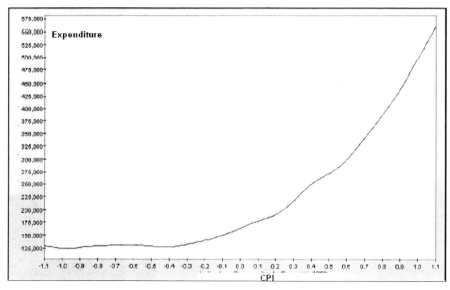

Graph 6.9 Nonparametric regression between the CIP and expenditures per adult equivalent
Source: Calculations using the QUID and ESAM II 2001/DPS survey data.

The preceding graph shows that the higher the CIP value, the higher the expenditure per head and per adult equivalent also, with the implication that households with high human capital, access to infrastuctures and goods of comfort, tend to be less poor from the monetary standpoint.

The following Table 6.12 supports the preceding conclusions, and shows a decline in the incidence of monetary poverty when going from the first to the last CIP quintile. Similarly, the incidence of multidimensional poverty decreases from the first to the last quintile of expenditure per head and per adult equivalent.

---

[18] Significant at the 1% level, Weight=weight*size.

Table 6.12 Nonmonetary poverty and expenditure per head

Quintile of expenditure per head and per adult equivalent	Incidence of multidimensional poverty/ Classification	Incidence of multidimensional poverty/ household of reference	CIP quintiles	Incidence of monetary poverty
1	93.7	92.6	1	73.3
2	83.4	82.3	2	72.5
3	69.0	67.6	3	59.1
4	42.6	40.8	4	30.5
5	17.4	16.9	5	7.2
Total	61.2	60	Total	48.5

Source: Calculations using the QUID and ESAM II 2001/DPS survey data.

To the question « How many monetary poor can we identify on the level of the nonmonetary poor, and vice-versa ?, » the following Table 6.13 provides some answers.

Table 6.13 Overlapping of nonmonetary poverty and monetary poverty

	Incidence of nonmonetary poverty – classification	Incidence of non-monetary poverty – household of reference	Incidence of monetary poverty
Group of the nonmonetary poor – classification	100%	98%	68%
Group of the nonmonetary poor – household of reference	100%	100%	68%
Group of the monetary poor	85%	84%	100%

Source: Calculations using the QUID and ESAM II 2001/DPS survey data.

Nearly 68% of the multidimensional poor are equally affected by monetary poverty. As to the monetary poor, more than 84% of them are also affected by multidimensional poverty. These results show that there actually exists some overlapping between these two concepts of poverty, although we may find that some nonmonetary poor completely escape monetary poverty, and vice versa. The following paragraph highlights this situation:

6.5.8 Extent of Double Poverty

The question here is to determine the proportion of households affected both by monetary and nonmonetary poverty, the proportion of those who are poor on the nonmonetary level and non-poor on the monetary level and vice versa, and those

Table 6.14 Extent of double poverty

		Method of classification					Method used for the household of reference				
		The multidimensional and monetary poor	The multidimensional poor and monetary non-poor	The multidimensional non-poor and monetary poor	The multidimensional non-poor and monetary non-poor	Total	The multidimensional and monetary poor	The multidimensional poor and monetary non-poor	The multidimensional non-poor and monetary poor	The multidimensional non-poor and monetary non-poor	Total
Area	Urban	16.8	7.1	20.8	55.3	100	15.7	6.6	21.9	55.8	100
	Rural	60.1	32.9	4.8	2.1	100	59.6	32.7	5.3	2.4	100
Total		41.6	19.6	6.9	31.8	100	40.8	19.2	7.7	32.3	100
Region	Dakar	4.7	3.9	28.9	62.9	100	4.0	3.4	29.6	63.0	100
	Ziguinchor	58.2	17.6	8.9	15.3	100	57.1	17.2	10.0	15.7	100
	Diourbel	57.5	23.3	4.0	15.1	100	57.0	23.2	4.5	15.3	100
	St Louis	37.7	36.5	3.5	22.2	100	37.0	35.9	4.2	22.9	100
	Tamba	53.1	36.3	3.1	7.6	100	52.6	36.0	3.6	7.8	100
	Kaolack	61.1	20.6	4.2	14.1	100	60.2	20.2	5.1	14.5	100
	Thiès	40.1	24.5	8.5	27.0	100	38.8	23.7	9.8	27.7	100
	Louga	33.7	46.7	2.5	17.2	100	33.3	46.1	2.9	17.7	100
	Fatick	43.7	44.0	2.6	9.7	100	43.3	43.6	3.0	10.1	100
	Kolda	65.1	28.9	1.4	4.2	100	65.0	28.8	1.5	4.7	100
Total		41.6	19.6	6.9	31.8	100	40.8	19.2	7.7	32.3	100
Sex	Male	44.9	19.8	6.3	29.0	100	44.1	19.5	7.1	29.3	100
	Female	27.5	18.9	9.6	44.0	100	26.7	18.4	10.4	44.5	100
Total		41.6	19.6	6.9	31.8	100	40.8	19.2	7.7	32.3	100
Size	1 person	2.9	32.1	0.4	64.6	100	2.9	31.7	0.4	65.0	100
	2 to 3	7.1	44.4	1.6	47.0	100	6.9	43.3	1.8	48.0	100
	4 to 6	29.2	33.5	3.5	33.9	100	28.8	33.0	3.9	34.3	100
	7 to 9	48.3	16.3	5.2	30.1	100	47.1	16.0	6.4	30.5	100
	10 to 12	52.8	10.7	7.6	28.8	100	51.4	10.5	9.0	29.1	100
	More than 12	54.0	5.8	15.4	24.8	100	53.3	5.7	16.1	24.9	100
Total		41.6	19.6	6.9	31.8	100	40.8	19.2	7.7	32.3	100

Table 6.14 (Continued)

		Method of classification					Method used for the household of reference				
		The multidimensional and monetary poor	The multidimensional poor and monetary non-poor	The multidimensional non-poor and monetary poor	The multidimensional non-poor and monetary non-poor	Total	The multidimensional and monetary poor	The multidimensional poor and monetary non-poor	The multidimensional non-poor and monetary poor	The multidimensional non-poor and monetary non-poor	Total
Matrimonial status	Monogamous	41.6	20.7	5.4	32.3	100	40.9	20.3	6.1	32.7	100
	Polygamous	47.9	18.8	8.1	25.1	100	46.9	18.5	9.1	25.5	100
	Single	22.2	17.2	6.0	54.5	100	22.2	17.2	6.0	54.6	100
	Widower	29.7	19.2	12.2	38.9	100	28.5	18.5	13.4	39.6	100
	Divorcee	25.7	10.0	12.5	51.9	100	25.2	9.8	13.0	52.0	100
Total		41.6	19.6	6.9	31.8	100	40.8	19.2	7.7	32.3	100
Activities	Agriculture	70.2	25.1	2.0	2.8	100	70.1	24.9	2.1	2.9	100
	Mines, quarries	27.4	17.9	9.2	45.5	100	26.1	17.0	10.5	46.4	100
	Construction	40.7	18.6	12.2	28.5	100	39.9	18.2	13.0	28.9	100
	Transport	28.7	19.4	8.6	43.3	100	27.6	18.5	9.7	44.2	100
	Commerce/Sales	25.7	21.8	8.0	44.5	100	24.8	21.2	8.9	45.1	100
	Services	24.0	17.0	10.2	48.8	100	23.2	16.5	11.0	49.3	100
	Education/health	8.4	8.5	6.9	76.2	100	8.4	8.5	6.9	76.2	100
	Administration	2.7	6.0	5.9	85.4	100	2.4	5.4	6.2	86.0	100
	Others	34.3	16.4	9.8	39.5	100	32.9	15.8	11.2	40.1	100
Total		41.6	19.6	6.9	31.8	100	40.8	19.2	7.7	32.3	100

Source: Calculations using the QUID and ESAM II 2001/DPS survey data.

who escape from these two forms of poverty – or double poverty. These different proportions are presented in the following Table 6.14:

More than 40% of Senegalese households are affected by double poverty, and about a third escape from it. The incidence of double poverty is particularly high in the rural area compared to the urban area. It remains widespread among rural households whose members not only lack financial means, but also infrastructures and a pleasant environment to live in, in addition to being unable to satisfy their basic needs (nutrition, education, health, drinking water, etc.). The proportion of those who escape from monetary poverty but who are under the yoke of nonmonetary poverty is particularly high. Thus, despite the fact that a number of rural households may have financial means at their disposal, they are still condemned to lead an indecent life for lack of infrastructures, a pleasant environment, and functional capacities.

In the urban area, the proportion of non-poor households on the nonmonetary level, but poor on the monetary level, is particularly high as compared to the rural area. This corroborates the daily financial problems faced by city dwellers, in spite of the existence of infrastructures, a more decent environment, and functional capacities. This state of affairs raises several questions linked, notably, to income redistribution policies, and to the inefficiency with which markets funtion, especially the market for labor.

Generally speaking, double poverty affects the poorest groups. Thus the regions of Kolda, Tambacounda, and Diourbel are the most affected, as well as large families, polygamous families, and farmers. Households managed by a woman are less affected by double poverty than those headed by a man.

6.6 Conclusion and Recommendations

Because of the multidimensional nature of poverty, the monetary approach alone is not always sufficient to account for the multiple phenomena which compromise the ablity of some populations to lead decent and happy lives. A multidimensional analysis therefore becomes necessary if we truly want to identify the poor, as well as the strategies more likely to combat this phenomenon more efficiently.

As applied to the case of Senegal, the multidimensional approach to poverty, which is based on the calculation of a composite indicator of poverty derived from multiple correspondence analysis by taking into account other dimensions of poverty such as education, health, drinking water, nutrition, housing, sanitation energy, communications, household durables, goods of comfort, and other assets, has permitted to draw important conclusions on poverty.

On the multidimensional level, all households are not affected by the same type of poverty. The most widespread forms of poverty are those linked to the vulnerability of human existence (inadequate human capital and indecent living conditions), to the shortage or absence of basic infrastructures, and to the lack of goods of comfort and household equipment.

The incidence of multidimensional poverty was estimated to be in the neighborhood of 60% relative to a household of reference able to satisfy a minimum of basic needs. Moreover, monetary poverty affects 48.5% of households. Whether on the monetary or nonmonetary level, the rural area is more affected by poverty than the urban area. In the latter area, monetary problems are predominant as compared to nonmonetary difficulties, whereas it is the reverse in the rural area. Despite the presence of human capital and infrastructures, urban households always find it very difficult to overcome monetary problems, which leads us to question the efficiency of markets, and notably that of the labor markets.

The regions of Tambacounda and Kolda remain the poorest, whereas the least poor remain the most urbanized cities such as Dakar and Thiès. Relative to the activity of the household manager, the results of the study point to farmers as being the most affected by poverty. As to the matrimonial status of the head of the household, polygamists are the most affected, as compared to monogamists, divorcees, and singles. Households managed by a woman generally have a slight advantage over those managed by a man. Monetary poverty as well as nonmonetary poverty also remain the monopoly of large families.

It should be noted that there exists a positive link between monetary and nonmonetary poverty, with a positive and significant correlation between the CIP and expenditure per adult equivalent. The majority of the monetary poor are also poor on the multidimensional level and vice versa.

From the economic policy standpoint, interventions of a general nature to increase labor productivity, in accordance with utilitarian theory, should be given priority in the urban area where poverty is more of a monetary nature, while for the rural area, which faces both forms of poverty though multidimensional poverty is relatively more pronounced there, an efficient combination of targeted interventions in accordance with the nonutilitarian approach, in addition to interventions of a general order, would rather be advisable.

Acknowledgments This research study was carried through thanks to a subsidy from the PEP (Poverty and Economic Policy) research network which is financed by the International Development Research Center (IDRC).We thank all those persons who, closely or from afar, have contributed to its successful conclusion. We deliver our thanks to all the members of the PEP network team and to IDRC. Our thanks also go to professors, Jean-Yves Duclos, Louis-Marie Asselin, Dorothée Boccanfuso, Luc Savard, John Cockburn, Abdelkrim Araar, Chris Scott, Bernard Decaluwé, Cosme Vodounou, Sami Bibi and Touhami Abdelkhalek for their enlightened contributions to this study.

Chapter 7
Case Study # 2 Dynamic Poverty Analysis in Vietnam 1993–2002: Multidimensional Versus Money-Metric Analysis

Louis-Marie Asselin, Vu Tuan Anh

7.1 Introduction

In 1986, 10 years after the country's reunification, the Doi Moi (renovation) was initiated in Vietnam as a process of reform from a centrally planned system to a market-based economy.[1,2] "The underlying strategy of doi moi was to introduce market principles to enhance the efficiency of the economy, while at the same time preserving a central role for the state in economic management. Implementation gathered momentum in 1989 when price controls were largely phased out and agriculture reverted to family farming as opposed to farming based on collectives."[3] Measures under this reform program concerned all economic sectors during the period 1989–1996: these included reforms in agriculture, prices, exchange rate, interest rate, fiscal sector, foreign trade and investment, financial sector, state enterprises, and the private sector. "Under the reform program, Vietnam has achieved rapid growth. From a low of 4% in 1987, the annual rate of growth has increased to over 9% in both 1995 and 1996, averaging 7.3% annually for the past decade. This has translated into annual per capita real income growth of about 5%. In US dollar terms, per capita income grew from barely $100 in 1987, to over $300 in 1996."[4]

How has this remarkable economic performance affected distribution and poverty in the country? "Poverty has been reduced by more than 35% since the launching of the doi moi reform process in 1986."[5] This assessment was based on two household

---

Louis-Marie Asselin and Vu Tuan Anh have benefited from the financial support of the IDRC MIMAP program.

[1] A first version of this case study has been published in Asselin and Vu Tuan Anh (2005), and a summary of this first version in Asselin and Vu Tuan Anh (2008). In this first version, the poverty types algorithm had been used only for a minimal sequence of poverty type sets (first factorial axis). In the present case study, the full poverty types algorithm is used, and thus all numerical results are changed.

[2] See UNDP & UNICEF (1996).

[3] World Bank (1997), p.15.

[4] loc. cit., p. 17.

[5] UNDP & UNICEF (1996), p.1.

surveys completed in 1993, including the first Vietnam Living Standards Survey which estimated the poverty headcount in 1993 at 58.1%.[6] More focus was then given to intensify poverty reduction and this was translated into the National Target Program for Hunger Eradication and Poverty Reduction (HEPR), which was formally established in 1998. This program was confirmed as a central component of the 10-year comprehensive poverty reduction and growth strategy designed after 2000 and formally approved in 2002.[7]

Such a preoccupation with poverty has raised a strong interest for measuring and monitoring the phenomenon in Vietnam. Starting in the 1990s, a sequence of Vietnam Living Standards Surveys were implemented – in 1992–1993, 1998 and 2002 – with ever-increasing sample sizes. Poverty measurement was done using the standard money-metric approach. For the 10-year period 1993–2002, results were quite spectacular: a near 30% point reduction in poverty as is shown in Graph 7.1.

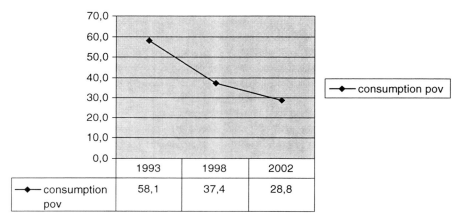

Graph 7.1 Vietnam consumption poverty rate 1993–2002

Sources: Government of Vietnam (1999), p.4, GSO (2004), p.25.

In the same period however, the international community had changed its way of looking at poverty. The concept of poverty had evolved from income or consumption poverty to a multidimensional view. This raises new technical challenges: How is poverty to be measured using multiple indicators? How are relevant indicators to be determined? How are these multiple measurements to be weighted in order to get a composite (integrated) measurement of family welfare, in view of identifying the poorest? Beyond the technical issues, there is also a policy issue: in Vietnam, during the same period 1993–2002, has multidimensional poverty been reduced as strikingly as it appears in Graph 7.1 for consumption poverty?

[6] Government of Vietnam (1999), p. 4.
[7] Socialist Republic of Vietnam (2002), p. 90.

In addition to this conceptual extension of poverty, an operational issue has become more and more evident: the limitations in the analytical power of standard household surveys designed to measure as accurately as needed the poor's standard of living, i.e., their monetary poverty. Policy makers ask for reliable poverty measurements with a very high level of disaggregation by geographic location as well as by socioeconomic groups, and with regular updates, annually if possible. Developing countries cannot meet these policy requirements given the high costs of usual standard household living standards surveys. Can this problem be overcome using sets of light poverty indicators while still reflecting a multidimensional concept of poverty?

These are the issues the present paper addresses.

7.2 Research Objectives

The present study aims to extend the dynamic money-metric analysis of the general decline of poverty in Vietnam during the period 1993–2002 by using a similar multidimensional poverty analysis, and to compare both approaches. The first study objective is formulated thus:

Objective #1: To verify the hypothesis that the Vietnam development and poverty reduction strategy has reduced multidimensional poverty as strikingly as consumption poverty during the period 1993–2002.

The assessment of consumption poverty reduction has led to discrimination between the levels and trends observed across rural/urban areas, geographical regions from North to South, ethnic groups, etc. A pattern of poverty decline has thus emerged. For example, it has been observed that

a) "Poverty remains a largely rural phenomenon. . . Between 1993 and 1998, poverty has declined in both rural and urban areas . . . from 66 to 45% in rural areas and from 25 to 9% in urban ones"[8]; "The poverty gap index also indicates that poverty is much deeper in rural than in urban areas . . . However, in both rural and urban areas the depth of poverty has declined during the 1993–1998 period."[9]

b) "Poverty has declined in all seven regions of Vietnam, though the rate of decline and incidence of poverty varies greatly across regions. . . The Northern Uplands, Central Highlands and North Central Coast are the three poorest regions. Poverty gap measures further suggest that poverty is deeper in the upland regions. The South East region, which includes Ho Chi Minh City, is the wealthiest region by a considerable margin. . . The most dramatic reduction in poverty has occurred in the Red River Delta. The Mekong Delta, conversely, shows the smallest improvement."[10]

---

[8] Government of Vietnam (1999), pp. 3, 11.

[9] Loc. cit., p. 12.

[10] Loc. cit. p. 3.

c) "Ethnic minorities in Vietnam are significantly poorer than the Kinh majority . . .
   Between 1993 and 1998, the poverty incidence for ethnic minorities has come
   down from 86 to 75%, but it still remains very high. In comparison, the poverty
   rate for the Kinh majority has fallen from 54 to 31% over this period. Thus the
   situation of the ethnic minorities is improving, but at a slower rate than the Kinh,
   and they are beginning to lag behind. In 1993, ethnic minority groups constituted
   13% of the overall population, but 20% of the poor. Their share in the total population has risen slightly to 14%, but they now account for 29% of all poor people
   in Vietnam."[11]
   Inequality analysis in terms of household expenditures (consumption) has shown
   that
d) "The pattern of expenditure growth has resulted in an increase in inequality in
   Vietnam between 1993 and 1998. The Gini coefficient for per capita expenditures
   has increased from 0.33 to 0.35."[12]
e) Inequality is higher in urban than in rural area[13] and lower in the Northern part
   of the country than in the Southern part, and "that the three regions that had
   the lowest inequality in 1993 – Northern Uplands, Red River Delta, and North
   Central Coast – have experienced a slight increase in inequality in the 1993–1998
   period, while the opposite is true for the other four southern regions."[14]

These analyses naturally suggest a second study objective:

Objective #2: To establish the extent by which the *pattern* of multidimensional
poverty and inequality dynamics in Vietnam can be compared to the consumption
poverty and inequality dynamics during the period 1993–2002.

To significantly alleviate the limitations in the analytical power across space and
time as well as the high costs of average living standard household surveys, a search
for light, feasible, relevant, and reliable poverty indicators is in order. Such indicators should cover the main dimensions of poverty as usually identified in the literature[15] and should be low cost for developing countries, in view of disaggregating the
poverty monitoring and analysis at the scale of small regions, and more frequently
than on a 5-year interval basis. The statistical processing of these sets of indicators
should be based on tools easily accessible. This is an operational objective looked
for here:

Objective #3: To demonstrate the feasibility and relevance of a sound methodology
for regularly monitoring multidimensional poverty at national and local levels in
developing countries.

The fulfillment of these objectives has strong policy implications. To achieve the
first two while talking in terms comparable to the money-metric terminology which

---

[11] Loc. cit., p. 32.

[12] Loc. cit., p.68.

[13] loc. cit., p. 72.

[14] Loc. cit., p. 74.

[15] Part I, Introduction.

policymakers are used to, there is a need to develop multidimensional poverty and inequality indices. This is a very big methodological challenge, precisely the one we are facing in the present study.

A methodology for measuring multidimensional poverty has been developed since 1999 by the CBMS research group in Vietnam, within the MIMAP network sponsored by IDRC. This methodology has been applied to different household survey data sets, some generated by the MIMAP program itself, some by the General Statistical Office of Vietnam. In particular, an important component of the methodology, a composite indicator of CBMS-type poverty indicators, has been applied to the three Vietnam Living Standards Surveys that were run during the period 1992–2002. It has been fully described in a recent paper (Asselin L.M. and Vu Tuan Anh, 2005), with the results coming out from the VLSS-1 (1992–1993) and VLSS-2 (1997–1998) surveys. Since then, data from the VLSS-3 (2002) survey have been made available, and the multidimensional methodology has been applied to this third country representative data set.

The present paper focuses on the dynamic analysis of poverty across three points in time during the period 1992–2002, as provided by the three VLSS surveys. It highlights the convergence and divergence of facts between money-metric and multidimensional analysis, the first one measuring the consumption poverty, the second one measuring the human and physical assets poverty.

7.3 Methodology

The 5-step methodology is developed as follows:

7.3.1 Step 1 – An Operational Concept of Multidimensional Poverty

First, a concept of multidimensional poverty is needed. However, there is no special technique to define such a concept. In making the process as participative as possible, some people have to share their philosophical view on the meaning of poverty, each participant referring to his own experience, thinking, and knowledge of the relevant literature. Some material provided in I-1 and Appendix A may help in such a social process. In the present case, the multidimensional poverty concept emerged at the end of the 1990s within the Vietnam MIMAP team involved in developing a CBMS.[16] The general objective of a CBMS is to develop the local capacity to measure poverty at the community level with a small set of indicators, in view of planning and monitoring local development aiming at poverty alleviation.

---

[16] See Vu Tuan Anh (2000). MIMAP: Micro Impact of Macroeconomic and Adjustment Policies. CBMS: Community-Based Monitoring System.

Thus, dimensions of poverty taken into account depend on ways local communities perceive poverty and on their development priorities.

Whatever the process is, the operationalization of the concepts materializes in a set of indicators. In Vietnam, a basic step was achieved with the conduct of a pilot test in 1999 using a simple one-page questionnaire in 4 provinces, 20 communes, and 22,770 households. Two of the four provinces were from the Northern region, Thai-Nguyen and Hai-Duong, while two were from the Southern region, Lam-Dong, and Tra-Vinh.[17] This short questionnaire was able to provide 11 nonmonetary indicators, presented in Table 7.1.

Table 7.1 MIMAP Vietnam CBMS: First set of 11 nonmonetary poverty indicators (1999)

#1	Underemployment: lacking jobs
#2	Hld with chronic sick
#3	Enough clothes in cold season
#4	Availability of mosquito nets
#5	Medical care unavailable
#6	Hld with illiterate adults
#7	Hld with children not going to school
#8	Hld with children malnourished
#9	Hld has no radio and no TV
#10	Housing: type of dwelling
#11	Drinking water

These indicators are categorical ordinal. A simple proxy to household total income was also in the questionnaire.

Analysis was done by computing a composite index of these 11 nonmoney-metric indicators, with a factorial methodology, the Multiple Correspondence Analysis. Main results coming from this MIMAP survey are given in Table 7.2.

Table 7.2 Mean poverty indicator by province

Region	Province	Multidimensional poverty indicator	Income per capita (proxy)
North	Thai Nguyen	3300	113
	Hai Duong	3234	140
	sub-total	3278	121
South	Lam Dong	2904	149
	Tra Vinh	2976	148
	sub-total	2956	148
Total		3091	138

Source: Table 5.2, Asselin L.-M. and Vu Tuan Anh (2008).

According to Table 7.2, the two Northern provinces are better off than the two Southern ones in terms of multidimensional poverty. This questions the usual perception that the South is better off than the North in terms of income, according to

---

[17] See Vu Tuan Anh (2000)

the first VLSS survey in 1992–1993. Even here, as a proxy to income, we have the same result: income welfare seems better in the South than in the North.

When these results came out of the multidimensional poverty analysis using CBMS data, the following issue was raised: the MIMAP–CBMS sample cannot be considered as representative of the whole of Vietnam. Could the robustness of this result be tested with household survey data representative of the whole country? This issue was in fact the starting point of the present study.

In the meantime, one more indicator – sanitation (toilet) – was added to those cited in Table 7.1. The indicator was added about 1 year later, when the CBMS approach was implemented in view of monitoring poverty in a specific poverty alleviation project, the ILMC (Improved Livelihood for Mountainous Communities) project in the province of Thanh Hoa.[18] On the other hand, the child nutrition indicator (# 8) was progressively abandoned for the CBMS, considering its dubious reliability when measured using a very short questionnaire.

The preoccupation with robustness and representativeness led to the consideration of staging large national household surveys with the objective of identifying the availability of some (if not all) of the 11 CBMS nonmonetary indicators of poverty in these databases. Fortunately, 8 of these 11 indicators could be constructed from important surveys implemented during the period 1993–2002. These eight indicators are given in Table 7.3.

Table 7.3 The eight Vietnam–CBMS indicators extracted from surveys representative at national level

Indicator no.	Title	Description
#1	Underemployment	A worker is considered as underemployed if he has missed a job for 3 months or more in the last year. At the household level, at least one main worker is underemployed.
#2	Chronic sickness	For a person, to be sick for at least one month out of a year. At the household level, at least one household member is chronically sick.
#3	Adult illiteracy	A person 15 year+ who cannot read, write and do simple calculations is illiterate. At the household level, at least one adult member is illiterate.
#4	Underschooling	A child 6–15 years old is not attending school. At the household level, at least one child is not going to school.
#5	Without radio, TV.	There is no radio or TV set owned by the household.
#6	Type of dwelling	Category of house, based on roof, walls, and floor material.
#7	Drinking water	Type of main source for drinking water.
#8	Sanitation	Type of toilet used by the household.

Source: Table 5.3, Asselin L.-M. and Vu Tuan Anh (2008).

---

[18] See Asselin M. (2005).

These eight indicators present a concept of human (#1 to #4) and physical (#5 to #8) assets household poverty. In this study, this poverty concept will be compared with the classical consumption poverty based on the money-metric expenditure approach. It should be noted that according to the terminology used in I-2.2.1, the first four indicators are obtained as poverty by inclusion, through endogenous transmission. Viewed from the standpoint of the Poverty Concept Structure defined in I-2.3, the present poverty concept is depicted in Table 7.4, where each of the eight indicators is localized in the appropriate subdimension cell. This table refers to the Poverty Matrix Structure provided as Table 7.5, a reproduction of Fig. 2.1.

Table 7.4 The poverty concept structure of the eight Vietnam-CBMS indicators

Vietnam CBMS poverty concept	01	02	03	04	05	06	07	08		(%)
D1									0	0
D2	1		1		1				3	38
D3			1						1	13
D4									0	0
D5	1	1							2	25
D6		1							1	13
D7	1								1	13
D8									0	0
D9									0	0
D10									0	0
									8	100

The poverty concept used here is thus a 5-dimension concept, with dominance first of education (38%) and second of water/sanitation (25%). Three other dimensions are then equally represented: health, employment, and housing.

If not explicitly represented in any of the eight indicators, income underlies some of them: particularly #5 radio, TV, and #6 type of dwelling depend directly on household income level (permanent income). Indicator #8 sanitation is influenced by household income but is also dependent on community infrastructure.

Table 7.5 Poverty matrix structure

	01	02	03	04	05	06	07	08
D1. Income	Income proxy	Ownership of durable goods	Typical expenditures	Perception of economic situation				
D2. Education	Primary enrolment	Secondary enrolment	Literacy	Drop-out rate	IEC resources (Info/Educ to Communic)	Access to school infrastructure services	Education level achieved	Pre-school
D3. Health	Infant/child mortality	Maternal mortality	Morbidity to handicap incidence	Access to health infrastructure services	Specific disease prevention treatment			
D4. Food/Nutrition	Malnutrition	Food security status						
D5. Water/Sanitation	Sources of drinking water	Sanitation facilities						
D6. Employment/labor	Unemployment inactivity	Underemployment	Categories of workers	Child labor	Wage rates			
D7. Housing (environment)	Housing characteristics	Home ownership	Sources of energy	Living environment				
D8. Access to productive assets	Land distribution	Irrigated land	Productive assets (agricultural & others)	Access to credit	Information technology	Production techniques		
D9. Access to markets	Price of basic commodities	Access to market infrastructure	Access to services	Access to roads				
D10. Participation/Social peace	Crime incidence	Domestic violence	Social participation	Participation in election	Access to public meeting infrastructure			

7.3.2 Step 2 Data

Three data sets representative at the country level were used in this study, the first three Vietnam Living Standard Surveys (VNLSS):

- VNLSS-1 in 1992–1993, with a sample of 4,800 households,
- VNLSS-2 in 1997–1998, with a sample of 6,002 households,
- VNLSS-3 in 2002, with the first sample of 30,000 households. This is the only sample with expenditures data[19] and made publicly available. Due to technical difficulties in matching household files, analysis was done with a random sub-sample of 22,702 households.

The eight Vietnam CBMS indicators were constructed from the relevant sections of the extensive questionnaires used in these surveys.

Due to the extreme differences in the questionnaires used in both the MIMAP surveys and VNLSS, adaptations have been required to extract from VNLSS an acceptable proxy for some indicators, namely

- Underemployment. Due to the complexity of the employment section in the VNLSS (main job, secondary job, self-employment, etc.), and to differences in the 1993, 1998, and 2002 questionnaires, many questions have been required to approximate the CBMS definition;
- Chronic sickness. This is defined as "persons having been sick for at least 15 days in the last 4 weeks." Adjustments had to be done for the VNLSS-3 survey, using information on hospitalization to develop a proxy since that survey used a different questionnaire;
- Adult illiteracy. Due to the lack of detail in the CBMS questionnaire, and to the different questionnaires used in the three VNLSS, the three capacities "read," "write," and "calculate" were retained for the sake of reliable comparison This requirement is higher than in many standard studies. On the other hand, it could have been closer to the expected results of functional literacy programs; and
- Underschooling in the range 6–15 has been taken to include the normal age at the end of the lower secondary level.

Official expenditure aggregates, provided in the raw data sets, were used to compare with the money-metric analysis of poverty and inequality.

7.3.3 Step 3 – Dynamic Multidimensional Poverty Profile

The idea behind the profile is to present the basic facts about the evolution of the eight indicators through the three periods 1993, 1998, and 2002, by correctly

---

[19] An additional 45,000 households' sample was drawn without expenditures. See GSO (2004).

estimating their distribution from the three corresponding VNLSS. Particular attention is then given to the percentage of households below each of the eight specific poverty thresholds. Such a poverty profile however, with many categorical indicators, becomes rapidly cumbersome and laborious to interpret if broken down by different socioeconomic classifications; this is why the presentation is limited at the country level to highlight the main trends. Meaningful comparisons with the money-metric analysis of poverty and inequality, a main objective of this study, are also quite difficult to make. Deeper analysis is thus greatly facilitated by going to some type of aggregation across poverty dimensions, which is achieved through steps 4 and 5.

7.3.4 Step 4 – Composite Indicator of Multidimensional Poverty and Dynamic Analysis

Steps 4 and 5 correspond to the two-step approach to poverty and inequality indices as described in Section 3.1. Step 4 is thus the first step of this approach, which consists of building a composite indicator of multidimensional poverty (CIP). The methodology used is the factorial technique called multiple correspondence analysis (MCA), extensively justified in Section 3.3.2 and described in Section 3.4. The central operation is the numerically positive recoding of the eight primary poverty indicators, which is done here with the VLSS-1 data for the base period 1993. Categorical weights are then kept constant through time for the periods 1998 and 2002. This means that, with the same weights, the household score for the composite indicator is computed from the two subsequent surveys: VNLSS-2 (1998) and VNLSS-3 (2002). There is no price issue.

Some policy analysis available exclusively with the MCA CIP is done before progressing to the second step. Analytical tools used are those developed in Section 4.1, particularly the Poverty State Elimination Efficiency (PSEE) diagram as defined in Section 4.1.2.

7.3.5 Step 5 – Multidimensional Poverty and Inequality Indices, and Dynamic Analysis

Step 5 is the second of the two-step approach to multidimensional poverty indices. The CIP absolute poverty line, defined in Section 4.2.1, is computed and FGT indices are constructed. A dynamic comparative analysis of multidimensional poverty in Vietnam is then developed, the comparison being with the standard money-metric analysis already available in the literature and recalculated here from the primary data for different kinds of socioeconomic groups.

A similar dynamic comparative analysis of multidimensional inequality is finally done, essentially using the Gini index.

7.4 Results and Analysis

First, the basic results are discussed, immediately followed by some policy insights (Section 7.4.1). Then the comparative analysis with the money-metric approach is presented for poverty (Section 7.4.2) and inequality (Section 7.4.3).

The focus is to illustrate poverty dynamics in Vietnam as revealed through two approaches: money-metric (consumption) and multidimensional (human and physical assets). The presentation is largely graphical, with short comments following. All money-metric results were checked and found to be fully consistent with the officially published figures for the three periods.

7.4.1 Basic Results and Policy Insights

7.4.1.1 A Primary Dynamic Poverty Profile Disaggregated Across Poverty Dimensions

Table 7.6 presents the estimated distributions of the eight primary poverty indicators for the three periods 1993, 1998, and 2002. Significant improvements are colored as yellow for poverty reduction and pink for welfare increase. It can be immediately seen that there is greater improvement in the period 1993–1998 than in the period 1998–2002. Only one dimension, health (chronic sickness), seems to have remained

Table 7.6 Vietnam multidimensional poverty profile 1993–2002

		1993	1998	2002 (%)
Underemployment	Underemployment	44.0%	28.9%	27.5%
	No underemployment	56.0%	71.1%	72.5%
Chronic sickness	With chronic sick	18.1%	20.6%	20.2%
	No chronic sick	81.9%	79.4%	79.2%
Adult illiteracy	Adults illiterate	37.5%	35.2%	19.0%
	Adults literate	62.5%	64.8%	81.0%
Underschooling 6–15	Child. not going school	15.1%	8.4%	9.0%
	Children going school	84.9%	91.6%	91.0%
Hld without radio, TV	Without radio, TV	53.0%	28.8%	24.3%
	With radio or TV	47.0	71.2%	75.7%
Type of dwelling	Temporary house	36.5%	25.0%	23.6%
	Semi-permanent house	47.0%	59.2%	59.2%
	Permanent house	16.5%	15.7%	17.2%
Drinking water	Pond, lake, river	19.3%	11.4%	9.7%
	Other water sources	1.8%	4.4%	3.3%
	Dug well	52.7%	43.2%	37.8%
	Piped, rain, drilled	26.2%	41.0%	49.2%
Sanitation (type of toilet used)	No toilet, other type	47.4%	33.4%	28.2%
	Simple toilet	33.8%	39.7%	24.6%
	Double-vault compost latrine	8.4	9.8%	22.0%
	Flush toilet septic tank	10.4%	17.0%	25.2%

stable during the 10-year interval. All other poverty dimensions were reduced in the same interval. Steady improvement in the 10-year interval is observed uniquely in the water/sanitation dimension, in both subdimensions (indicators).

The only other significant improvement during the period 1998–2002 is with the education indicator (or adult illiteracy to be precise) which appears to have decreased dramatically. Thus, the trend in consumption poverty reduction revealed in Graph 7.1 seems globally observed in multidimensional poverty, for seven primary indicators.

This can be seen more easily in Graphs 7.2 and 7.3 exhibiting the shaded categories of Table 7.6 which are those categories below the poverty threshold specific to each indicator. Globally, poverty seems to have been reduced more in physical than in human assets. Except for illiteracy, improvements are stronger in the period 1993–1998 than in 1998–2002, a phenomenon also observed in Graph 7.1 for consumption poverty.

To advance further in the analysis, a poverty profile as seen in Table 7.6 and associated graphs should be broken down according to different socioeconomic classifications of households. Obviously it then becomes a quite heavy analysis process and is not presented here. But such disaggregations have effectively been done for the period 1993–1998, the most remarkable in poverty reduction, and results are briefly reported here.[20]

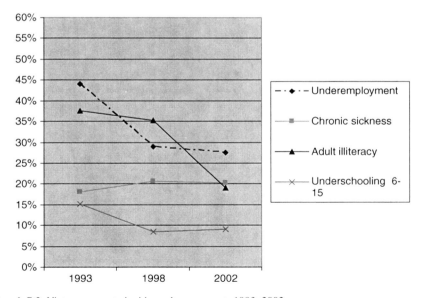

Graph 7.2 Vietnam poverty incidence human assets 1993–2002

---

[20] The numerous two-way tables thus generated can be provided to the interested reader on request. More detailed results have already been published in L.-M. Asselin and Vu Tuan Anh (2005).

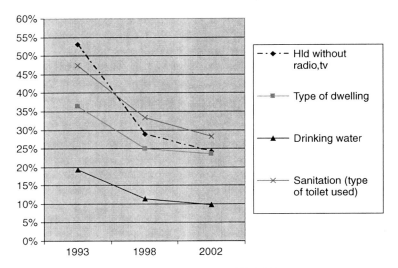

Graph 7.3 Vietnam poverty incidence physical assets 1993–2002

Disaggregations of the profile are across the following nine socioeconomic classifications:

a) geographical location;

- rural/urban;
- seven regions: Northern Mountains (1), Red River Delta (2), North Central Coast (3), South Central Coast (4), Central Highlands (5), South East (6), Mekong River Delta (7);
- North (regions 1 and 2), Center (regions 3, 4 and 5), South (regions 6 and 7).

b) social characteristics:

- ethnicity (Kinh, minorities);
- household size (5 or less, more than 5);
- gender of household head;
- main activity (farm, non-farm).

c) money-metric poverty:

- relative income poverty: relatively poor households are those below half the median expenditure per capita; and
- expenditure quintile.

Cross-classified with the eight indicators, the nine classification variables generate 72 two-way tables for each period. A significance test was done for the distribution differences in each of the 72 two-way tables. This test is the Pearson chi-squared test adjusted to take into account the effects of the complex sample design on this well-known test in the i.i.d. case.[21] In 1993, almost all disaggregations (61 over 72) are significant at least at the $p_{.05}$ level, while most of them are significant at the $p_{.001}$ level. Chronic sickness alone accounts for 6 of the 11 non-significant cases, the regional distribution of sickness here being an exception.

1993 Poverty Profile Disaggregation

Geographically, all types and forms of poverty, except chronic sickness, are more acute in rural than in urban areas. The level of sickness is the same in both areas. Regionally, from North to South, there are significant differences in all types and forms of poverty, except for underemployment. All other forms of poverty are dominant in the South, except chronic sickness which is more acute in the Center. However, if we refine the regional analysis within the North–Center–South main division, all eight indicators are significantly distributed. In the North, education and health poverty, as well as temporary housing, are stronger in the Northern Uplands than in the Red River Delta (Hanoi). On the other hand, underemployment largely dominates in the Red River Delta, where it reaches the highest rate (53.5%) in the country, while the lowest rate is observed in the Uplands. In the South, all types and forms of poverty are more acute in the Mekong River Delta than in the South East (HCMC). In fact, four of the eight poverty indicators take their country highest value in the Mekong River Delta.

Socially, we observe that the ethnic minority groups are less literate and have lower quality dwelling and sanitation facilities than the Kinh. On the other hand, the incidence of underemployment is higher among the Kinh. Female-headed households are better off relative to underemployment, schooling, safe water, and sanitation, while male-headed households are better off in terms of literacy and communication means. Except for chronic sickness where farming households do not differ, they are significantly poorer than non-farming ones in all other forms of poverty. A large household size implies more individual poverty (a fact that comes as no surprise), according to the nature of the indicators. On the other hand, larger households are better equipped in terms of means of communication, while their sanitation facilities seem to be less satisfactory.

Economically, income poverty is directly associated with illiteracy, no communication facilities, temporary housing, unsafe water, and bad sanitation facilities. Relative income poverty does not significantly affect children's schooling, but there is a significant drop in underschooling for the richest households (5th quintile). The same is observed regarding underemployment: it drops significantly only for the richest households. Income poverty has no significant effect on chronic sickness.

---

[21] The statistic then follows an F-distribution. See Rao J.N.K. and Scott A.J., *On chi-squared tests for multiway contingency tables with cell proportions estimated from survey data*, The Annals of Statistics, 1984, Vol. 12, No.1, 46-60. We use the test as implemented in the STATA procedure **svytab**.

1993–1998 Changes Across Socioeconomic Groups

If the 1993–1998 changes are analyzed more deeply by looking at the disaggregated profiles in both years, it is observed that

- the −24.2% improvement in communication facilities has occurred more in Central Highlands (−35.8%) and less in Northern Mountains (−14.8%) as well as among the minorities (−12.6%);
- underemployment has decreased significantly in two of the three regions having the highest rates, North Central Coast (−27.2%) and Red River Delta (−23.8%), with the third region, the Mekong River Delta, remaining high with a small decrease of only −4.1%;
- sanitation has improved strongly in the North Central Coast, but less than the average in Mekong River Delta, where it was and remains the most deficient. Minorities have performed particularly well in this aspect;
- reduction in temporary housing has been particularly noteworthy in Central Highlands (−30.8%), but very low in the Mekong River Delta (−6.2%), which remains by far the most deficient region in this regard;
- adult illiteracy has decreased significantly in the Central Highlands (−17%), where it had the highest rate in 1993. It is at the same level in 1998 than the Mekong River Delta, whose improvement has been only −3.7%; and
- chronic sickness has decreased remarkably in the South Central Coast (−15.2%), but more than doubled in the South East (+9.9%) and almost doubled in the Red River Delta (+9.6%).

From this analysis of disaggregated multidimensional profiles, it can be concluded that the dynamics of multidimensional poverty would be easier to observe with some aggregation across poverty dimensions through a composite indicator of poverty (CIP).

7.4.1.2 CIP Computation and Base-Year 1993 Analysis

A Multiple correspondence analysis (MCA) has been run for the base year 1993 on the eight indicators of Table 7.3. The main, detailed results are presented in Appendix D. Table D.1 gives the 21 categorical scores (quantifications) for the first eight factorial axes, which, according to Table D.3, account for 73.7% of the total inertia given by the formula $I_{tot} = \frac{J}{K} - 1$ of Section 3.4.4. Table D.1 is necessary to assess, for each factorial axis, the fundamental requirement of Axis Consistency in view of applying the Poverty Types Algorithm developed in Section 3.4.4. The algorithm allows the construction of the CIP through an important intermediary output, the identification of a small set of factorial poverty axis and poverty types, which deserves a specific static analysis for the base-year (Poverty Types Identification and Analysis across Socioeconomic Groups). A second part (CIP and Comparative Analysis of Multidimensional versus Consumption Poverty) uses the CIP intensively for a detailed comparative analysis of multidimensional versus consumption poverty, always for the base year 1993.

Poverty Types Identification and Analysis Across Socioeconomic Groups

By examining the categories scores on axis #1, it can already be seen that this axis meets the FAOC-G property (I-3.4.1), as shown in Graph 7.4.

These results on the first axis demonstrate that there exists a *minimal sequence of poverty type sets* (I-3.4.4) with the number of axis L = 1. Looking only at axis #1 as a poverty axis, Graph 7.4 clearly shows that

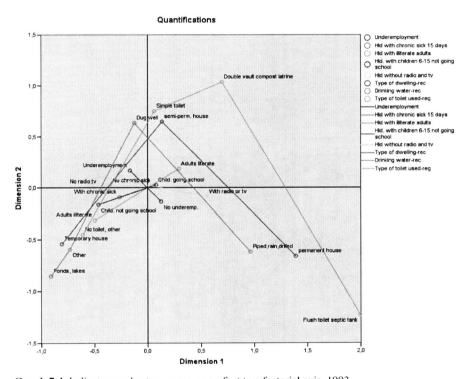

Graph 7.4 Indicators and category scores on first two factorial axis, 1993

– poverty is associated with unsafe drinking water (ponds, lakes), temporary houses, no toilet, illiterate adults, unschooled children, no radio/TV, underemployment, and chronic sickness
– basic welfare (non-poverty) is associated with safe drinking water (piped, rain, drain), permanent house, good sanitation (flush toilet, septic tank), literate adults, all children going to school, possession of radio or TV, full employment, no chronic sickness.

However, Graph 7.4 reveals more details:

a) discrimination between households on axis #1 is dominated by some indicators of physical assets (water, sanitation, housing); some human asset indicators like employment, sickness, schooling appear very weak; and

b) quite clearly axis #2 is not a poverty axis (Section 3.4.4, poverty sets identification), since many indicators are inconsistent on this axis (water, sanitation, housing), and still others are globally inconsistent (radio–TV and employment in a direction opposite to schooling and sickness).

Thus, it can be hypothesized that much more poverty information (inertia) and discriminating power could be kept in the composite indicator of poverty by analyzing more deeply the first two axes and exploring further the axes with the poverty types algorithm. This is done with Table 7.7, which provides an admissible sequence of poverty sets (Section 3.4.4) with $L = 4$ factorial axes.

Table 7.7 Poverty types algorithm applied to first eight factorial axes

	Discrimination measures Axis							
	1	2	3	4	5	6	7	8
Underemployment	0.021	0.023	0.031	0.496	0.031	0.084	0.196	0.000
Hld with chronic sick	0.015	0.001	0.439	0.068	0.007	0.067	0.215	0.000
Hld with illiterate adults	0.146	0.056	0.108	0.098	0.001	0.012	0.016	0.036
Hld. with child not going school	0.038	0.004	0.132	0.275	0.000	0.190	0.133	0.124
Hld without radio and TV	0.250	0.010	0.060	0.016	0.030	0.075	0.113	0.177
Type of dwelling-rec	0.566	0.378	0.029	0.006	0.061	0.003	0.001	0.336
Drinking water-rec	0.421	0.461	0.218	0.070	0.299	0.409	0.183	0.115
Type of toilet used-reg	0.632	0.535	0.103	0.080	0.573	0.147	0.064	0.101
8*50% eigenvalue	1.045	0.734	0.560	0.554	0.502	0.493	0.461	0.444
Before eliminating intersections	2.089	0.061	0.089	0.770	0.038	0.268	0.540	0.036
		0.033	0.710	0.182	0.032	0.162	0.134	0.301
After eliminating intersections-2	2.089						0.411	
After eliminating intersections-3	2.015						0.196	
			0.602					
After eliminating intersections-4	2.015			0.770			0.000	
			0.439					
After eliminating intersections-5	2.015			0.770				
			0.439					
After eliminating intersections-6	2.015			0.770				
			0.439					
After eliminating intersections-7	2.015			0.770				
			0.439					
After eliminating intersections-8	2.015			0.770				
			0.439					

The computation of the algorithm is quite obvious from its functioning as described in Section 3.4.4 and Table 7.7. The discrimination measures forming the computing basis are given as an output of the MCA procedure and are provided (albeit with different names such as contribution, etc.), by any software supporting MCA.[22] Once these numerous discrimination measures are exported in a spreadsheet like Excel, the computation becomes easy. Nevertheless some explanation may help to understand the process:

a) the whole first column is dark gray since the property FAOC-G is satisfied, with the preferred orientation (poverty with negative scores on the left)[23] But appears also in the same first column a very low discriminating power for three human asset indicators: "underemployment," "households with chronic sick," and "households with children not going school." But those three cannot be eliminated from the first poverty set unless another poverty set where these indicators have more discriminating power can be found;
b) axis #2 does not identify any poverty set: the dark gray and light gray subsets of consistent indicators do not meet the 50% threshold requirement 0.734;
c) axis #3 identifies an important poverty set (light gray) that includes the four human asset indicators. The sickness indicator dominates, and is thus taken off the first poverty set, like "underemployment" and "children not going school." But "household with illiterate adult" remains in the first poverty set;
d) axis #4 identifies a poverty set with two indicators, "underemployment" and "children not going school," which are then taken off the preceding poverty set (axis #3) because their discriminating power is much stronger;
e) axis # 5 does not identify any poverty set, and the algorithm can stop here since, according to Table D.3, 52.2% of the total inertia is taken into account. An admissible sequence is thus achieved;
f) for illustrative purposes, the algorithm is pursued until axis 8. Another poverty set is identified on axis 7, but it can be easily checked that all identified indicators are already more discriminating in the preceding ones.

It can be seen from Table 7.7 that by finding three poverty types with the algorithm, the composite indicator of poverty (CIP) will summarize 54% more inertia (poverty information: $2.015 + 0.439 + 0.770 = 3.224$) than the CIP based only on the first axis, 2.089.

After completing this process, the composite indicator of poverty (CIP) is computed according to the generalized definition (26), Section 3.4.4:

---

[22] Computations are made here with the SPSS procedure HOMALS.

[23] It must be emphasized that axis orientation is completely irrelevant in determining the position of the factorial axis. This orientation can be changed for any axis, the only impact being a change in the sign of the factorial scores on the axis. In applying the poverty types algorithm it is important to identify the poverty sets according to the orientation with which there is consistency, so that recoding the indicators (see Section 3.4.2) in view of aggregation in the CIP, all recoded indicators come with consistent signs (positive). The consistency orientation is identified here with the dark gray color (poverty on left side) and light gray color (poverty on right side).

$$C_i = \frac{\sum_{l=1}^{L^*} \sum_{k \epsilon k_l^*} \sum_{jk=1}^{Jk} W_{jk}^{+l,k} I_{i,jk}^k}{k} \qquad (7.1)$$

The first step involves the positive rescaling of each indicator, based on its category scores relative to the relevant poverty axis. This operation gives the required weights $W_{jk}^{+l,k}$ as given in Table 7.8.

Table **7.8** Category weights for the eight primary indicators

Indicator	Category	Weight
Underemployment	Underemployment	0
	No underemployment	3811
Hld with chronic sick	With chronic sick	0
	No chronic sick	4595
Hld with illiterate adults	Adults illiterate	0
	Adults literate	1544
Hld. with children 6–15 not going school	Child. not going school	0
	Child. going school	3927
Hld without radio and TV	No radio, TV	0
	With radio or TV	1988
Type of dwelling	Temporary house	0
	Semi-permanent. House	1845
	Permanent house	4302
Drinking water	Ponds, lakes	0
	Other	348
	Dug well	1534
	Piped, rain, drilled	3667
Type of toilet used	No toilet, other	0
	Simple toilet	1315
	Double-vault compost latrine	2559
	Flush toilet septic tank	5098

The light gray cells in the column "Weight" of Table 7.8 identify the specific poverty thresholds determined a priori.

The three poverty types identified respectively on factorial axis #1, #3, and #4 deserve further analysis.

The first poverty type includes five of the eight indicators:

• Household without radio and TV;
• Type of dwelling;
• Drinking water;
• Type of toilet used;
• Household with illiterate adults.

Since the first four indicators group together the household physical assets plus the literacy of the household head, an appropriate name for this poverty type could be «Enabling home.»

The second poverty type, with only the "Chronic sickness" indicator can be named «Health.»

The third poverty type includes two indicators:

- Underemployment
- Households with children 6–15 not going school.

When no poverty exists for both these indicators, it means that adults in the households are fully employed at work and that children are busy where they should be, at school. In this sense, all household members are correctly using and developing their human capital, and the name «Human capital mobilization» could be appropriate for this poverty type.

The interesting issue for policy purposes is to try to identify some association between different socioeconomic groups and the three poverty types. The poverty type algorithm tells us that the relevant factorial planes where the specific groups can be visualized are those given by axis #1, #3, and #4, respectively identified as the first, second, and third poverty axis. This visualization is done in Graphs 7.5 and

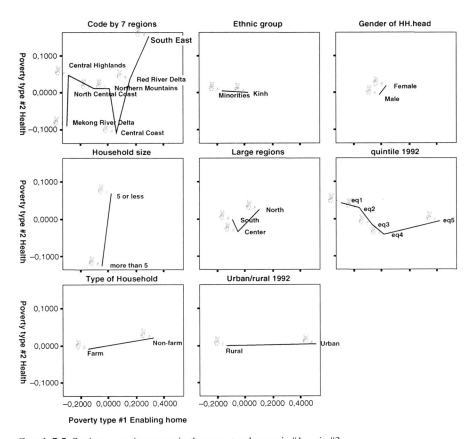

Graph 7.5 Socioeconomic groups in the poverty plane axis #1–axis #3

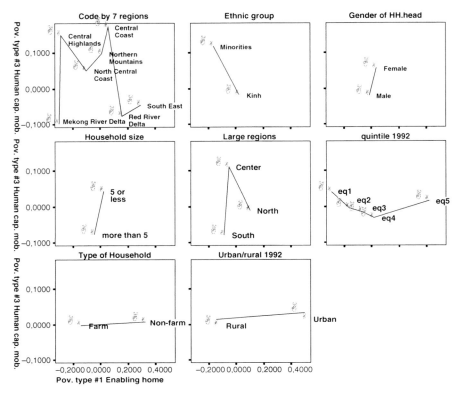

Graph 7.6 Socioeconomic groups in the poverty plane axis #1–axis #4

7.6, with eight of the nine socioeconomic classifications described in Section 4.1.1: rural/urban, 7 regions, 3 large regions (North–Center–South), ethnic groups, household size, gender of household head, and farm/non-farm, expenditure quintile.

Before analyzing Graphs 7.5 and 7.6, results from the between group F-test for each classification (8) and each poverty type (3) should be kept in mind:

- Enabling home type is highly significant ($<.000$) for all classifications, except for gender of household head where it is moderately significant ($<.05$).
- Health type is not significant for three classifications: gender of household head, ethnic group, rural/urban; moderately significant ($<.05$) for farm/non-farm; and highly significant ($<.000$) in the four other cases.
- Human capital mobilization type is highly significant ($<.000$) for all classifications, except for rural/urban and farm/non-farm, where it is not significant.

To reduce the first type of poverty (Graphs 7.5 and 7.6), «Enabling home» (housing, water, sanitation, radio/TV, literacy), programs should target:

a) large farming households in rural areas,

b) initially in the South, particularly in the Mekong River Delta,
c) subsequently in the Center, particularly in the Central Highlands,
d) with special attention to minorities.

It is observed that such types of households belong to the lowest-income quintiles (1 and 2) in the country.

To reduce the second type of poverty (Graph 7.5), «Health» (chronic sickness), programs should target

a) large households,
b) mainly in the Central Coast (Center) and in the Mekong River Delta (South).

It is observed that such types of households belong mainly to the highest-income quintiles (3, 4, and 5) in the country.

To reduce the third type of poverty (Graph 7.6), «Human capital mobilization» (employment, schooling), programs should target

a) male-headed large households,
b) mainly in the whole South, both the Mekong River Delta and South East,
c) secondly in the Red River Delta (North),
d) with special attention to the Kinh.

It is observed that such types of households belong mainly to the middle-income quintiles (3, 4) in the country.

Some interesting facts emerge from this analysis:

– the rural/urban factor is concerned only with the first type of poverty;
– the Mekong River Delta is concerned with the three types of multidimensional poverty; and
– only the first type of poverty, «Enabling home,» is monotonically increasing with income poverty. For targeting the two other types of poverty, if designed policies intend to prioritize the low-income quintiles, a proxy to household income is required. The household first factorial score becomes an interesting candidate.

To get a more synthetic view of multidimensional poverty and advance further in its comparison with income (consumption) poverty, the CIP provided by (7.1) above is now required.

CIP and Comparative Analysis of Multidimensional Versus Consumption Poverty

Graphs 7.7, 7.8, 7.9, and 7.10 compare both measurements of poverty, the multidimensional CIP and the consumption indicator (expenditure/cap), for the socioeconomic groups determined by the eight classifications used previously. The arithmetical mean per household is used. According to the F-test, all eight classifications are

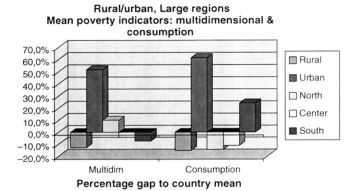

Graph 7.7 Socioeconomic groups comparisons Vietnam 1993 multidimensional versus consumption poverty: R/U and North-Center–South

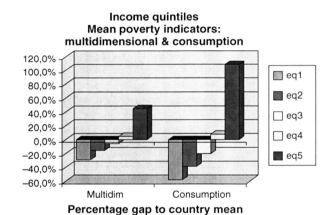

Graph 7.8 Socioeconomic groups comparisons Vietnam 1993 multidimensional versus consumption poverty: Quintiles

highly significant (<.000) for both indicators. The graphs present the gap between the group mean and the country mean, in percentage.

Two facts come out of Graph 7.7:

1) multidimensional and consumption poverty are stronger in rural than in urban areas, the gap being more pronounced for consumption poverty;
2) for the three large regions – North, Center, and South – the poverty profile is completely reversed for multidimensional and consumption poverty. Multidimensional poverty increases from North to Center and South, while the reverse

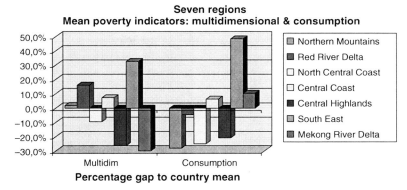

Graph 7.9 Socioeconomic groups comparisons Vietnam 1993 multidimensional versus consumption poverty: Seven regions

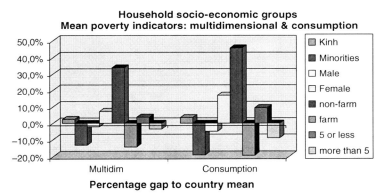

Graph 7.10 Socioeconomic groups comparisons Vietnam 1993 multidimensional versus consumption poverty: Household groups

is true for consumption poverty. Moreover, differentials are much stronger for consumption poverty.

This regional discordance can be seen more clearly in Graph 7.9, the highlights of which are as follows:

- in terms of multidimensional poverty, the Mekong River Delta is the worst region, while it is the Northern Mountains for consumption poverty;
- in terms of multidimensional poverty, the South East (Ho Chi Minh area) is the best off region, followed by the Red River Delta (Hanoi area) and the Central Coast;
- in terms of consumption poverty, the South East remains the best off, followed by the Mekong River Delta and Central Coast; and
- the Central Highlands is among the worst regions for both kinds of poverty.

According to income quintiles (Graph 7.8), multidimensional poverty increases in a monotonous way from lowest to highest quintiles, but with much less pronounced differentials than for the consumption indicator.

From Graph 7.10 it is observed that the profile is similar for different household characteristics, for both kinds of poverty. The less performing groups are minorities, male-headed households, large households, and farming households. In all cases, however, differentials are more pronounced in terms of consumption poverty.

To summarize, there is a large concordance between multidimensional and consumption poverty according to different socioeconomic classifications, but there is an important discordance for the regions, from North to South, and differentials tend to be usually stronger for consumption than for multidimensional poverty.

7.4.2 Comparative Dynamic Poverty Analysis 1993–2002

To compare the evolution of multidimensional and consumption poverty across time, similar concepts and tools shall be used. What is needed for multidimensional poverty is some measures like most standard poverty indices and FGT indices. With the CIP, a very important step is achieved: a unidimensional basic welfare measurement, which is positive, and is similar to an income (expenditure) variable. What is missing is a poverty line for the CIP. In this study, this line is first defined, followed by comparative analysis.

7.4.2.1 An Absolute Multidimensional Poverty Line

The definition adopted here is presented in Section 4.2.1. It relies on the concept of union-poverty, where multidimensional-poor is a household poor in at least one of the eight primary indicators listed in Table 7.8 (Section 4.1.2.1). Using this pure concept of union poverty, the poverty headcount in Vietnam is at 91.8% in 1993.

To operationalize this definition of union poverty, the CIP poverty line is defined as the average of the poverty thresholds specific to the primary indicators. To be strictly below this line is a necessary and sufficient condition to be union-poor, in case all primary indicators are pure poverty indicators (Section 2.1 and Section 4.2.1). But here, three of the eight indicators are extended poverty indicators: type of dwelling, drinking water, and type of toilet used. Thus the absolute poverty line allows for compensation: it is a «compensated» absolute poverty line. Its numerical value, from Table 7.8, is: $\bar{C} = 2421,625$.

Table 7.9 presents the computation of the compensating power (Section 4.2.1) of the absolute poverty line, which is 21%.

To have a CIP below $\bar{C}$ is still a sufficient condition for being union-poor, but not more necessary: a household can compensate for being poor, e.g., in literacy, by having a permanent house, and so on. The compensated poverty headcount in 1993, determined with the absolute poverty line, is then 79.6%. The poverty analysis can now proceed to multidimensional poverty indices.

Table 7.9 The compensating power of the absolute poverty line in 1993

		Weight	Frequency	Compensation needed	Compensation available
Under-employment	Underemployment	0	5 789 830	22 065 042 130	
	No underemp.	3811	5 331 346		
Hld with chronic sick	With chronic sick	0	2 395 285	11 006 334 575	
	No chronic sick	4595	8 725 891		
Hld with illiterate adults	Adults illiterate	0	4 772 936	7 369 413 184	
	Adults literate	1544	6 348 240		
Hld. with children 6–15 not going school	Child. not going school	0	2 069 056	8 125 182 912	
	Child. going school	3927	9 052 120		
Hld without radio and tv	No radio, tv	0	6 668 591	13 257 158 908	
	With radio or tv	1988	4 082 271		
Type of dwelling-	Temporary house	0	5 040 385	9 299 510 325	
	semi-perm. house	1845	5 293 139		
	permanent house	4302	787 652		1 935 260 964
Drinking water	Ponds, lakes	0	2 662 734	926 631 432	
	Other	348	232 181		
	Dug well	1534	6 407 020		7 598 725 720
	Piped, rain, drilled	3667	1 819 241		6 038 060 879
Type of toilet used	No toilet, other	0	6 312 972	8 301 558 180	
	Simple toilet	1315	4 055 820		
	Double vault compost latris	2559	623 068		775 096 592
	Flush toilet septic tank	5098	129 316		489 202 428
Absolute poverty line		**2421,625**		80 350 831 646	16 836 346 583
				Compensating power	**21,0%**

7.4.2.2 FGT Indices Across Time for Multidimensional and Consumption Poverty

On the basis of the category weights computed using the 1993 data (given in Table 7.8) the composite indicator of poverty (CIP) is first computed for each household appearing in the 1998 and 2002 databases. Weights and the absolute poverty line are kept constant. Using the CIP and its poverty line $\bar{C}$, well-known FGT indices can now be computed as usual, in each of the three periods. The analysis is done first at the country level, and then according to different socioeconomic disaggregations.

Country Level

The very first graph presented in the introduction (see Graph 7.1: Consumption Poverty Rate 1993–2002) can now be completed using a second line presenting the multidimensional poverty rate (headcount), referred to here as the "human and physical asset" poverty rate, on the basis of the name given previously to the poverty concept represented by the eight primary indicators, and to the corresponding CIP. Graph 7.1 thus becomes Graph 7.11.

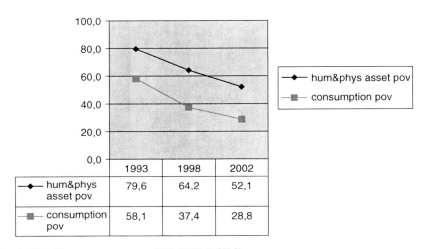

Graph 7.11 Vietnam poverty rate 1993–2002 (FGT-0)

There is first evidence: the incidence of multidimensional poverty is much higher, by a significant 20% points. The explanation lies in the very different poverty concepts. There is no surprise that a multidimensional concept, with the basic require-

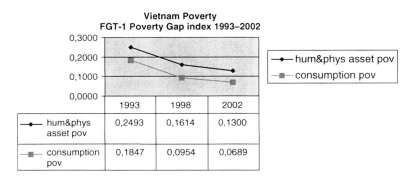

Graph 7.12 Vietnam multidimensional poverty gap index 1993–2002

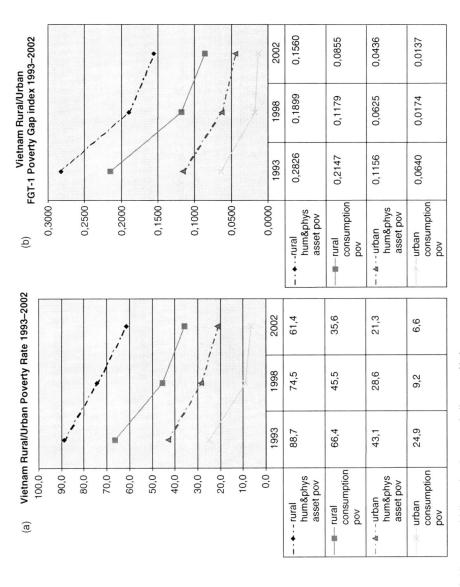

Graph 7.13 Vietnam multidimensional poverty indices rural/urban

ment that all dimensions be satisfied (before some possible compensation), can be expected to produce a higher poverty level than a concept based on a minimal food basket.

As consumption poverty, multidimensional poverty has significantly decreased over the period 1993–2002, almost at the same absolute rate, 27% points instead of 30. This seems a remarkable convergent fact at the country level, given the two very different poverty concepts.

But what about the depth of poverty? Graph 7.12 provides the answer: multidimensional poverty is deeper, but moves in the same declining pattern, with the same absolute reduction close to 0.12 over the 10-year period. However, it is easily verified that the differential between both indices (more or less 0.06) is due to the difference in the poverty rate itself revealed in Graph 7.11: in 1993, the average poverty gap per poor people is 0.318 for consumption and 0.313 for human and physical assets. Again, in terms of reduction of the depth of poverty, a high convergence is depicted in Graph 7.12 at the country level.

For the incidence of poverty (Graph 7.13-A), the pattern of decline is similar for both poverty types in both rural and urban areas, except for a general level differential of approximately 20% points, which is noticed at the country level. Absolute rural/urban differentials are comparable as well as absolute declines.

Regarding the depth of poverty, Graph 7.13-B calls for the same assessment: decline patterns are similar.

Again, in the rural and urban poverty comparisons and trends across time, there is convergence between the two different poverty measurements.

North–Center–South

With Graphs 7.14-A and 7.14-B there appears a regional discordance between the patterns of both kinds of poverty. In 1993, they are consistent with the inverse ranking of North, Center, and South already revealed in Graph 7.7 (CIP and Comparative Analysis of Multidimensional versus Consumption Poverty) relative to the means of both indicators: less multidimensional poverty in the North, but more consumption poverty than in the South. The Center always stands closer to the poorest of both extreme regions Again as in Graph 7.7, there remain larger regional gaps in 1993 for consumption than for multidimensional poverty.

Since the North has performed better than the South in both types of poverty reduction, especially during the 1993–1998 period, the changes in the poverty patterns have gone in opposite directions: the North–South gap has increased in terms of multidimensional poverty from 1993 to 2002, but has decreased for consumption poverty. Due to its low performance in the reduction of consumption poverty in the period 1998–2002, the Center has clearly moved from its middle position in 1993 to the worst position in 2002, a move which has not occurred in terms of multidimensional poverty for which it remained closely connected to the South.

Regarding the depth of poverty, the story is slightly different, as seen in Graphs 7.15-A and 7.15-B. The same inverse ranking of North–Center–South is

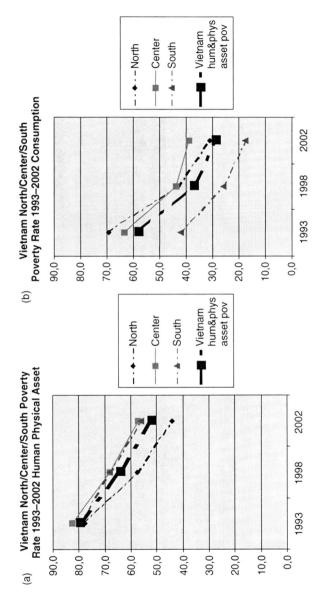

Graph 7.14 Vietnam multidimensional poverty rate North–Center–South

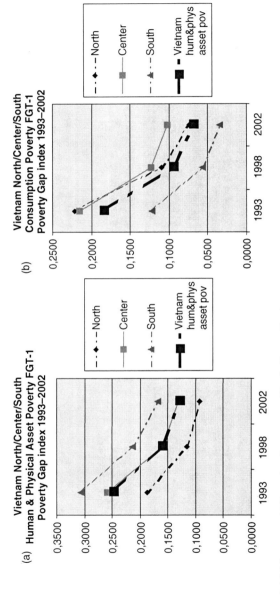

Graph 7.15 Vietnam multidimensional poverty gap North–Center–South

observed: deepest multidimensional poverty is in the South where, on the other hand, consumption poverty is the least deep. But the initial pattern in 1993 is quite different: the differential depth gaps are as strong in multidimensional and consumption poverty. Especially for the multidimensional poverty, the decreasing trends are different: the South has better reduced the poverty depth, so that the initial gaps have decreased in 2002, contrary to the corresponding poverty rates. The depth story remains similar to the rate one for consumption poverty.

This regional analysis North–Center–South can be refined further by looking at the detailed results for Vietnam's seven regions, as defined at the beginning of the 10-year period. These results are presented graphically in Appendix E, for the FGT-0 and FGT-1 indices. Without going into a complete analysis, it can be observed that

- the positive gap between multidimensional and consumption indices increases from Northern to Southern regions, which means that multidimensional poverty is much more pervasive than consumption poverty in the South, compared to the North;
- the most striking decrease in both sorts of poverty happened in the Red River Delta (Hanoi region) especially in the first period 1993–1998, and in the South East (Ho Chi Minh region), in this case exclusively during the 1993–1998 period; and
- divergent decrease rates are observed in the Northern Mountains (both periods), in the North Central Coast, the Central Highlands, and the South East for the second period.

Ethnicity

Poverty distributions and trends in poverty across the majority Kinh (86%) and the minority (14%) ethnic groups are presented in Graphs 7.16-A, B, C, and D. It can be observed that

- Minorities are poorer in terms of the poverty rate, whatever the sort of poverty (A and B);
- the poverty rate gap between both ethnic groups is much higher with consumption than with multidimensional poverty;
- for both sorts of poverty, the poverty rate has decreased significantly for the Kinh, while it has remained almost constant for the Minorities, during the period 1993–2002. This is an important convergent fact;
- poverty is much deeper for the Minorities than for the Kinh, whatever the sort of poverty (C and D), but the differential is much higher with consumption poverty;
- the more striking convergent fact is that the trends in the depth of poverty are similar for both sorts of poverty: the Kinh experienced a very significant decline over the whole period 1993–2002. The Minorities experienced a decline in the first period 1993–1998, followed by an increase in 1998–2002; this rising was

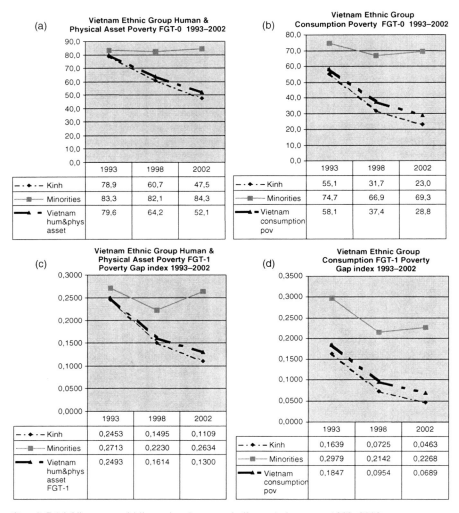

Graph 7.16 Vietnam multidimensional poverty indices ethnic groups 1993–2002

nevertheless steeper for multidimensional poverty, so that over the 10-year period there was really no gain for them.

The Minorities have really thus been left behind with the remarkable poverty reduction in Vietnam during the period 1993–2002, and both approaches to poverty agree on this.

7.4.3 Comparative Dynamic Inequality Analysis 1993–2002

The CIP is a numerical and positive indicator of multidimensional basic welfare. Usual inequality indices can thus be calculated and compared with the consumption

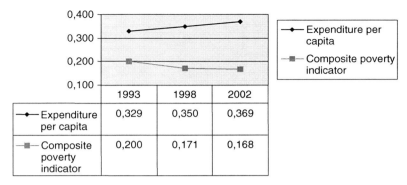

Graph 7.17 Vietnam Gini coefficient for consumption and multidimensional poverty 1993–2002

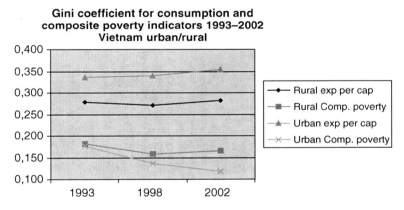

Graph 7.18 Vietnam Gini coefficient for consumption and multidimensional poverty 1993–2002 urban/rural

inequality. The Gini coefficient is used for this end and results are presented in Graphs 7.17, 7.18, 7.19, and 7.20.

7.4.3.1 Country Level

Graph 7.17 provides the basic facts: inequality in the CIP is much lower than for the consumption indicator, 0.200 compared to 0.329 in 1993. More importantly, inequality in the CIP decreases over the period 1993–2002, while consumption inequality increases. In 2002, the CIP Gini coefficient is less than half of the consumption Gini coefficient.

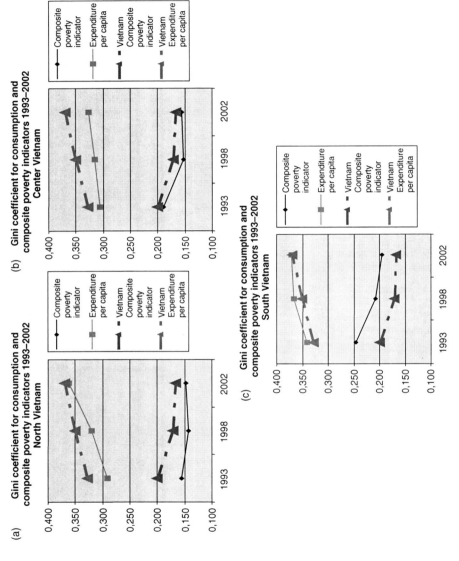

Graph 7.19 Vietnam Gini coefficient for consumption and multidimensional poverty 1993–2002 North–Center–South

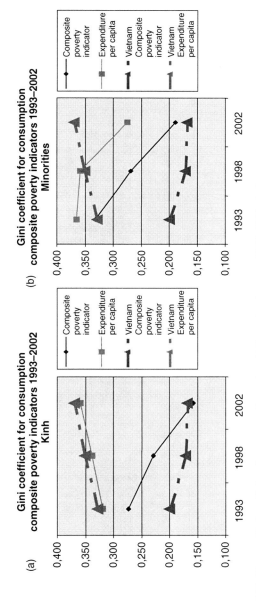

Graph 7.20 Vietnam Gini coefficient for consumption and multidimensional poverty 1993–2002 ethnic groups

7.4.3.2 Rural/Urban

An additional divergent fact shows up in Graph 7.18: rural inequality is significantly lower than urban inequality for consumption, while the inverse situation – more rural inequality – develops for the multidimensional basic welfare. Moreover, while rural inequality follows the same trend for both indicators, remaining almost constant, urban inequality decreases strongly for the composite welfare and increases moderately for consumption over the 10-year period.

7.4.3.3 North–Center–South

Graphs 7.19-A, B, and C present the regional evolution of inequality for both kinds of welfare, compared with both Gini coefficients at the country level.

It comes out that

- the opposite trends in inequality exist in each of three large regions, and are more pronounced in the first than in the second period;
- there is more inequality in the South, for both sorts of welfare;
- the lowest inequality in multidimensional welfare is in the North, but the Center has caught up in terms of inequality by 1998;
- the lowest inequality in consumption was in the North in 1993 but was supplanted by the Center at the end of the 10-year period;
- the strongest increase in consumption inequality happened in the North, so that at the end of the 1993–2002 periods, the region caught up with the South;
- the strongest decrease in multidimensional inequality happened in the South, but it still remained the most unequal region in 2002; and
- at the beginning of the 10-year period, the regional ranking in increasing inequality was North–Center–South. This remained the same for multidimensional inequality at the end of the period. The ranking changed to Center–North–South for consumption inequality.

7.4.3.4 Ethnicity

It should first be kept in mind that Minorities have really been left behind in the striking poverty reduction achieved in Vietnam from 1993 to 2002, and even that the depth of both sorts of poverty is increasing within these small communities (Section 7.4.2.2, Graphs 7.16). Here, Graphs 7.20-A and B highlight important facts regarding the dynamics of inequality within the two ethnic groups, especially

- in 1993, Minorities were more unequal than Kinh in both sorts of welfare, but the situation has dramatically changed in 2002: Minorities are much more equal than Kinh in consumption and have almost caught up with them in terms of a significantly lowered multidimensional inequality; and

- contrary to the divergent trends in inequality generally observed in all parts of the country (including among the Kinh majority), the Minorities have experienced significant reduction in both consumption and multidimensional inequality. This fact has to be connected with the increasing depth of poverty for the Minorities, which bring the poor closer and farther from the poverty lines.

To conclude on the inequality analysis, there is important divergence between both approaches to poverty, mainly in the trends, but also on the levels of inequality. However, the generally lower levels of multidimensional inequality call for some qualification. A technical factor could be part of the explanation: that multidimensional poverty is measured with discrete variables having a very small number of categories. Thus the number of possible values for the CIP is finite, e.g., there are here 1,536 possible values with 8 indicators and 21 categories. With a sample of 4,800 households in the VNLSS-1 (1993), less than 50% of these values (in fact, only 699 values) are really observed, for an average of 7 households per observed value. Some inter-household variation, normally observed with a continuous variable like expenditures, disappears partly in the discrete case, and can contribute to lower inequality indices. This is why more attention should be given to trends in inequality and comparisons across socioeconomic groups.

7.4.4 Policy Insights

7.4.4.1 Poverty Reduction Unitary Gains (PRUG)

The measurement of multidimensional poverty used here, built on an internal analysis of the complex structure of associations between subdimensions and multiple poverty states, indicates that the elimination of a specific poverty state translates into an increase in the basic welfare as captured by the CIP. This fact deserves more attention, in view of identifying the most rewarding poverty state eliminations. A first, synthetic view on this issue is obtained through the poverty reduction unitary gain (PRUG, Section 4.1.2), which consists of a simple graphical representation of Table 7.8. This representation is done in graphs 7.21-A to 7.21-C, where primary indicators are grouped according to the three poverty types underlying the CIP. Due to the basic ordering consistency requirement, all lines must obviously be increasing. The absolute poverty line is added to each graph. This line represents the average gain per indicator required to get a household out of union poverty, and serves here as a visual reference to assess the relative ordering of the numerous unitary gains. Due to the specific poverty thresholds appearing in Table 7.8 and identified here (see the legends on the right of the Graphs 7.21), the poverty line lies at the average of the ordinates of the eight poverty states #2. The poverty line represents also the unique basic welfare level of all households if there were no compensation effects and if poverty was completely eliminated. The slope of each line segment corresponds to the welfare gained by moving from the lowest state to the superior one.

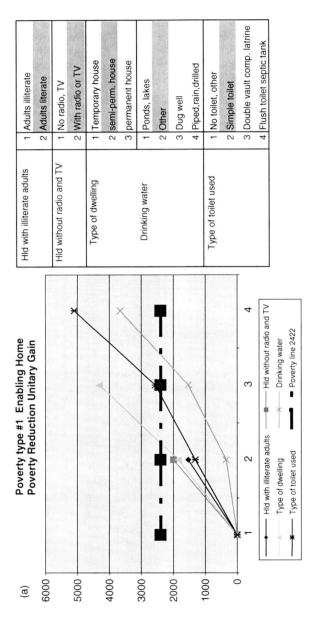

		Adults illiterate
Hld with illiterate adults	1	Adults illiterate
	2	Adults literate
Hld without radio and TV	1	No radio, TV
	2	With radio or TV
Type of dwelling	1	Temporary house
	2	semi-perm. house
	3	permanent house
Drinking water	1	Ponds, lakes
	2	Other
	3	Dug well
	4	Piped,rain,drilled
Type of toilet used	1	No toilet, other
	2	Simple toilet
	3	Double vault comp. latrine
	4	Flush toilet septic tank

Graph 7.21 Vietnam poverty reduction unitary gain in each poverty subdimension

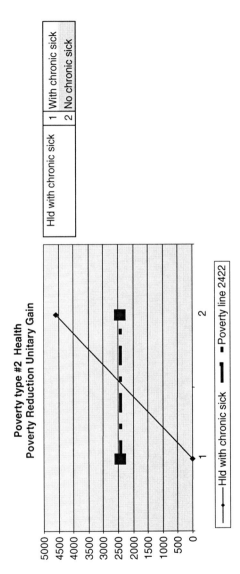

Graph 7.21 (Continued)

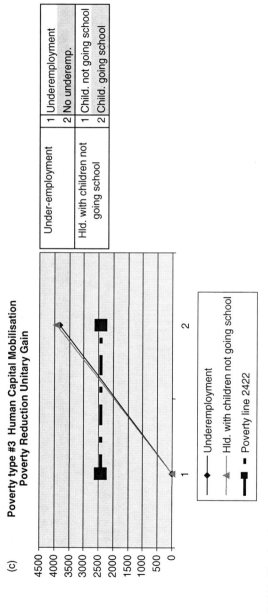

Graph 7.21 (Continued)

From graphs 7.21-A, B, and C, it is observed that

- interventions limited to the elimination of extreme poverty, i.e., going from poverty state #1 to #2, offer a much higher unitary gain in the case of poverty types #2 and #3, the decreasing ranking in most rewarded eliminations being:
  - chronic sickness;
  - underschooling, underemployment (same level);
  - not having a radio or TV set;
  - temporary housing;
  - adult illiteracy;
  - having no toilet;
  - ponds and lakes as sources of drinking water.

- in the case of the only poverty type where compensation is possible – enabling home – lines are convex for the three concerned subdimensions. This means that the very last possible improvement is the most rewarding: getting a permanent house, accessing piped, rain, or a drilled water source, getting a flush toilet-septic tank. It should be noticed that nothing in the technique imposes this convexity, as lines could as well be concave.

In this regard, three remarks are called for.

First, it must be noticed that some convexity phenomena like those observed here can raise important ethical issues for poverty reduction policy makers. Let us suppose that there are two groups of households below the poverty line. Households in both groups suffer from illiteracy and from having a temporary house, but have a radio or TV set. A first subgroup is also poor in terms of access to drinking water and in sanitation, while the second subgroup already benefits from dug well water and a double-vault compost latrine. Supporting the first subgroup just to eliminate drinking water and sanitation poverty would not take them over the poverty line, while helping the better-off second subgroup to improve on their safe water and sanitation access would obviously take them over the poverty line. The scenario of needing to choose which group to support could be an obvious ethical dilemma for policy makers.

Second, a clear view of unitary gains should be accompanied by a cost analysis to really inform policy choices: what is the cost of moving from a poverty state A to the state B?

Third, to measure the aggregate basic social welfare gain obtained through eliminating different subdimensions of poverty requires that actual poverty distributions as estimated in Table 7.6 (Section 7.4.1.1) be joined with the PRUG graphs (see Section 4.1.2).

7.4.4.2 Poverty State Elimination Efficiency (PSEE)

Aggregate gains in basic welfare depend on poverty distributions, which vary obviously through space and time. These are easily measurable, as a result of the pos-

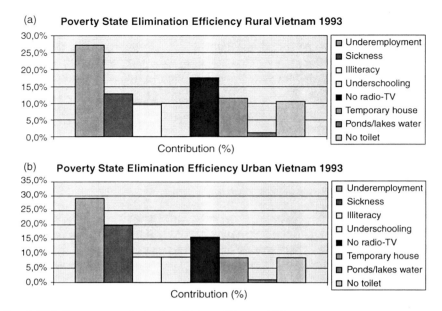

Graph 7.22 Poverty state elimination efficiency Vietnam 1993

itive recoding of the primary indicators and the CIP built on this basis. Due to the structure of the CIP, the required aggregate gains for eliminating all primary poverty states are additive across subdimensions of poverty (Section 4.1.2). PSEE Graphs 7.22 and 7.23 present these gains as percentages of the total required gains, first for the base year 1993, and then for the final year 2002. These percentages correspond to the potential aggregate gain in multidimensional welfare, and equivalently in multidimensional poverty reduction, by eliminating specific poverty states below the relevant poverty threshold. Since for all eight subdimensions (indicators) the specific poverty threshold corresponds to the poverty state #2, it is sufficient to refer here to only one eliminated poverty state in each subdimension, which is the first one. There are two graphs for each period, according to the rural/urban distinction. In some sense, they are the demand side expressing priorities in poverty elimination. As for the preceding analysis of unitary gains, the full picture of efficiency cannot be achieved without costing each poverty state elimination, which unfortunately could not be done here.

No graph is given at the country level simply because there is almost no difference with the rural graph, since Vietnam is approximately 80% rural in 1993 and 76% in 2002.

According to graph 7.22-A, the priorities for rural Vietnam in 1993 would have been

1. eliminate underemployment;
2. far behind, access social communication means (radio, TV); and
3. eliminate chronic sickness.

All other poverty states come together as a group, except eliminating ponds/lakes as unsafe drinking water, since the latter appears as a less urgent intervention. The ranking is thus not the same as the one based on unitary gains, especially since underschooling falls far below the top three priorities.

In urban areas, the only important change in ranking is that chronic sickness supplants communication means as the second priority in eliminating poverty states (Graph 7.22-B).

It should be noticed that the three poverty types are represented in the first three priorities: human capital mobilization with eliminating unemployment, health with eliminating chronic sickness, and enabling home with accessing means of communication.

The issue of accessing radio/TV as communication means deserves further attention. It has to be interpreted in the strict sense as an *indicator*, which means something intended to represent a larger and more profound dimension. Here, «radio/TV» represents the first poverty type which, as already observed previously (Graphs 4.4 and 4.5), is strongly associated with the income dimension of poverty. Moreover, compared to its four other companion indicators (illiteracy, housing type, drinking water source, and sanitation), it is certainly the most strongly identifiable with a private good, a durable good closely associated to the consumption level. In this regard, housing is obviously a private, long-term investment. Thus, looking at «radio/TV» as an income indicator, the second priority in rural area, and third in urban area, can be interpreted as income generation.

Ten years later, in 2002, important changes have occurred, as seen in graphs 7.23-A and 7.23-B. Sickness elimination, i.e., health, largely supplants communication means (income generation) as the second priority in rural areas, with employment remaining as first priority. Accessing communication means has become no more important than housing conditions and sanitation.

In urban areas however, health becomes the first preoccupation, significantly supplanting the elimination of underemployment. Also, as in rural areas, acquiring communication means (income generation) is no more important than other dimensions of the enabling home poverty type; in fact, it appears as the fourth priority after the elimination of temporary housing.

This efficiency analysis of different poverty reduction policies can be developed further by bringing back into the picture the analysis of poverty types across socioeconomic groups presented above in "Poverty Types Identification and Analysis across Socioeconomic Groups". Such a connection provides relevant indications in regard to targeting the most efficient policies.

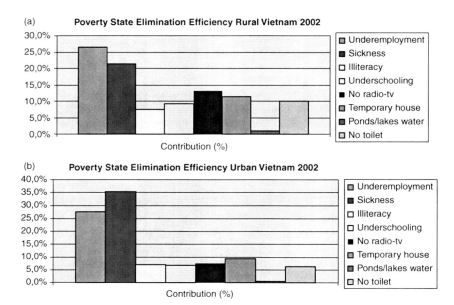

Graph 7.23 Poverty state elimination efficiency Vietnam 2002

7.5 Conclusion

A 5-dimension measurement of poverty in Vietnam has been developed, on the basis of eight categorical ordinal indicators. These dimensions are education, health, water/sanitation, employment, and housing. A composite indicator of multidimensional poverty (CIP) has been constructed using a specific factorial technique – multiple correspondence analysis (MCA). The CIP has been computed for each household of the VNLSS 1 (1993), 2 (1998), and 3 (2002) databases, and an absolute multidimensional poverty line has also been constructed for this study.

The hypothesis raised as the first research objective has been effectively verified. During the period 1993–2002, multidimensional poverty has decreased in Vietnam as strikingly as consumption poverty, by –27% at the country level compared to –30% for the consumption poverty headcount. The important decrease in the depth of poverty is almost the same in both kinds of poverty, between –0.11 and –0.12. The level of multidimensional poverty is higher, essentially due to a very different, larger scope, and more demanding concept of poverty (since it is based on union poverty). But this result regarding the central hypothesis appears as a very significant fact of empirical convergence.

A second study objective was to establish if patterns of poverty and inequality dynamics were also the same for both kinds of poverty. The answer is no, the patterns are different. Yet this assessment calls for an important qualification, since there are many convergent and divergent facts.

For the poverty analysis, there is convergence for the rural/urban decreasing and relative level patterns, but very different achievements for the Kinh/Minorities. Also, both sorts of poverty have steadily decreased, at different rates, in all seven regions. Best performing regions are the Red River Delta and the South East. An official report quoted above asserts that for the period 1993–1998, "(Thus) the situation of the ethnic minorities is improving, but at a slower rate than the Kinh, and they are beginning to lag behind."[24] Our analysis shows that for both sorts of poverty, the situation of the Minorities has dramatically deteriorated during the period 1998–2002: the Minorities experienced no reduction in the poverty headcount, which remains very high at 70 and 80% for consumption and multidimensional poverty, respectively, and an increased depth in poverty. Divergence is essentially seen at the regional level. Universally, there is less multidimensional poverty in the North and less consumption poverty in the South. Due to the differences in the decreasing poverty rates, the gap between the North and the South has increased in multidimensional poverty and decreased in consumption poverty.

The most important divergence facts are observed in inequality. Generally, at the country level and in most disaggregations across socioeconomic groups, inequality in multidimensional welfare (CIP) is much lower than in consumption. More importantly however, multidimensional inequality decreases while consumption inequality increases during the 1993–2002 period.

From a policy standpoint, a disaggregation of the basic welfare improvements required for eliminating poverty completely shows that in 2002, priority should be given to health and employment, then to income generation.

Finally, regarding the third operational objective pursued in this applied research, it seems that a sound methodology of multidimensional poverty measurement is feasible and relevant. Measurement is based on light categorical indicators that are available to a participative implementation at the local level, as demonstrated by their primitive CBMS origin recalled in Section 7.3.1. This opens the way to a more regular monitoring of poverty reduction policies, with a high disaggregation potential.

---

[24] Government of Vietnam (1999), p. 32.

References

1. Anderson T.W. (1958), *An Introduction to Multivariate Statistical Analysis*, John Wiley & Sons, New York.
2. Asselin L.-M. and A. Dauphin (1999), *Poverty Measurement, A Conceptual Framework*, CECI, MIMAP Training Session on Poverty Measurement and Analysis, Laval University, Quebec, August 1999.
3. Asselin L.-M. (2002a), *Multidimensional Poverty, Theory*, IDRC, MIMAP Training Session on Multidimensional Poverty, Laval University, Quebec, June 2002.
4. Asselin, L.M. (2002b), *Pauvreté Multidimensionnelle*, CRDI, IMG.
5. Asselin M. (2005), Technique d'évaluation d'impact des projets de réduction de la pauvreté suivant une approche multidimensionnelle. Application vietnamienne. Master degree thesis in rural economics, Laval University, Québec. Unpublished.
6. Asselin, L.-M. and V.T. Anh (2005), *Multidimensional Poverty in Vietnam 1993–1998 According to CBMS Indicators, Vietnam Socio-Economic Development Review*, Spring 2005, no. 41
7. Asselin L.-M. and V.T. Anh (2008), *Multidimensional Poverty Measurement with Multiple Correspondence Analysis*, in *Quantitative Approaches to Multidimensional Poverty Measurement*, N. Kakwani and J. Silber ed., Palgrave.
8. Benzécri, J.P. (1980), *L'Analyse Des Données, Analyse Des Correspondances*, Exposé élémentaire, Dunod.
9. Benzécri J.P. and F. Benzécri (1980), *L'analyse des données, Analyse des correspondances*, Dunod, Paris.
10. Betti G., B. Cheli, A. Lemmi and V. Verma (2007), *The Fuzzy Approach to Multidimensional Poverty*, in *Quantitative Approaches to Multidimensional Poverty Measurement*, N. Kakwani and J. Silber ed., Macmillan Press, Palgrave. Forthcoming.
11. Bibi Sami (2002), *Measuring Poverty in a Multidimensional Perspective: A Review of Littérature*, Faculté des Sciences Economiques et de Gestion de Tunis, CIRPEE, Université Laval, Québec, Canada.
12. Bourguignon F. and S.R. Chakravarty (1999), *A Family of Multidimensional Poverty Measures*, in *Advances in Econometrics, Income Distribution and Scientific Methodology*, Essays in honor of Camilo Dagum, D.J. Slottje ed.: Physica-Verlag GmbH & Co.
13. Bry, X. (1995), *Analyses Factorielles Simples*, Economica, Paris.
14. Chakravarty, S.R., D. Mukherjee and R.R. Ranade (1997), On the Family of sub-groups and factor decomposable measures of multidimensional poverty in D.J. Slottje ed., *Research on Economic Inequality*, vol. 8, JAI Press, London
15. Daffé, G. and M.S. Badji (2003), Le profil de pauvreté féminine au Sénégal, Programme de recherche MIMAP/Sénégal-CREA.
16. Direction de la statistique et de la prévision (DPS) (2001), Plan d'échantillonnage de l'enquête QUID 2001/ESAM II.

17. DPS (1988), Population du Sénégal : structure par âge et par sexe en 1988 et projection de 1998 à 2015. Dakar.
18. DPS (1995), Enquêtes Sénégalaises Auprès des ménages. Rapport préliminaire, Dakar.
19. DPS (1997), Enquêtes Démographiques et de Santé III. Rapport, Dakar.
20. DPS (1998), Situation économique du Sénégal. Dakar.
21. DPS (2003), Comptes révisés du Sénégal 1996.2001 Dakar.
22. Duclos J.Y., D. Sahn and S. Younger (2002), Comparaison robuste de la pauvreté multidimensionnelle, CIRPEE & Cornell University.
23. Duclos, J.Y. and A. Araar (2004), Poverty and Equity: Measurement, Policy and Estimation with DAD.
24. Duclos J.Y. and A. Araar (2006), *Poverty and Equity: Measurement, Policy and Estimation with DAD*, Springer and IDRC, 393 p.
25. Duclos J.Y., D. Sahn and S. Younger (2006), *Using an Ordinal Approach to Multidimensional Poverty Analysis,* in *Quantitative Approaches to Multidimensional Poverty Measurement*, N. Kakwani and J. Silber ed., Macmillan Press, Palgrave. Forthcoming.
26. Escofier, B. and J. et Pagès (1990), Analyses factorielles simples et multiples, objectifs méthodes et interprétation, DUNOD, 284 P.
27. Fatou, C. and R. et Kane (2002), Profil de la pauvreté au Sénégal : approche monétaire, Programme de recherche MIMAP/ Sénégal-CREA.
28. Filmer D. and L. Pritchett (2001), *Estimating Wealth Effects without Expenditure Data-or Tears,* Demography, vol. 38, no. 1, pp. 115–132
29. Foster Greer J.J. and E. Thorbecke (1984), A class of decomposable poverty Measures, Econometrica.
30. Gendreau, F. (1998), Crises, pauvreté et changement démographiques dans les pays du sud.
31. General Statistical Office (2004), *Results of the Survey on Households Living Standards 2002*, Statistical Publishing House, Hanoi
32. Government of Vietnam (1999), Vietnam Development Report 2000, Attacking Poverty.
33. Greenacre, M. and J. Blasius (1994), *Correspondence Analysis in the Social Sciences, Recent Developments and Applications*, Academic Press, Harcourt Brace & Company Publishers.
34. Ki, J.B. and K. Akakpo (2001), Dimensions spatiales de la pauvreté humaine au Sénégal, Mémoire de fin d'étude, ENEA-STADE.
35. Kolenikov S. and G. Angeles (2004), *The Use of Discrete Data in PCA: Theory, Simulations, and Applications to Socioeconomic Indices*, Working paper, Carolina Population Center, University of North Carolina at Chapel Hill, October 20, 2004.
36. Krugman, P. and M. Obstfeld (1995), Economie internationale, 2è éditions, Nouveaux horizons les Prémisses, ECONOMICA.
37. Lachaud J.P. (2000), Dépenses des ménages, développement humain et pauvreté au Burkina Faso : Substitution ou complémentarité ? Document de travail no 49, Université Montesquieu-Bordeaux IV, Centre d'économie de développement.
38. Lebart L., A. Morineau and M. Piron (1990), *Statistique exploratoire multidimensionnelle,* 3rd edition, Dunod, Paris.
39. Lebart, L., A. Morineau and M. Piron (1995). Statistique exploratoire multidimensionnelle, DUNOD, PARIS.
40. Maasoumi E. (1986), *The Measurement and Decomposition of Multi-Dimensional Inequality*, Econometrica, vol. 54, no. 4, pp. 991–997.
41. Maasoumi E. (1999), *Multidimensional Approaches to Welfare Analysis*, Chap. 15 in J. Silber ed., *Handbook of Income Inequality Measurement*, Kluwer Academic Publishers, 437–477.
42. Meulman, J.J. (1992), The integration of multidimensional scaling and multivariate analysis with optimal transformations, Psychometrika, vol. 57, no. 4, pp. 539–565.
43. Ministère de l'Economie et des Finances du Sénégal (2002), Document de Stratégie de Réduction de la Pauvreté (DSRP), Dakar.
44. PNUD (1990), Rapport mondial sur le développement humain. PNUD.

45. Ravallion, M. (1994a), *Poverty Comparisons, Chur,* Harwood Academic Publishers, Switzerland.
46. Ravallion M. (1994b), *Poverty comparisons,* The World Bank, Harwood Academic Publishers, Switzerland.
47. Rawls J. (1971), *A Theory of Justice,* Harvard University Press.
48. Rényi A. (1966), *Introduction à la théorie de l'information,* appendice à *Calcul des probabilités,* Dunod, Paris.
49. Sahn D.E. and D.C. Stifel (2000), *Poverty Comparisons Over Time and Across Countries in Africa,* World Development, vol. 28, no. 12, pp. 2123–2155.
50. Sen A, (1976), *Poverty : An Ordinal Approach to Measurement,* Econometrica, vol. 44, no. 2, 219–231.
51. Sen A. (1982), *Equality of What?,* in *Choice, Welfare and Measurement,* MIT Press.
52. Sen, A. (1985), *Commodities and Capabilities.* Amsterdam North Holland.
53. Sen A. (1992), *Inequality Reexamined,* Harvard University Press, 4th printing 1997.
54. Sen A. (1999), *Development as Freedom,* Anchor Books, New York, 366 p.
55. Shorrocks A.F. (1980), *The class of additively decomposable inequality measures,* Econometrica, vol. 48, no. 3, 613–625.
56. Socialist Republic of Vietnam (2002), *The Comprehensive Poverty Reduction and Growth Strategy,* Hanoi, May 2002.
57. Streeten P. et al. (1981), *First Things First, Meeting Basic Human Needs in Developing Countries,* Oxford University Press.
58. Tabachnick B.G. and L.S. Fidell (2001), *Using Multivariate Statistics,* fourth edition, Allyn and Bacon.
59. Taylor C. (1989), *Sources of the Self, The Making of the Modern Identity,* Harvard University Press, Cambridge, 601 p.
60. Theil H. (1967), *Economics and Information Theory,* North Holland Publishing Company, Amsterdam.
61. UNDP and UNICEF (1996), Catching Up, Capacity Development for Poverty Elimination in Viet Nam, Hanoi, October 1996.
62. Volle, M. (1993), *Analyse des données,* Paris 1993.
63. Vu Tuan Anh (2000), Poverty Monitoring in Vietnam, Annual MIMAP meeting held in Palawan, Philippines, September 2000. IDRC, Ottawa, mimeo.
64. World Bank (1997), Vietnam, Deepening Reform for Growth, An Economic Report, Report No. 17031-VN, October 31, 1997.

Appendix A
Poverty Measurement: A Conceptual Framework

A.1 Poverty, An Equity Issue

A.1.1 Basic Considerations

The concept of poverty takes its origin in social ethics, which can be seen as a central part of political philosophy, domain of philosophical thinking looking for a theory of social arrangements. If we want to see a link with more familiar subjects of economic theory, we can say that this area of philosophical research belongs to the foundations of the theory of social choice. Social ethics is also deeply rooted in the more global subject of moral philosophy, a theory of the Good.

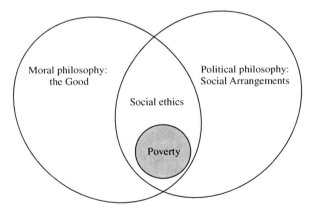

Graph A.1 Philosophical roots of the concept of poverty

Appendix A is a revised and expanded version of Part I of Asselin and Dauphin, Poverty Measurement, A Conceptual Framework, CECI, MIMAP Training Session on Poverty Measurement and Analysis, Laval University, Quebec, August 1999.

Why should we consider that the concept of poverty is primarily an ethical concept? Essentially, to think about poverty means to identify individual situations which are judged unacceptable, meaning unfair or unjust, in a given society. Thus the concept of poverty arises basically from normative considerations with respect to equity. Within the corpus of political philosophy, the theory of justice is the most appropriate domain on which to rely for the development of the concept of poverty. The most influential modern theorist in this domain of political philosophy is certainly John Rawls,[1] whom Amartya Sen mentions as an important reference for his own work on the theory of equity.[2]

The search for a fair society is in fact a search for some form of equity among the members of this society, an equitable position being defined by the equality of all members relatively to « things » which need to be specified. Poverty, which corresponds to an unacceptable degree of inequality, cannot be analyzed without referring to our conception of the desired equality in the framework of the social arrangement.[3] In view of developing a concept of poverty, it is first required to position ourselves in regard to social equality. We choose here to take as an important basis of our reflection on the equity issue the analytic framework developed by Amartya Sen, without necessarily adopting his personal choices relative to social justice and poverty definitions.

The central question in the definition of social justice is « equality of what? ». That is the space question. Here, a great diversity is obviously possible in the objects (variables) taken in this space of equality. This diversity can be reduced by considering the nature of the space of equality, whether it is a space of *achievements* (e.g., calories and nutrients provided by daily food consumption), a space of *freedoms* to achieve (e.g., capacity to decide how many calories and nutrients will be obtained through daily food consumption), or a space of *resources* determining a set of freedoms to achieve (e.g., disposable income, monetary or in-kind, giving the capacity to decide how many calories and nutrients will be obtained through daily food consumption).[4] The specification of the space of equality, including its nature (resources, freedoms, or achievements), expresses a philosophical view on social justice, and on this basis, schools of thought can be distinguished. That will be done in the next sections.

But at the very beginning, the idea of equality has to face an important difficulty – the basic heterogeneity of human beings:

---

[1] John Rawls, *A Theory of Justice,* Harvard University Press, 1971.

[2] Amartya Sen, *Inequality Reexamined,* Harvard University Press, 1992, 4th printing 1997, p. XI.

[3] A. Sen, loc. cit., p. 9: «The theory of inequality evaluation has close links with that of assessment of poverty, and the choice of space becomes a central concern in identifying the poor and in aggregating the information about the states of those identified».

[4] It should be clear that this classification is not absolute, but relative to how the proponent of a space of equality qualifies this space. Thus, for instance, income could be presented as an achievement per se, the freedom to choose his income level being determined, among other resources, by human capital. But income is usually viewed as a variable in the resource space, and for any other variable, there is usually a first natural classification as resource, freedom, or achievement.

We differ from each other not only in external characteristics (e.g. in inherited fortunes, in the natural and social environment in which we live), but also in our personal characteristics (e.g. age, sex, proneness to illness, physical and mental abilities). The assessment of the claims of equality has to come to terms with the existence of pervasive human diversity.[5]

This structural diversity has a strong effect on the meaning and consequences of equality in a given space. With a same level of freedom, different persons will not necessarily realize the same achievements. In better-off households, it can happen, due to cultural factors, that some or even all household members suffer from malnutrition. People having the same resources do not have necessarily an equal freedom to the same achievements: due to metabolic differences, the same aliments are not transformed into equal amounts of nutrients, so that an equal income does not ensure access to the same quality of nutrition for different persons. To sum up,

One of the consequences of «human diversity» is that equality in one space tends to go, in fact, with inequality in another.[6]

A.1.2 A Traditional School: Utilitarianism as the Best Known Form of Welfarism

Welfarism in general and utilitarianism in particular see value, ultimately, only in individual utility, which is defined in terms of some mental characteristic, such as pleasure, happiness, or desire.[7]

This characterization of welfarist theories seems largely shared in the economic community:

[The welfarist approach] aims to base comparisons of well-being, and public policy decisions, solely on individual "utilities".
. . .
The essence of the approach is the concept of a *preference ordering* over goods, generally taken to be representable by a "utility function", the value of which is deemed to be a sufficient statistic for assessing a person's well-being.[8]

Sen adds:

In so far as utility is meant to stand for individual well-being, it provides a rather limited accounting of that . . .[9]

To go farther in the characterization of welfarism and of its dominant form, utilitarianism, Sen takes the viewpoint of the informational basis:

---

[5] Amartya Sen, loc. cit., p.1.

[6] Loc. cit., p. 20.

[7] Loc. cit., p. 6.

[8] Martin Ravallion, *Poverty comparisons,* The World Bank, Harwood Academic Publishers, 1994, pp. 4–5.

[9] Amartya Sen, loc. cit., p. 6.

Most theories of justice can also be usefully analysed in terms of the information used in two different – though interrelated – parts of the exercise, viz. (1) the selection of *relevant personal features* and (2) the choice of *combining characteristics*. To illustrate, for the standard utilitarian theory, the only intrinsically important "relevant personal features" are *individual utilities*, and the only usable "combining characteristic" is *summation*, yielding the *total* of those utilities. The set of *welfarist* theories, of which utilitarianism is a particular example, retains the former part (viz. takes utilities as the only relevant features) but can use other combining characteristics, e.g., utility-based maximin (or lexicographic maximin), summation of concave transforms of utilities (such as summing the logarithms of utilities).[10]

This specific social theory has a long history:

> During much of modern moral philosophy the predominant systematic theory has been some form of utilitarianism. One reason for this is that it has been espoused by a long line of brilliant writers who have built up a body of thought truly impressive in its scope and refinement. We sometimes forget that the great utilitarians, Hume and Adam Smith, Bentham and Mill, were social theorists and economists of the first rank; and the moral doctrine they worked out was framed to meet the needs of their wider interests and to fit into a comprehensive scheme.[11]

We can see that utilitarianism, viewed as a theory of social arrangement, is not primarily and explicitly a theory of equality. But from its beginning, especially with Adam Smith's conception of the invisible hand, it was understood that the best social achievement could be reached as a result of everybody pursuing his own utility. By giving a larger opportunity to everyone to maximize his personal utility, an aggregate social utility, resulting from a combination of all the individual utilities, could be increased. In this idea lies the double root of maximization, as a characteristic of welfarist theories, and of some form or another of equality as a by-product of this maximization process, perceived as a social objective. Welfarist theories are then naturally «growth» theories.

To be more specific about the space in which equality emerges as a by-product of welfare (social utility) maximization, we have to consider how, since Adam Smith, economic theory, as a more and more autonomous field within moral philosophy, formalized progressively the welfarist approach.

> In his pioneering contribution to measuring inequality in terms of social-welfare loss, Hugh Dalton (1920) used a simple utilitarian social-welfare function. Social welfare was taken to be the sum-total of individual utilities, and each individual utility was taken to be a function of the income of that individual. The same utility function was taken to apply to all individuals.[12]

Even without the restrictive condition of the same utility function for all, but with the basic utilitarian characteristic of a social welfare function additive with equal weights for all individual members, the welfarist maximization program requires that all marginal utilities be equal. So, the space of individual marginal utilities

---

[10] Loc. cit., pp. 73–74.

[11] John Rawls, loc. cit., p. VII.

[12] Amartya Sen, loc. cit., p. 95.

is the first one where equality is required by this approach. With the additional simplifying assumption made by Dalton, the equality condition, then valid for individual utilities, can be transposed in the space of individual incomes. We should bear in mind that since Adam Smith, social optimality was explained by economic considerations developed through resources allocation determining the individual income constraint. This resource space, income, emerged as a more familiar space for specifically economic thinking, in contrast with the utility space which can be perceived as the space where economic theory remains connected to the more global social science realm.

After Dalton, utilitarianism was to develop its equality reflection in the income space:

> Since Dalton's measure of inequality operates on utilities as such, it is very exacting on the measurability and interpersonal comparability of individual utilities. It is, in fact, not easy to talk about percentage shortfalls of utility sum-totals from the maximal sum-total (e.g., "The sum of *utilities* is reduced by 17 per cent"). Atkinson's (1970b) index of inequality, in contrast, operates on incomes, and measures the social loss involved in unequal income distribution in terms of shortfalls of equivalent incomes. Atkinson measures the inequality of a distribution of incomes by the percentage reduction of total income that can be sustained without reducing social welfare, by distributing the new reduced total exactly equally.[13]

So, we can retain that utilitarianism, the dominant form of welfarism as an approach to social arrangement theory, while being naturally more an economic growth theory than an equalitarian theory, has developed as a by-product equalitarian considerations in the achievement space of individual marginal utilities, and more operationally in classical (and neoclassical) economics in the resource space of individual incomes.

A.1.3 A Pragmatic and Humanitarian Reaction to Utilitarianism: The Basic-Needs Approach

The basic-needs approach is not shaped within a conceptual revision of welfarism and utilitarianism. It is not a proposition for a theory of equality different from the one derived from these dominant economic paradigms.

> Of concern here [is] which objective is more important: reduction in inequality or meeting basic needs; egalitarianism or humanitarianism... reducing inequality is a highly complex, abstract objective, open to many different interpretations and therefore operationally ambiguous... Removing malnutrition in children, eradicating disease, or educating girls are concrete, specific achievements that meet the basic needs of deprived groups, whereas reducing inequality is abstract... In the case of equality however, no one knows how to achieve (and maintain) it, how precisely to define it, or by what criteria to judge it .[14]

---

[13] Loc. cit, p.96.

[14] P. Streeten et al., *First Things First, Meeting Basic Human Needs in Developing Countries,* Oxford University Press, 1981, pp. 17–18.

The basic-needs approach emerged explicitly in the seventies as a reaction to welfarism in the area of anti-poverty policies:

> In formulating policies aimed at reducing poverty, a good deal of attention has been paid in the economic literature to restructuring patterns of production and income so that they benefit the poor. But similar attention has not been devoted to the consumption side. This imbalance is restored if the basic needs objective is placed at the center of the development dialogue where it belongs.[15]

This reaction was also against the welfarist growth strategy [the maximization strategy] as the basic policy to eradicate poverty. This policy was based on three justifications[16]:

- market forces would spread the benefits of growth widely;
- market forces would spread the benefits of growth speedily;
- progressive taxation, social services, and other government actions would spread the benefits downward.

> None of the assumptions underlying these three justifications turned out to be universally true. Except for a very few countries, with special initial conditions and policies, there was no automatic tendency for income to be widely spread. Nor did governments always take corrective action to reduce poverty; after all, governments were themselves often formed by people who had close psychological, social, economic, and political links with the beneficiaries of the concentrated growth process, even though their motives were often mixed. And it certainly was not the case that a period of enduring mass poverty was needed to accumulate capital. It was found that small-scale farmers saved at least as high a proportion of their income as the big landowners and were more productive, in terms of yield per acre, and that entrepreneurial talent was widespread and not confined to large firms. Prolonged mass poverty was therefore not needed to accumulate savings and capital and to stimulate entrepreneurship.[17]

The basic-needs approach is a direct approach to the problem of poverty seen as an unacceptable degree of social inequity, with a sense of urgency:

> Emphasis on basic needs must be seen as a pragmatic response to the urgent problem of world poverty; as the ultimate objective of economic development, it should shape national planning for investment, production, and consumption.[18]

Even if the basic-needs approach was more operationally defined toward the end-seventies, it has a long history in economics:

> Much of what goes under the label of «basic needs» has been contained in previous work on growth with equity, employment creation, integrated rural development, and redistribution with growth. In particular, the emphasis on making the poor more productive has remained an important component of the basic needs approach. Its distinct contribution consists in deepening the income measure of poverty by adding physical estimates of the particular

---

[15] Loc. cit., pp. VII–VIII.

[16] Loc. cit., p. 9.

[17] Loc. cit., pp. 10–11.

[18] Loc. cit., p. IX.

goods and services required to achieve certain results, such as adequate standards of nutrition, health, shelter, water and sanitation, education, and other essentials.[19]

The British economist Rowntree, in his famous study «Poverty: A Study of Town Life,» published in 1901, is usually recognized as the first author having seriously analyzed and measured the concept of basic needs. Rowntree has worked essentially on three categories of basic needs: food, house rent, and household sundries consisting of boots, clothes, and fuel. Interestingly, Rowntree used different methods to set up the minimum requirements in each category. For food, he resorted to nutritional standards established by nutritionists for males, females, adults, and children. But for household sundries, he resorted to a qualitative approach by asking people their views on what were to be considered basic requirements. For house rent, he simply took what households were in fact paying.

In reference to Sen's analytic framework, the basic-needs approach positions the equity debate in a space of achievements, not of resources. It looks for a «concrete specification of human needs in contrast (and as a supplement) to abstract concepts» and places «the emphasis is on ends in contrast to means.»[20] Which are these basic achievements?

[They are] at present considered to be in six areas: nutrition, primary education, health, sanitation, water supply, and housing and related infrastructure.[21]

Elsewhere in Streeten, the results to be achieved are described as «adequate standards of nutrition, health, shelter, water and sanitation, education and other essentials.»[22] Clothing is also mentioned frequently as a possible area (p. 25). In fact, as can be seen from the quotations, the list of basic achievements is usually an open list and there are important debates about what should be this list.[23] It is important to understand that «basic needs are not primarily a welfare concept.»[24] So, in the space of achievements, they do not overlap with utility, the achievement looked at by welfarists. For the basic-needs school, the achievement space is multi-dimensional and has a kind of structure generated from priorities defined among the different results to be achieved.

Since the basic-needs approach, as we have seen, differentiates itself from the welfarist school essentially in the area of poverty eradication policies, we can conclude with some policy considerations. The basic-needs approach suggests and facilitates selective policies. «The crucial factual assumption is that leakages, inefficiencies, and "trickle-up" (which make the better-off the ultimate beneficiaries of

---

[19] Loc. cit., p. 3.

[20] Loc. cit., p. 34.

[21] Loc. cit., p. 92.

[22] Loc. cit., p. 3.

[23] See loc. cit., chapter 1, Interpretations, pp. 25–26.

[24] Loc. cit., p. 3.

anti-poverty policies) are smaller in a selective system than in a general system.»[25]
With a strong preoccupation for more targeted interventions,

> A basic needs approach calls for decentralization to the village and district level so that
> plans can be adapted to variable local conditions and the power and efforts of the poor
> can be mobilized. At the same time, such decentralization often concentrates power in the
> hands of the local elite, who block policies that would benefit the poor. In the interest of
> the rural poor, decentralization therefore has to be balanced by the retention of power in the
> central government. It is not an easy task to design an administrative and political structure
> which is both decentralized for adaptability and flexibility and centralized explicitly for the
> protection of the poor and the politically weak. Voluntary organizations can also make an
> important contribution by offering guidance to local leaders on the special needs of the
> poor.[26]

But more proactive state interventions to ensure the satisfaction of the basic needs
for everybody could have economic effects which are not to be overlooked:

> A major difficulty of a basic needs approach is that efforts to meet basic needs in a short
> time, in a society that previously pursued non-basic needs policies, will create disequilib-
> rium in several markets, with macroeconomic repercussions.[27]

The issue is then to judge if meeting the basic needs of the population is more
important than avoiding some turbulence in the economic aggregates.

A.1.4 A Theoretical and Humanist Reaction to Utilitarianism: The Capability Approach

The capability approach to equity developed by Sen relies intellectually for a large
part on the Rawlsian theory of justice as mentioned earlier. Rawls's conception has
itself been developed in opposition to utilitarianism:

> Those who criticized them [the brilliant utilitarianist writers Hume, Adam Smith, Bentham,
> Mill, etc.] failed, I believe to construct a workable and systematic moral conception to
> oppose it... What I have attempted to do is to generalize and carry to a higher order of
> abstraction the traditional theory of the social contract as represented by Locke, Rousseau,
> and Kant. In this way I hope that the theory can be developed so that it is no longer open to
> the more obvious objections often thought fatal to it. Moreover, this theory seems to offer
> an alternative systematic account of justice that is superior, or so I argue, to the dominant
> utilitarianism of the tradition. My ambitions for the book will be completely realized if it
> enables one to see more clearly the chief structural features of the alternative conception of
> justice that is implicit in the contract tradition and points the way to its further elaboration.
> Of the traditional views, it is this conception, I believe, which best approximates our consid-
> ered judgments of justice and constitutes the most appropriate moral basis for a democratic
> society.[28]

---

[25] Loc. cit., p. 38.

[26] Loc. cit., p. 58.

[27] Loc. cit., p. 58.

[28] John Rawls, loc. cit., pp. VII–VIII.

Rawls has then developed a specific contract theory, «Justice as Fairness,» on which we come back below.

A social contract theory is structurally an ethical theory completely different from a teleological one, like utilitarianism.

> The two main concepts of ethics are those of the right and the good ... The structure of an ethical theory is, then, largely determined by how it defines and connects these two basic notions. Now it seems that the simplest way of relating them is taken by teleological theories: the good is defined independently from the right, and then the right is defined as that which maximizes the good.[29]

For utilitarianism, utility is defined as the good, and what is right is to maximize the sum of individual utilities. In contrast, as a contract theory,

> [Justice as fairness] is a deontological theory, one that either does not specify the good independently from the right or does not interpret the right as maximizing the good ... Justice as fairness is a deontological theory in the second way. The question of attaining the greatest net balance of satisfaction never arises in justice as fairness; this maximum principle is not used at all.[30]
> ... in justice as fairness the concept of right is prior to that of the good. In contrast with teleological theories, something is good only if it fits into ways of life consistent with the principles of right already on hand.[31]

To consider justice as fairness just as a special and partial case of a social contract theory, first a set of principles is explicitly stated and agreed to by all members of the society, and this defines what is right. What is good and needs not to be maximized is conditional on this set of principles, which is the central component of the social contract.

A.1.5   A Specific Social Contract Theory: Justice as Fairness

But what is justice as fairness as a particular case of a social contract theory, the one proposed by Rawls (1971)? Let us have a quick overview.

> There are two principles of justice, which are first expressed that way: First: each person is to have an equal right to the most extensive basic liberty compatible with a similar liberty for others. Second: social and economic inequalities are to be arranged so that they are both (a) reasonably expected to be to everyone's advantage, and (b) attached to positions and offices open to all.[32]
> ... it should be observed that the two principles ... are a special case of a more general conception of justice that can be expressed as follows.

---

[29] Loc. cit., p.24.

[30] Loc. cit., p. 30.

[31] Loc. cit., p. 396.

[32] Loc. cit., p. 60.

> All social values – liberty and opportunity, income and wealth, and the bases of self-respect – are to be distributed equally unless an unequal distribution of any, or all, of these values is to everyone's advantage.[33]

For the principles of justice to constitute a real social contract, they must be agreed to by all members of the society. To reach this universal agreement, Rawls uses a special mechanism or condition, which he calls *the original position of equity* (OPE). This condition stipulates that

> They [the principles of justice] are the principles that free and rational persons concerned to further their own interests would accept in an initial position of equality as defining the fundamental terms of their association ... These principles are to regulate all further agreements; they specify the kinds of social cooperation that can be entered into and the forms of government that can be established.
> . . .
> In justice as fairness the original position of equality corresponds to the state of nature in the traditional theory of the social contract. This original position is not, of course, thought of as an actual historical state of affairs, much less as a primitive condition of culture. It is understood as a purely hypothetical situation characterized so as to lead to a certain conception of justice. Among the essential features of this situation is that no one knows his place in society, his class position or social status, nor does any one know his fortune in the distribution of natural assets and abilities, his intelligence, strength, and the like. I shall even assume that the parties do not know their conceptions of the good or their special psychological propensities. The principles of justice are chosen behind a veil of ignorance. This ensures that no one is advantaged or disadvantaged in the choice of principles by the outcome of natural chance or the contingency of social circumstances. Since all are similarly situated and no one is able to design principles to favor his particular condition, the principles of justice are the result of a fair agreement or bargain ... This explains the propriety of the name «justice as fairness»: it conveys the idea that the principles of justice are agreed to in an initial situation that is fair.[34]

Now, these two principles of justice need to be more precise if they are to allow a real social arrangement. In particular, the space where equality is to be assessed, according to the second principle, has to be specified. Seeing the social arrangement as being first a kind of distributive mechanism, Rawls introduces a set of *primary goods*, to begin some operationalization of his second principle.

> Injustice, then, is simply inequalities that are not to the benefit of all. Of course, this conception is extremely vague and requires interpretation.
>
> As a first step, suppose that the basic structure of society distributes certain primary goods, that is things that every rational man is presumed to want. These goods normally have a use whatever a person's rational plan of life. For simplicity, assume that the chief primary goods at the disposition of society are *rights and liberties, powers and opportunities, income and wealth* ... These are the social primary goods. Other primary goods such as health and vigor, intelligence and imagination, are natural goods; although their possession is influenced by the basic structure, they are not so directly under its control.[35]

---

[33] Loc. cit., p. 62.

[34] Loc. cit., pp. 11–12.

[35] Loc. cit., p. 62.

We can see that the Rawlsian space of equality includes the economic domain with income and wealth, but is much larger than only economic. Now, the primary social goods constitute the basis of individual *expectations.*[36]

> Thus in applying the second principle I assume that it is possible to assign an expectation of well-being to representative individuals holding these positions.[37]

Even with these operational complements, the implementation of the second principle of justice is conditional to the interpretation given to it, and here Rawls clearly differentiates two basic approaches: the principle of efficiency and the difference principle.

> At this point it is necessary ... to explain the principle of efficiency. This principle is simply that of Pareto optimality (as economists refer to it) formulated so as to apply to the basic structure. I shall always use the term «efficiency» instead because this is literally correct and the term «optimality» suggests that the concept is much broader than it is in fact. To be sure, this principle was not originally intended to apply to institutions but to particular configurations of the economic system, for example, to distributions of goods among consumers or to modes of production. The principle holds that a configuration is efficient whenever it is impossible to change it so as to make some persons (at least one) better off without at the same time making other persons (at least one) worse off.[38]

It is important to see that this efficiency approach is marked with indifference and indeterminacy. Indifference, because in a socially efficient state, we do not mind about eventually strong inequality between individual expectations. Indeterminacy, in the sense that if there exists more than one efficient social state, there is no principle allowing to choose among them.

Using the efficiency principle generates two possible interpretations of the second principle of justice: a system of natural liberty and a system of liberal equality. They are described so:

> In the system of natural liberty the initial distribution is regulated by the arrangements implicit in the conception of careers open to talents (as earlier defined). These arrangements presuppose a background of equal liberty (as specified by the first principle) and a free market economy. They require a formal equality of opportunity in that all have at least the same legal rights of access to all social positions. But since there is no effort to preserve an equality, or similarity, of social positions, except insofar as this is necessary to preserve the requisite background institutions, the initial distribution of assets for any period of time is strongly influenced by natural and social contingencies.[39]
>
> . . .
>
> The liberal interpretation of the two principles seeks, then, to mitigate the influence of social contingencies and natural fortune on distributive shares. To accomplish this end it is necessary to impose further basic structural conditions on the social system. Free market arrangements must be set within a framework of political and legal institutions which reg-

---

[36] Loc. cit., Section 15.

[37] Loc. cit., p. 64.

[38] Loc. cit., pp. 66–67.

[39] Loc. cit., p. 72.

ulates the overall trends of economic events and preserves the social conditions necessary for fair equality of opportunity.[40]

So, both systems rely essentially on the free market system as a distributive mechanism, the first one strongly believing that it is efficient by itself, the second one stating that it is not and that it needs to be corrected by state interventions. In both cases, individual differences are not explicitly recognized.

With the difference principle, individual differences are directly acknowledged, either in natural endowment or in social position. Inequality in the distribution of social primary goods can be considered as just under two different interpretations of the second principle of justice, depending on whether the focus is on natural endowment only (Natural Aristocracy) or on whether it extends to social position (Democratic Equality).

> On this view [natural aristocracy] no attempt is made to regulate social contingencies beyond what is required by formal equality of opportunity, but the advantages of persons with greater natural endowments are to be limited to those that further the good of the poorer sectors of society. The aristocratic ideal is applied to a system that is open, at least from a legal point of view, and the better situation of those favored by it is regarded as just only when less would be had by those below, if less were given to those above. In this way the idea of "noblesse oblige" is carried over to the conception of natural aristocracy.[41]

> The democratic interpretation . . . is arrived at by combining the principle of fair equality of opportunity with the difference principle. This principle removes the indeterminateness of the principle of efficiency by singling out a particular position from which the social and economic inequalities of the basic structure are to be judged. Assuming the framework of institutions required by equal liberty and fair equality of opportunity, the higher expectations of those better situated are just if and only if they work as part of a scheme which improves the expectations of the least advantaged members of society. The intuitive idea is that the social order is not to establish and secure the more attractive prospects of those better off unless doing so is to the advantage of those less fortunate.[42]

It is immediately seen that a Pareto-efficient social state could be rejected with the difference principle if transferring some primary goods from the better-off to the worse-off improves the situation of the latter.

Among the four possible interpretations of the second principle of justice, Rawls commits himself to the difference principle and to the system of Democratic Equality.

After a long development of all these basic constituents of the social contract named Justice as Fairness, he arrives at a final statement of the two principles of justice.

First Principle

Each person is to have an equal right to the most extensive total system of equal basic liberties compatible with a similar system of liberty for all.

---

[40] Loc. cit., p.73.

[41] Loc. cit., p. 74.

[42] Loc. cit., p. 75.

Second Principle
Social and economic inequalities are to be arranged so that they are both:

(a) to the greatest benefit of the least advantaged, consistent with the just savings
    principle, and
(b) attached to offices and positions open to all under conditions of fair equality
    of opportunity.[43]

To these principles correspond two priority rules:
First Priority Rule (The Priority of Liberty)

The principles of justice are to be ranked in lexical order and therefore liberty can be
restricted only for the sake of liberty.

. . .

Second Priority Rule (The Priority of Justice over Efficiency and Welfare)

The second principle of justice is lexically prior to the principle of efficiency and to
that of maximizing the sum of advantages; and fair opportunity is prior to the difference
principle.[44]

A.1.6 An Adjustment and Complement to Justice as Fairness: The Capability Approach to Equity

In proposing his own approach to the evaluation of inequality, Sen also recognizes
his relationship with Rawls's theory of justice:

Indeed, my greatest intellectual debt is undoubtedly to John Rawls. I am led by his reasoning over quite a bit of the territory, and even when I go in a different direction (e.g.,
focusing more on the "extents" of freedoms, rather than on the "means"-what Rawls calls
the "primary goods"), that decision is, to a considerable extent, based on an explicit critique
of Rawls's theory.[45]

The main criticism addressed by Sen to Rawls is relative to informational issues:

A particularly important contrast is that between capability-based evaluation and Rawls's
(1971) procedure of focusing on the holding of "primary goods" (including resources such
as incomes, wealth, opportunities, the social bases of self-respect, etc.). This is a part of his
"Difference Principle", which is an integral component of the Rawlsian theory of "justice
as fairness". While my own approach is deeply influenced by Rawls's analysis, I argue
that the particular informational focus on which Rawls himself concentrates neglects some
considerations that can be of great importance to the substantive assessment of equality-and
of efficiency.[46]

---

[43] Loc. cit., p. 302.

[44] Loc. cit., pp. 302–303.

[45] Amartya Sen, *Inequality Reexamined*, Harvard University Press, 1997, p. XI.

[46] Loc. cit., p. 8.

Rawls himself had already admitted his focus on means by choosing the primary goods as the space of equality, and had anticipated the criticisms he would receive on this aspect of his theory:

> It may be objected that expectations should not be defined as an index of primary goods anyway but rather as the satisfactions to be expected when plans are executed using these goods. After all, it is in the fulfillment of these plans that men gain happiness, and there-fore the estimate of expectations should not be founded on the available means. Justice as fairness, however, takes a different view. For it does not look behind the use which persons make of the rights and opportunities available to them in order to measure, much less to maximize, the satisfactions they achieve.[47]

Rawls is opposed to discuss equality in the space of achievements, as do basically the welfarists and the basic-needs supporters. Sen is not opposed to analyze equality in a different space than achievements, and he recognizes that Rawls's theory "can also be interpreted . . . as taking us in the direction of the overall freedom actually enjoyed rather than being confined to the outcomes achieved."[48]

According to Sen, what is missing in the Rawlsian approach, at least in the infor-mational domain, is an intermediate space between the space of resources and the space of achievements. This is precisely the space of freedoms. This will become the essential complement by Sen to the Rawlsian approach to equity. But why did Sen pay so much importance to distinguish between the primary goods and the extents of freedoms? Basically, because there exists a fundamental diversity between human beings.

> The importance of the contrast [between the two approaches] once again turns on the fundamental diversity of human beings. Two persons holding the same bundle of primary goods can have very different freedoms to pursue their respective conceptions of the good (whether or not these conceptions coincide). To judge equality-or for that matter efficiency-in the space of primary goods amounts to giving priority to the "means" of freedom over any assessment of the "extents" of freedom, and this can be a drawback in many con-texts. The practical importance of the divergence can be very great indeed in dealing with inequalities related to gender, location, and class, and also to general variations in inherited characteristics.[49]

Sen's personal views on equity will be developed by giving specific contents to the space of freedoms and to the space of achievements. For the former, he will introduce the term *capabilities*, which specifies the *extents* of freedoms, and for the latter, the notion of *functionings* will describe the *type of outcomes* expected from capabilities.

The term "functionings" is first required to define what *well-being* means:

> The well-being of a person can be seen in terms of the quality (the "well-ness", as it were) of the person's being. Living may be seen as consisting of a set of interrelated "functionings", consisting of *beings* and *doings*. A person's achievement in this respect can be seen as the vector of his or her functionings. The relevant functionings can vary from such elementary

---

[47] John Rawls, loc. cit., p. 94.

[48] Amartya Sen, loc. cit., p. 80.

[49] Loc. cit., pp. 8–9.

things as being adequately nourished, being in good health, avoiding escapable morbidity and premature mortality, etc., to more complex achievements such as being happy, having self-respect, taking part in the life of the community, and so on. The claim is that functionings are *constitutive* of a person's being, and an evaluation of well-being has to take the form of an assessment of these constituent elements.[50]

The term "capabilities" is then defined by reference to functionings:

> Closely related to the notion of functionings is that of the *capability* to function. It represents the various combinations of functionings (beings and doings) that the person can achieve. Capability is, thus, a set of vectors of functionings, reflecting the person's freedom to lead one type of life or another. Just as the so-called "budget set" in the commodity space represents a person's freedom to buy commodity bundles, the "capability set" in the functioning space reflects the person's freedom to choose from possible livings.[51]

Specific functionings (e.g., being adequately nourished) relate to specific capabilities (e.g., the capability to be adequately nourished). To continue with the "budget set" analogy, axes in the functioning space correspond to specific capabilities, the extent of which is represented by the axis segment contained in the capability set.

The link between capabilities and well-being requires some explanation, since it has a double aspect.

> The relevance of a person's capability to his or her well-being arises from two distinct but interrelated considerations. First, if the achieved functionings constitute a person's well-being, then the capability to achieve functionings (i.e., all the alternative combinations of functionings a person can choose to have) will constitute the person's freedom-the real opportunities-to have well-being. This "well-being freedom" may have direct relevance in ethical and political analysis.
> . . .
> The second connection between well-being and capability takes the direct form of making *achieved* well-being itself depend on the *capability* to function. Choosing may itself be a valuable part of living, and a life of genuine choice with serious options may be seen to be-for that reason-richer. In this view, at least some types of capabilities contribute *directly* to well-being, making one's life richer with the opportunity of reflective choice.[52]

Sen insists on what differentiates the capability approach from better-known ones.

> In either form, the capability approach differs crucially from the more traditional approaches to individual and social evaluation, based on such variables as *primary goods* (as in Rawlsian evaluative systems), *resources* (as in Dworkin's social analysis), or *real income* (as in the analyses focusing on the GNP, GDP, named-goods vectors). These variables are all concerned with the instruments of achieving well-being and other objectives, and can be seen also as the means to freedom. In contrast, functionings belong to the constitutive elements of well-being. Capability reflects freedom to pursue these constitutive elements, and may even have . . . a direct role in well-being itself, in so far as deciding and choosing are also parts of living.[53]

---

[50] Loc. cit., p. 39.

[51] Loc. cit., p. 40.

[52] Loc. cit., p. 41.

[53] Loc. cit., p. 42.

But as utility is also acknowledged as a constituent of well-being, it must be emphasized that

> ...the capability approach differs from utilitarian evaluation (more generally "welfarist" evaluation) in making room for a variety of doings and beings as important in themselves (not just *because* they may yield utility, nor just to the *extent* that they yield utility). In this sense, the perspective of capabilities provides a fuller recognition of the variety of ways in which lives can be enriched or impoverished.[54]

Why should the capability space be chosen as the evaluation space for equality, instead of the functioning space?

> Furthermore, freedom of choice can indeed be of direct importance for the person's quality of life and well-being. The nature of this connection may be worth discussing a bit more. Acting freely and being able to choose are, in this view, directly conducive to well-being, not just because more freedom makes more alternatives available. This view is, of course, contrary to the one typically assumed in standard consumer theory, in which the contribution of a set of feasible choices is judged exclusively by the value of the best element available.[55]
>
> ...
>
> For example, "fasting" as a functioning is *not* just starving; it is *choosing to starve when one does have other options*. In examining a starving person's achieved well-being, it is of direct interest to know whether he is fasting or simply does not have the means to get enough food. Similarly, choosing a life-style is not exactly the same as having that life-style no matter how chosen, and one's well-being does depend on how that life-style happened to emerge.[56]

In fact, by developing the concept of freedom in a set of specific capabilities, Sen remains fundamentally in line with the Rawlsian focus on liberty for social justice analysis and evaluation.

The Rawlsian framework is too weak in its informational basis to address the issue of poverty, especially in the perspective of measurement. Sen's extension provides this basis and, in fact, it goes through some convergence with the basic-needs approach. All functionings and corresponding capabilities do not have the same weight in social equity assessment and we are thus brought to the identification of basic capabilities.

In a previous work, Sen had analyzed and criticized the insufficiencies of other approaches to cover the concept of «needs.»

> My contention is that *even* the concept of *needs* does not get adequate coverage through the information on primary goods and utility .
>
> ...
>
> It is arguable that what is missing in all this framework is some notion of "basic capabilities": a person being able to do certain basic things.
>
> ...
>
> There is something still missing in the combined list of primary goods and utilities. If it is argued that resources should be devoted to remove or substantially reduce the handicap of the cripple despite there being no marginal utility argument (because it is expensive),

---

[54] Loc. cit., pp. 43–44.

[55] Loc. cit., p. 51.

[56] Loc. cit., p. 52.

despite there being no total utility argument (because he is so contented), and despite there being no primary goods deprivation (because he has the goods that others have), the case must rest on something else. I believe what is at issue is the interpretation of needs in the form of basic capabilities. This interpretation of needs and interest is often implicit in the demand for equality. This type of equality I shall call "basic capability equality".[57]

This point of view is reemphasized ten years later:

In the context of some type of welfare analysis, e.g., in dealing with extreme poverty in developing economies, we may be able to go a fairly long distance in terms of a relatively small number of centrally important functionings (and the corresponding basic capabilities, e.g., the ability to be well-nourished and well-centered, the capability of escaping avoidable morbidity and premature mortality, and so forth). In other contexts, including more general problems of economic development, the list may have to be much longer and much more diverse.[58]

The capability definition of poverty then follows naturally:

...it is possible to argue for seeing poverty as the failure of basic capabilities to reach certain minimally acceptable levels. The functionings relevant to this analysis can vary from such elementary physical ones as being well-nourished, being adequately clothed and sheltered, avoiding preventable morbidity, etc., to more complex social achievement such as taking part in the life of the community, being able to appear in public without shame, and so on. These are rather "general" functionings, but-as was discussed earlier-the specific form that their fulfilments may take would tend to vary from society to society.[59]

A.1.7 A More Comprehensive Evaluation Framework: Taylor's Moral Philosophy

Looking for the conceptual basis of poverty as an equity issue, we are thus led to the world of moral philosophy. Sen's reaction to utilitarianism relies on Rawls's political philosophy, himself identified as Kantian. Regarding the moral philosophy of these different schools of thought, it would be useful to position each of them into a more comprehensive intellectual framework. Charles Taylor's largely praised work, *Sources of the Self*, opens a perspective on moral philosophies characterization which seems deeply relevant for the particular subject dealt with here.

Right at the beginning Taylor worries about the narrow focus given to morality in much contemporary moral philosophy, saying that "This moral philosophy has tended to focus on what it is right to do rather than on what it is good to be, on defining the content of obligation rather than the nature of good life."[60] Obviously

---

[57] Amartya Sen, "Equality of What? ", in *Choice, Welfare and Measurement*, MIT Press, 1982, pp. 367–368.

[58] Amartya Sen, *Inequality Reexamined,* Harvard University Press, 1997, p. 44–45.

[59] Loc. cit., pp. 109–110.

[60] Charles Taylor, *Sources of the Self, The Making of the Modern Identity*, Harvard University Press, Cambridge, 1989, p. 3.

he is aiming here particularly at Rawls, and such strong assertion requires arguments developed in the whole book.

Taylor's fundamental distinction is between ontological and sociobiological moral philosophies. An ontological moral philosophy considers that our moral reactions or intuitions "involve «strong evaluation», that is, they involve discriminations of right or wrong, better or worse, higher or lower, which are not rendered valid by our own desires, inclinations or choices, but rather stand independent of these and offer standards by which they can be judged."[61] Thus, "a moral reaction is an assent to, an affirmation of, a given ontology of the human."[62] Consequently, an ontological moral philosophy will articulate such an implicit ontology of the human. On the contrary, a sociobiological moral philosophy assimilates our moral reactions to «gut» reactions like nausea. This type of account is characteristic of "an important strand of modern naturalist consciousness."[63] This strand "has tried to hive this second [ontological] side off and declare it dispensable or irrelevant to morality."[64] Among the motives for this position is "the great epistemological cloud under which all such accounts lie for those who have followed empiricist or rationalist theories of knowledge, inspired by the success of modern natural science . . . This stance may go along with a sociobiological explanation for our having such reactions, which can be thought to have obvious evolutionary utility and indeed have analogues among other species."[65] And Taylor sums up his basic distinction like this: "The whole way in which we think, reason, argue and question ourselves about morality supposes that our moral reactions have these two sides: that they are not only «gut» feelings but also implicit acknowledgements of claims concerning their objects. The various ontological accounts try to articulate these claims. The temptations to deny this, which arises from modern epistemology, are strengthened by the widespread acceptance of a deeply wrong model of practical reasoning, one based on an illegitimate extrapolation from reasoning in natural science."[66]

Now, how do this general criticism and this distinction apply in the particular cases of Utilitarianism and Kantianism?

In fact, Taylor includes both schools of thought under a same criticism developed in a chapter entitled *Ethics of Inarticulacy*, the qualifier *inarticulacy* being applied to any nonontological moral philosophy, as seen above for sociobiological theories. "Utilitarianism and Kantianism organize everything around one basic reason. And as so often happens in such cases, the notion becomes accredited among the proponents of these theories that the nature of moral reasoning is such that we ought to be able to unify our moral views around a single base. John Rawls, following J.S. Mill, rejects what he describes as the «intuitionist» view, which is precisely a view which

---

[61] Loc. cit., p.4.

[62] loc. cit., p. 5.

[63] Loc. cit., p. 5.

[64] Loc.cit., p.5.

[65] loc. cit., pp. 5–6.

[66] Loc. cit., p. 7.

allows for a plurality of such basic criteria."[67] Taking such a position, these theories refrain to articulate the qualitative distinctions which define the good, i.e., the type of discriminations mentioned above which "underlies our ethical choices, leanings, intuitions.".[68] "Much of this philosophy [modern moral philosophy] strives to do away with these distinctions altogether, to give no place in moral life to a sense of the incomparably higher goods or hypergoods." This criticism of inarticulacy is then specified for utilitarianism and Kantianism.

"Utilitarianism is the most striking case. A good, happiness, is recognized. But this is characterized by a polemical refusal of any qualitative discrimination. There is no more higher or lower; all that belongs to the old, metaphysical views. There is just desire, and the only standard which remains is the maximization of its fulfillment. The critic can't help remarking how little utilitarians have escaped qualitative distinctions, how they in fact accord rationality and its corollary benevolence the status of higher motives, commanding admiration. But there is no doubt that the express theory aims to do without this distinction altogether."[69]

According to such a naturalist theory, "Morality is conceived purely as a guide to *action*. It is thought to be concerned purely with what it is right to do rather than what it is good to be... Moral philosophies so understood are philosophies of obligatory action... A satisfactory moral theory is generally thought to be one that defines some criterion or procedure which will allow us to derive all and only the things we are obliged to do."[70] Again utilitarianism and Kantianism undergo the same criticism: "So the major contenders in these stakes are utilitarianism, and different derivations of Kant's theory, which are action-focussed and offer answers exactly of this kind. What should I do? Well, work out what would produce the greatest happiness of the greatest number. Or work out what I could choose when I have treated other people's prescriptions as if they where my own (Hare). Or think what norm would be agreed by all the people affected, if they could deliberate together in ideal conditions of unconstrained communication (Habermas)."[71]

Having said that, Kant's theory obviously differs from utilitarianism while remaining in a specific sense a philosophy generating ethics of inarticulacy. "Kant's theory in fact rehabilitates one crucial distinction, that between actions done from duty and those done from inclinations. This is grounded on a distinction of motives: the desire for happiness versus respect for the moral law. Kant deliberately takes this stance in opposition to utilitarian thought... Following Rousseau, he breaks with the utilitarian conception of our motives as homogeneous. But nevertheless Kant shares the modern stress on freedom as self-determination. He insists on seeing the moral law as one which emanates from our will. Rational agents have a status that nothing else enjoys in the universe... Everything else may have a price, but only

---

[67] Loc. cit., p. 76.

[68] Loc. cit., p.77.

[69] loc. cit., pp. 78–79.

[70] Loc. cit., p. 79.

[71] Loc. cit., p. 79.

they have «dignity». And so Kant strongly insists that our moral obligations owe nothing to the order of nature. He rejects vigorously as irrelevant all those qualitative distinctions which pick out higher and lower in the order of the cosmos or in human nature. To take these as central to one's moral views is to fall into heteronomy. It has therefore been easy for the followers of Kant to take this rejection of qualitative distinctions in the order of being for a rejection of any distinction at all, and to forget or put into the shade Kant's doctrine of the dignity of rational agents."[72]

For modern moral philosophies of obligatory action, "the focus is on the principles, or injunctions, or standards which guide *action*, while visions of the good are altogether neglected . . . Contemporary philosophers, even when they descend from Kant rather than Bentham (e.g., John Rawls), share this focus."[73] Kantians as well as utilitarians are then led to share "a procedural[74] conception of ethics . . . For the utilitarians, rationality is maximizing calculation . . . For the Kantians the definitive procedure of practical reason is that of universalization."[75] Then Taylor identifies two sources of such a procedural approach to ethics, the modern epistemology already mentioned and the allegiance to modern freedom. "To make practical reason substantive implies that practical wisdom is a matter of seeing an order which in some sense is in nature. This order determines what ought to be done. To reverse this and give primacy to the agent's own desires or his will, while still wanting to give value to practical reason, you have to redefine this in procedural terms . . . This modern idea of freedom is the strongest motive for the massive shift from substantive to procedural justifications in the modern world."[76]

Finally, Taylor concludes with a very severe judgment of inarticulacy on the theories of obligatory action, exemplified with Rawls's theory of justice. "The more one examines the motives . . . of these theories of obligatory action, the stranger they appear. It seems that there are motivated by the strongest moral ideals, such as freedom, altruism and universalism. These are among the central moral aspirations of modern culture, the hypergoods which are distinctive to it. And yet what these ideals drive the theorists towards is a denial of all such goods. They are caught in a strange pragmatic contradiction, whereby the very goods which move them push them to deny or denature all such goods. They are constitutionally incapable of coming clean about the deeper sources of their own thinking. Their thought is inescapably cramped.

A common slogan of Kant-derived moral theories in our day serves also to justify the exclusion of qualitative distinctions. This is the principle of the priority of the right over the good. In its original form, as a Kantian counter-attack against utilitarianism, as an insistence that morality couldn't be conceived simply in terms of outcomes but that moral obligation also had to be thought deontologically, it

---

[72] Loc. cit., p. 83.

[73] Loc. cit., p. 84.

[74] In opposition to *substantive*.

[75] Loc. cit. p. 86.

[76] Loc. cit., p. 86.

can be seen as one moral theory among others and, in its anti-utilitarian thrust, highly justified. But it also can be used to downgrade not just the homogeneous good of desire-fulfilment central to utilitarian theory but also any conception of the good, including the qualitative distinctions underlying our moral views. Rawls, for instance, seems to be proposing in *A Theory of Justice* that we develop a notion of justice starting only with a «thin theory of the good», by which he means what I am calling weakly valued goods. But this suggestion is on the deepest level incoherent. Rawls does, of course, manage to derive (if his arguments in rational choice theory hold up) his two principles of justice. But as he himself agrees, we recognize that these are indeed acceptable principles of justice because they fit with our intuitions. If we were to articulate what underlies these intuitions we would start spelling out a very «thick» theory of the good. To say that we don't «need» this to develop our theory of justice turns out to be highly misleading. We don't actually spell it out, but we have to draw on the sense of the good that we have here in order to decide what are adequate principles of justice. The theory of justice which starts from the thin theory of the good turns out to be a theory which keeps its most basic insights inarticulate . . ..»[77]

At this point, it seems that the Taylor's categories regarding moral philosophies, ontological and sociobiological, strong evaluation, qualitative distinctions, hyper-goods, inarticulacy, moral theories of obligatory action, etc., shed a very relevant light on specific characteristics of philosophies playing an important role in the schools of thought involved in the debate about poverty and its measurement. We have with Taylor a very provocative and stimulating standpoint on the philosophical background of Sen's capability theory, Kantianism, and especially Rawls's theory. A way is opened to pursue the analysis by a careful examination of the extent to which Sen's own moral philosophy differs from Rawls's.

A.2 Conclusion

We have first argued that poverty is an equity issue and that it belongs to political philosophy, more specifically to ethics and ultimately to moral philosophy.

We have also opted for Sen's analytical framework to differentiate approaches to equity, involving a distinction between resource, freedom, and achievement spaces, combined with the basic recognition of human diversity.

A dominant doctrine since two centuries, in the western industrialized world, is a welfarist theory better known as *utilitarianism*. It has been developed as a strictly economic view of the best social arrangement, usually dominated by two concepts: growth and efficiency. Equity is a by-product of aggregate utility maximization, and consists largely of equal marginal individual utilities. From an achievement space reduced to utility, the marginalist analysis transposes equity considerations in the income space as a resource space: income determines the utility level. Poverty

---

[77] Loc. cit., pp.88–89.

is then defined as a socially unacceptable level of income and poverty alleviation policies will mostly try to increase the *productivity* of the poor.

In contrast to utilitarianism or welfarism stands *social contract theory* which also has old historical roots. John Rawls, with his theory of justice, is the most influential modern philosopher having explored and systematized this approach to ethics. Equity (or justice) is directly and explicitly considered as to what should be the basis of the social arrangement and has priority over growth and efficiency considerations. On these grounds, Amartya Sen proposes a *capability* approach to equity. The space in which equality should be looked for is the freedom space, consisting of a set of specific capabilities defined in reference to corresponding types of achievements called «functionings.» Poverty is then defined in reference to a subset of capabilities identified as «basic capabilities,» and by unacceptable deficiencies in these basic capabilities. Poverty alleviation policies will then look for *empowerment* of the poor.

The *basic-needs school* transposes the equity debate from social theory to the policy area, and goes directly to the poverty issue. Some types of poverty must be identified and eradicated within a short-term perspective. Without rejecting the productivity approach to poverty alleviation favored by welfarists, it identifies a small set of achievements corresponding to the satisfaction of some basic needs and requires that poverty alleviation policies ensure as quickly as possible that everybody achieves these basic satisfactions. Strictly speaking, this school is guided neither by welfarist objectives nor by freedom considerations, but essentially by humanitarian preoccupations.

In the practical work of identifying and measuring poverty in a society, a lot of methodological choices will have to be done, in which will be revealed the social philosophy supporting these choices. It could be the ethical philosophy of one of the approaches here discussed, or a hybrid of them. Taylor's philosophical framework can shed light on the intellectual and moral characteristics of these ethical philosophies.

It is important to be as conscious as possible of the ethical and moral paradigm dissimulated in apparently inoffensive technical choices, since, through policies leaning on these measurement techniques, the entire social structure can be deeply affected.

Appendix B
Lists of Indicators of Some Local, National, and International Poverty Measurement Initiatives

B.1 Indicator List # 1 Philippines CBMS Community Level

D1 : Income

1   Proportion of hlds. with income above poverty threshold
2   Proportion of hlds. with income above food threshold

D2 : Education

3   Elementary participation rate (6–12 yrs)
4   Secondary participation rate (13–16 yrs)
5   Literacy rate (10 yrs and above)
6   No.. of pre/elem/sec/vocat/ schools
7   Distance from village to nearest pre/elem/sec/vocat/
8   No. of elementary schools

D3 : Health

9   Infant mortality rate (0–1 yr)
10   Child mortality rate (1–6 yr)
11   Number of health/family planning/daycare centers, clinics
12   Distance from village to nearest health/family planning/daycare centers, clinics
13   Number of drugstores
14   Distance from village to nearest drugstore

D4 : Food / Nutrition

15   Prevalence of malnutrition (0–5 yrs)
16   Proportion of hlds. eating 3 meals a day

D5 : Water / Sanitation

17   Proportion of hlds. With access to potable water
18   Number hlds using types of sources of water
19   Village served by a water station/company
20   Proportion of hlds. with access to sanitary toilet facilities
21   Community garbage disposal available in the village

D6 : Labor / Employment

22   Employment rate (15 yrs+ working over total labor force)

D7 : Housing (living environment)

23   Proportion of hlds. living in non-makeshift housing
24   Proportion of hlds. who are not squatters
25   Distance from nearest electrical station/company
26   Number of hlds served by electrical station/company

D8 : Access to productive assets

27   Presence of credit institutions in the village

D9 : Access to markets

28   Distance from village to nearest market
29   Distance from village to nearest post office
30   Distance from village to nearest police station
31   Distance from village to nearest bank
32   Distance from village to nearest public transport
33   Distance from village to nearest concrete/asphalt road

D10 : Participation/Social peace

34   Number of crimes past 12 months / type of crime
35   Number of individuals suffering from domestic violence
36   Total number of registered voters
37   Distance from village to nearest multi-purpose hall

B.2 Indicator List # 2 Burkina Faso CBMS Community Level

D1 : Income

1   Proportion of hlds with bicycles/motorcycles/cars
2   Proportion of hlds with radio, TV, fans, refrigerators
3   Proportion of hlds with different types of kitchen tools
4   Loincloths ("pagnes") bought last 6 months per capita

D2 : Education

5   Elementary net enrolment rate by sex
6   Secondary net enrolment rate, by sex
7   Literacy rate (10 yrs and above) by sex
8   Drop out rate (6 yrs and above) by sex
9   Proportion of hlds.without radio/TV
10   Number of primary schools / literacy centres
11   Number of classrooms
12   Number of Islamic schools (medersa)
13   Distance to nearest prim. school /literacy centre /medersa
14   Proportion of population. according to education level attained, by sex
15   Success rate to the CEP exam
16   Continuation rate from elem. to sec. level

D3 : Health

17   Child mortality rate (0–5 yr)
18   Proportion of sick last 30 days by sex
19   Frequency of consultations by type of health workers
20   Frequency of preventive consultations type
21   Distance from village to nearest health center
22   Distance from village to nearest maternity hospital
23   Distance from village to nearest drugstore
24   Presence of nurse in the village
25   Presence of trained midwife in the village
26   Presence of traditional midwife in the village

D4 : Food / Nutrition

27   Average no. of meals/day, adults and children
28   Weekly frequency of tô, rice, meat, fish consumption
29   Level food grains stocks (remaining duration before next harvest)

D5 : Water / Sanitation

30   Proportion of hlds. With access to potable water
31   Proportion of hlds. With access to sanitary toilet facilities
32   Proportion of persons using soap for body and clothes wash

D6 : Labor / Employment

33   Dependency ratio

D7 : Housing (living environment)

34   Proportion of hlds. by type of roof/floor material
35   Proportion of hlds. by type of lighting
36   Proportion of hlds. by type of bed for head of hld.

D8 : Access to productive assets

37   Proportion of hlds. with credit for last agric. season
38   Type of agricultural tools/machines used
39   Type of cultivation techniques used

D10 : Participation/Social peace

40   Proportion of persons 10y+ member in an organization, by sex

B.3 Indicator List # 3 Burkina Faso PRSP the 24 Priority Indicators (Region Level)

D1 : Income

1   Rate of grain self sufficiency for farming households
2   Grain production per capita for farming households

D2 : Education

3   Primary school gross enrolment rate

4   Entry rate at CP1 grade by sex
5   Completion rate of primary cycle by sex
6   Adult literacy rate (15+)

D3 : Health

7   Immunization rate: BCG, DTCP3, measles yellow fever
8   Proportion of births attended by skilled health personnel
9   Child mortality rate (0-5 yr)
10   HIV prevalence

D4 : Food / Nutrition

11   Rate of underweighted newborn
12   Prop. of underweight children (weight/age) 0-5 yr

D5 : Water / Sanitation

13   Proportion of hlds. with access to safe water
14   Proportion of hlds. with access to sanitary toilet facilities

D6 : Labor / Employment

15   Unemployment rate
16   Proportion of labour force with occasional work or precarious job

D7 : Housing (living environment)

17   Proportion of hlds. with access to electricity
18   Proportion of hlds. with improved hearth
19   Distribution of hlds. by material used for roof, walls, floor

D8 : Access to productive assets

20   Proportion of hlds with yoke cultivation
21   Proportion of hlds with specific cultivation equipment
22   Proportion of hlds. with credit

D9 : Access to markets

23   Time to reach nearest market infrastructure

D10 : Participation/Social peace

24   Proportion of persons in community organization, by sex

B.4 Indicator List # 4 CWIQ Standard Indicators

D1: Income

1   Proportion of hlds owning selected household items
2   Distribution of hlds. by perception of change in eco. sit last year

D2: Education

3   Primary school enrolment rate
4   Secondary school enrolment rate
5   Primary school drop out rate by age/gender

6   Secondary school drop out rate by age/gender
7   Distribution of hlds. by time to reach nearest prim/second school
8   Proportion of students not satisfied by reasons of dissatisfaction.
9   Proportion of children 6-18 ever attended by reason not att.

D3: Health

10   Proportion of sick last 4 wks by type of sickness/injury
11   Distribution of hlds. by time to reach nearest health facility
12   Proportion of sick not satisfied by serv. by reason of dissatisfaction.
13   Proportion of sick did not consult by reason not consulting
14   Proportion of consultations by type of health care provider
15   Distribution of births last 5 yrs by place of birth
16   Distribution of births last 5 yrs by person delivered the child

D4: Food / Nutrition

17   Proportion of stunted children (height/age)
18   Proportion of wasted children (weight/height)
19   Proportion of underweight children (weight/age)
20   Distribution of hlds by difficulty satisfying food needs

D5: Water / Sanitation

21   Distribution of hlds. by source of water
22   Distribution of hlds. by time to reach nearest water supply
23   Distribution of hlds. by type of toilet

D6: Labor / Employment

24   Mean no. hld members by age group & dependency ratio
25   Distribution of population by work status (15 yr+)
26   Distribution of unemployed population by reason
27   Distribution of economically inactive population by reason
28   Distribution of underemployed population by employment status
29   Distribution of underemployed population by activity
30   Distribution of underemployed population by employer
31   Distribution of working population by employment status
32   Distribution of working population by employer
33   Distribution of working population by activity

D7: Housing (living environment)

34   Distribution of hlds. by material used for roof and walls
35   Distribution of hlds. by fuel used for lighting and cooking
36   Distribution of hlds. by housing tenure
37   Proportion of hlds. without access to electricity

D8: Access to productive assets

38   Distribution of hlds. by changes in land holding last yr
39   Proportion of hlds. owning certain assets

D9: Access to markets

40   Distribution of hlds. by time to reach nearest food market
41   Distribution of hlds. by time to reach nearest public transport.

B.5 Indicator List # 5 MDG's Human Poverty Goals (1 to 7) Country Level

D1 : Income

1	1a. Proportion of population below $1 a day
2	1b. National poverty headcount ratio
3	2. Poverty gap ratio at $1 a day (incidence × depth of poverty)

D2: Education

4	6. Net enrolment ratio in primary education
5	9. Ratio of girls to boys in primary education
6	20. Ratio of school attendance of orphans/non-orphans aged 10–14
7	9. Ratio of girls to boys in secondary education
8	8. Literacy rate of 15- to 24-year-olds
9	10. Ratio of literate females to males among 15- to 24-year-olds
10	7a. Proportion of pupils starting grade 1 who reach grade 5
11	7b. Primary completion rate

D3: Health

12	13. Under-five mortality rate
13	14. Infant mortality rate
14	16. Maternal mortality ratio
15	18. HIV prevalence among 15- to 24-year-old pregnant women
16	21. Prevalence and death rates associated with malaria
17	23. Prevalence and death rates associated with tuberculosis
18	17. Proportion of births attended by skilled health personnel
19	46. Proportion of population with access to affordable, essential drugs on a sustained basis
20	19a. Condom use at last high-risk sex
21	19b. % of aged 15-24 with comprehensive correct knowledge of HIV/AIDS
22	19c. Contraceptive prevalence rate (15-49 w)
23	22. Proportion of population in malaria-risk areas using effective malaria prevention/treatment
24	24. Proportion of tuberculosis cases detected and cured under DOTS
25	15. Proportion of one-year-old children immunized against measles

D4: Food / Nutrition

26	4. Prevalence of underweight in children (under five years of age)
27	5. Proportion of population below minimum level of dietary energy

D5: Water / Sanitation

28	30. Proportion of population with sustainable access to improved water source
29	31. Proportion of population with access to improved sanitation (R/U)

D6: Labor / Employment

30	45. Unemployment rate of 15- to 24-year-olds, male and female and total

D7: Housing (living environment)

31   11. Share of women in wage employment in the non agricultural sector
32   32. Proportion of households with access to secure tenure
33   29. Proportion of population using solid fuels
34   25. Proportion of land area covered by forest

D8: Access to productive assets

35   47. Telephone lines and cellular subscribers per 100 people
36   48a. Personal computers in use per 100 people
37   48b. Internet users per 100 people

D10: Participation/Social peace

38   12. Proportion of seats held by women in national parliament

B.6 Indicator list # 6 Multiple indicator cluster survey (UNICEF)

D1: Income

1   Household availability of Insecticide Treated Nets (ITNs)

D2: Education

2   Prop. of child of primary-school entry age entering school at that age
3   6. Net primary school attendance rate
4   9.Ratio of girls to boys in primary education
5   20. Ratio of school attendance of orphans/non-orphans aged 10–17
6   Net secondary school attendance rate
7   9.Ratio of girls to boys in secondary education
8   8.Literacy rate of 15- to 24-year-olds (women)
9   7a. Proportion of pupils starting grade 1 who reach grade 5
10   Transition rate to secondary
11   7b. Primary completion rate
12   Support for learning (% 0–59 m with family support)
13   Father's support for learning (% 0–59 m with father's support)
14   Home-based school readiness (% children)
15   Support for learning: children's books (3 or more)
16   Support for learning: non-children's books (3 or more)
17   Support for learning: materials for play
18   Non-adult care:0–59 months left alone or in the care of another child
19   Preschool attendance (36–59 months)
20   School readiness: 1st grade with preschool the previous year

D3: Health

21   Under-Five Mortality Rate
22   Infant Mortality Rate
23   Maternal Mortality Ratio
24   Night blindness in pregnant women

25   Prop. children aged 2–9 years with at least one type of disability
26   Prevalence of orphans (0–17 y)
27   Prevalence of vulnerable children (0–17 y): chronically ill parents
28   Prop. children 0–17 y not living with a biological parent
29   Proportion of births attended by skilled health personnel
30   Proportion of live births that were weighed at birth
31   Antenatal Care last birth since 24 months (15–49 w)
32   19c.Contraceptive prevalence rate (15–49 w)
33   Antibiotic treatment of suspect pneumonia (0–59 months)
34   Care seeking for suspect pneumonia (0–59 months)
35   DPT3 immunization coverage (1 y old)
36   Measles immunization coverage (12–23 months)
37   TB immunization coverage (12–23 months)
38   Hepatitis B coverage (12–23 months)
39   Polio3 immunization coverage (12–23 months)
40   Hib coverage (12–23 months)
41   Fully immunized children
42   Neonatal tetanus protection (0–11 months)
43   ORT use (0–59 months)
44   Received (ORT or increased fluids) and continued feeding (0–59 m)
45   22. Bed net use (under fives)
46   22. Anti-malarial treatment (under fives)
47   Intermittent Preventive Treatment (pregnant women)
48   Iodized salt consumption
49   Vitamin A supplementation (under fives)
50   Vitamin A supplementation (post-partum mothers)
51   Children consuming Vitamin A fortified foods
52   19a.Condom use at last high-risk sex
53   19b.% 15–24 with comprehensive correct knowledge of HIV/AIDS
54   Women 15–49 who know where to be tested for HIV
55   Women 15–49 who have been tested for HIV
56   Knowledge of mother- to-child transmission of HIV (15–49)
57   PMTCT counseling coverage
58   PMTCT testing coverage

D4: Food / Nutrition

59   Underweight prevalence under 5y
60   Underweight prevalence under 5y
61   Stunting prevalence under 5y
62   Wasting prevalence under 5y
63   Birth weight below 2.5 kg
64   Exclusive breastfeeding rate (< 6 months)
65   Continued breastfeeding rate (12–15 months and 20–23 months)
66   Timely complementary feeding rate (6–9 months)

67   Frequency of complementary feeding (6–11 months)
68   Adequately fed infants (0–11 months)
69   Timely initiation of breastfeeding (within 1 hr. birth)

D5: Water / Sanitation

70   Use of improved drinking water sources
71   Proportion of households that treat their water to make it safer to drink
72   Use of adequate sanitary means of excreta disposal
73   Sanitary disposal of child's feces

D6: Labor / Employment

74   Prop. children 5–14 y in child labour activities, student/non student

D7: Housing (living environment)

75   29. Proportion of population using solid fuels

D10: Participation/Social peace

76   Prevalence of female genital cutting (FGC) (w 15–49 y)
77   Prevalence of extreme form of FGC (infibulation, etc) (w 15–49 y)
78   FGC prevalence-daughters (w 15–49 y)
79   Approval for FGC (w 15–49 y)
80   Child discipline: punishment severity
81   Birth registration, proportion 0–59 months

Appendix C
Classification Principle and Algorithm

The principle consists of forming homogenous classes by minimizing the within-class dispersion, and by maximizing between-class dispersion. The two functions on which the algorithm is based are the following: (1) the reallocation function: it partitions, i.e. it assigns each individual in cluster E to attraction centers formed by the cores. It is defined by the following equation :

$$\pi(X, A_j) = \frac{1}{n_j} \sum_{X' \in A_j} d(X, X')$$

where n_j is the number of core elements. The recentering function calculates the new cores from the already formed classes:

$$V(A_j, P_j) = \frac{1}{N_j} \sum_{X \in P_j} \pi(X, A_j),$$

where Nj is the number elements in the class.

The execution of the algorithm proceeds as follows:

1. Ramdom initialization of the first K cores;
2. Assignment: Calculation of the class of each cluster point;
3. Update of the centers (or class attributes);
4. Calculation of the new centers of each class (barycenter);
5. Test of convergence: The execution of the algorithm ends when the partitioning stops, i.e. when the within-class inertia criterion converges. It is defined by the following equation:

$$I_w = \sum_{j=1}^{K} \sum_{X \in P_j} d^2(X, G_j),$$

where Gj is the center of gravity of the class defined by equation:

$$G_j = \frac{\sum\limits_{o_i \in E} \mu_i o_i}{\sum \mu_i}.$$

Histogram of the First 5 Eigen Values of the Preliminary MCA

```
+--------+--------+------------+------------+------------------------------
----------------------------------------+
| NUMBER |  EIGEN  | PERCENTAGE | CUMULATIVE |                             |
|        |  VALUE  |            | PERCENTAGE |                             |
-----------------------------------------------------------------------
|   1    | 0.2915  |   10.29    |   10.29    |                             |
*****************************************************************|
|   2    | 0.0820  |    2.89    |   13.18    | **************              |
|   3    | 0.0664  |    2.34    |   15.52    | ***********                 |
|   4    | 0.0646  |    2.28    |   17.80    | *********                   |
|   5    | 0.0550  |    1.94    |   19.74    | *******                     |
```

Histogram of the First 5 Eigen Values of the Final MCA

```
+--------+--------+------------+------------+-------------------+
| NUMBER |  EIGEN  | PERCENTAGE | CUMULATIVE |                   |
|        |  VALUE  |            | PERCENTAGE |                   |
-----------------------------------------------------------------------
|   1    | 0.3426  |   30.94    |   30.94    |                   |
*****************************************************************|
|   2    | 0.0879  |    7.94    |   38.88    | **************    |
|   3    | 0.0634  |    5.73    |   44.61    | ***********       |
|   4    | 0.0548  |    4.95    |   49.56    | *********         |
|   5    | 0.0515  |    4.65    |   54.21    | *********         |
```

Table C.1 Coordinates, contribution, and square cosines of the final MCA (illustrative variables)

Variables	Coordinates Axis 1 (CIP value)	Variables	Coordinates axis 1 (CIP value)
Area		Main activity	
Urban	0.82	Agriculture	−0.81
Rural	−0.68	Mines, quarries	0.37
Region		Construction	0.08
Dakar	1.13	Transport	0.32
Ziguinchor	−0.17	Commerce/sales	0.33
Diourbel	−0.46	Services and others	0.46
St Louis	−0.24	Education/health	0.98
Tamba	−0.74	Administration	1.17
Kaolack	−0.46	Other activities	0.26
Thiès	0.04	Size	
Louga	−0.51	1 person	0.57
Fatick	−0.49	2–3 persons	0.22
Kolda	−0.84	4–6 persons	−0.01
Sex		7–9 persons	−0.08
Male	−0.10	10–12 persons	−0.09
Female	0.37	More than 12 persons	−0.10

Table C.1 (continued)

Variables	Coordinates Axis 1 (CIP value)	Variables	Coordinates axis 1 (CIP value)
Age class		Matrimonial status	
20–24 years	−0.10	Monogamous	−0.02
25–29 years	−0.04	Polygamous	−0.16
30–34 years	−0.08	Single	0.50
35–39 years	0.01	Widower	0.33
40–44 years	0.03	Divorcee	0.53
45–49 years	0.10	Other	−0.08
50–54 years	0.11		
55–59 years	−0.03		
60–64 years	−0.09		
65–and more	−0.06		

Histogram of the First Index nodes of the Classification

```
★ ★ ★ ★    13217    13213    1956 252271.91     0.00403    ★ ★
★ ★ ★ ★    13219    13214    1741 262003.23     0.00871    ★ ★ ★
★ ★ ★ ★    13218    13220    2916 507075.91     0.01326    ★ ★ ★ ★ ★
★ ★ ★ ★    13222    13221    3697 514276.16     0.05069    ★ ★ ★ ★ ★ ★ ★ ★ ★ ★ ★
★ ★ ★ ★    13223    13224    66131021352.13     0.25020
★ ★ ★ ★ ★ ★ ★ ★ ★ ★ ★ ★ ★ ★ ★ ★ ★ ★ ★ ★ ★ ★ ★ ★ ★ ★ ★ ★ ★ ★ ★ ★ ★ ★ ★ ★ ★ ★ ★ ★ ★ ★ ★ ★ ★ ★ ★ ★ ★ ★ ★ ★ ★ ★ ★ ★ ★ ★ ★ ★ ★ ★ ★ ★
```

The disconetion between the first and the second knot shows the pertinence of the cutout*** into classes.

Appendix D
Multiple Correspondence Analysis on 1993 Data: Main Results

Table D.1 Vietnam 1993 multiple correspondence analysis factorial scores

		Household distribution (%)	Categories scores on the first 8 factorial axes							
			1	2	3	4	5	6	7	8
Underemployment	Underemployment	44.0	−0.167	0.169	0.197	−0.792	0.198	0.326	−0.499	0.009
	No underemployment	56.0	0.126	−0.138	−0.155	0.627	−0.156	−0.256	0.393	−0.010
Hld with chronic sick	With chronic sick	18.1	−0.265	−0.072	1.407	0.557	−0.182	−0.551	−0.985	0.044
	No chronic sick	81.9	0.055	0.012	−0.312	−0.121	0.040	0.122	0.219	−0.012
Hld with illiterate adults	Adults illiterate	37.5	−0.496	−0.307	0.423	0.405	0.043	−0.139	−0.162	−0.246
	Adults literate	62.5	0.293	0.180	−0.255	−0.240	−0.026	0.084	0.098	0.145
Hld. with children 6-15 not going school	Child. not going school	15.1	−0.462	−0.155	0.861	−1.238	0.003	−1.030	0.863	0.831
	Child. going school	84.9	0.079	0.024	−0.154	0.223	−0.001	0.184	−0.153	−0.150
Hld without radio and TV	No radio, TV	53.0	−0.456	0.112	−0.232	0.107	−0.165	0.261	−0.326	0.412
	With radio or TV	47.0	0.560	−0.084	0.266	−0.150	0.190	−0.296	0.359	−0.442
Type of dwelling	Temporary house	36.5	−0.808	−0.545	−0.221	0.048	−0.106	0.070	0.045	0.359

Table D.2 (continued)

		Household distribution (%)	Categories scores on the first 8 factorial axes							
			1	2	3	4	5	6	7	8
	Semi-perm. house	47.0	0.135	0.649	0.105	−0.076	0.235	−0.022	−0.013	−0.589
	Permanent house	16.5	1.390	−0.660	0.188	0.121	−0.436	−0.092	−0.058	0.874
Drinking water	Ponds, lakes	19.3	−0.911	−0.853	0.236	−0.222	−0.207	0.250	0.527	−0.656
	Other	1.8	−0.733	−0.646	−3.443	0.076	3.958	−4.609	−2.097	0.327
	Dug well	52.7	−0.127	0.636	0.011	0.246	−0.137	−0.082	0.091	0.240
	Piped, rain, drilled	26.2	0.963	−0.619	0.034	−0.330	0.162	0.288	−0.428	−0.027
Type of toilet used	No toilet, other	47.4	−0.611	−0.453	−0.043	−0.013	0.289	0.178	0.076	−0.085
	Simple toilet	33.8	0.062	0.745	−0.178	−0.214	−0.804	−0.440	−0.163	−0.117
	Double-vault compost latrine	8.4	0.697	1.055	1.043	0.872	1.916	0.883	0.679	1.046
	Flush toilet septic tank	10.4	1.995	−1.230	−0.070	0.064	−0.254	−0.095	−0.359	−0.092

Table D.3 Factorial axes contributions

Axis	Eigenvalue	%	Cum%
1	0.2612	16.1	16.1
2	0.1835	11.3	27.4
3	0.1401	8.6	36.0
4	0.1385	8.5	44.5
5	0.1255	7.7	52.2
6	0.1233	7.6	59.8
7	0.1151	7.1	66.9
8	0.1111	6.8	73.7
Total (13 axis)	1.625		100.0

Appendix E
Poverty Analysis. Results for the Seven Regions of Vietnam

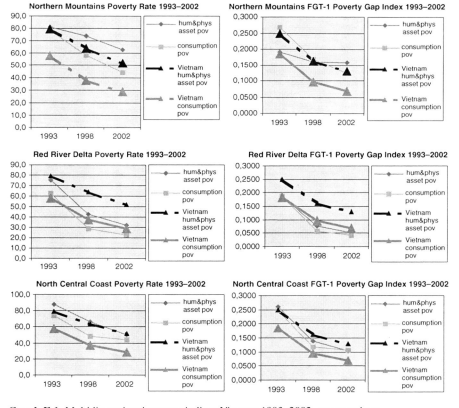

Graph E.1 Multidimensional poverty indices Vietnam 1993–2002, seven regions

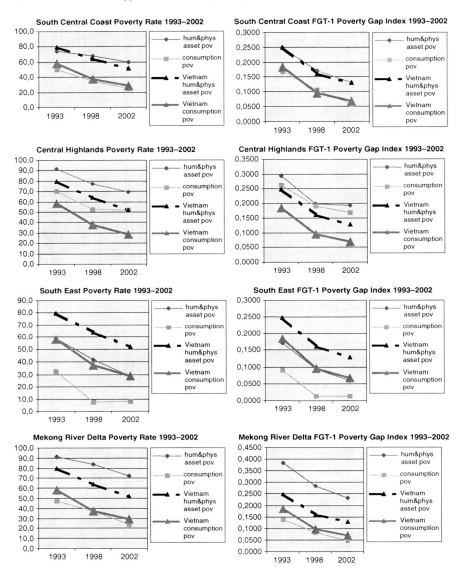

Graph E.2 (continued)

Index

Breinigsville, PA USA
24 August 2009
222800BV00004B/1/P